TECHNOMANIFESTOS

TECHNOMANIFESTOS

VISIONS FROM THE INFORMATION REVOLUTIONARIES

ADAM BRATE

TEXERE

NEW YORK / LONDON

Copyright © 2002 Adam Brate

Published in 2002 by

TEXERE LLC
55 East 52nd Street
New York, NY 10055

Tel: +1 (212) 317 5511
Fax: +1 (212) 317 5178
www.etexere.com

In the UK

TEXERE Publishing Limited
71–77 Leadenhall Street
London EC3A 3DE

Tel: +44 (0)20 7204 3644
Fax: +44 (0)20 7208 6701
www.etexere.co.uk

This publication is designed to provide accurate and authoritative information in regard to the subject matter covered. It is sold with the understanding that the publisher is not engaged in rendering legal, accounting, or other professional services. If legal advice or other expert assistance is required, the services of a competent professional person should be sought.

Designed by The Book Design Group

Library of Congress Cataloging in Publication Data has been applied for.

ISBN 1–58799–103–9

Printed in the United States of America

This book is printed on acid-free paper.

10   9   8   7   6   5   4   3   2   1

TECHNOMANIFESTOS

JAKARTA, Indonesia, May 21, 1998—President Suharto resigns in the face of nationwide protests and rioting by hundreds of thousands of people, led by tens of thousands of students. The students organized across 40 universities within a few days, using the Internet. The protests reached every corner of the 17,000 islands of Indonesia through the electronic communications network that had been established, ironically, as a cash cow for Suharto's children.

LIMA, Peru, November 20, 2000—President Alberto Fujimori faxes his resignation from Japan, humiliated by videotapes exposing corruption and graft involving top officials. More than 2,000 videotapes recorded by his top intelligence officer were confiscated, then shown on national television, continuing to fascinate and horrify the Peruvian public for months.

MANILA, Philippines, January 20, 2001—Four days of mass protests force President Joseph Estrada to resign. The protests are dubbed People Power 2, in reference to the People Power protests of 1986 that toppled Ferdinand Marcos. This time, the demonstrations are coordinated through 160 million text messages sent over cellular phones.

Each of these revolutions is part of the Information Revolution, the great social and technological movement of the information age. Its visionaries strive to establish the means by which everybody can pursue the democratic ideals of creative and political freedom. The revolution is becoming more powerful as technologies become cheaper and smaller and universal.

The Information Revolution is founded on the technologies of the post–World War II era: electronic communications networks, digital media, and computers. They are a ubiquitous component of our environment, a literal and figurative web of electricity running through our homes, below our streets, across the skies, before our eyes. Information technologies are part of our habitat. We can scale their peaks, mine their resources, build castles or shrines on their slopes, or leave them wild and forbidding. The Information Revolution presents a series of choices for us to make.

The technomanifestos excerpted and discussed in this book are the writings of the scientists, mathematicians, engineers, and activists who have shaped technologies for individual and collective empowerment. These are the innovators who emphasize technology's beneficial social impact over its commercial import, although they made the computer software companies and dot com enterprises possible.

The ideas expressed in the manifestos of the information revolutionaries are related to and, in many ways, as important as those expressed in the Declaration of Independence, the U.S. Constitution, and the Federalist Papers. The founding papers of the American Revolution delineated a new political system based on the basic principle of freedom. The technomanifestos introduce a new set of social and technological ideals inspired by the same principle. Like the framers of the Constitution, the information revolutionaries have a potent agenda: to release the power of the people. They build technologies to free people of the industrial age systems that turn them into tools.

Since the Industrial Revolution, many people in the West have led two lives—a personal life and a work life. The personal realm is generally founded on the strengths that underlie intimate relationships and personal well-being: trust, love, individuality, respect, joy, creativity, and cooperation. The work and business realm is typically founded on other principles: efficiency, structure, competition, the scientific method, and the belief that everything can be reduced to its measurable components. Work, the foundation of our economic and political structure, has thus been divorced of human frailties. It has also been divorced of human strengths.

Many of the visionaries featured in this book realize that the advances of the Industrial Revolution have come at the expense of the personal sphere. The economies of the United States and Europe have been built on the efficiency of the assembly line, which requires many people to spend their lives doing the same task every day with little pleasure or creativity. The rise of the bureaucracy occurred as the concept of the assembly line moved into the world of ideas. The corporation, the governmental institution, and even the classroom are factories of thought that have run on the machinery of administrative drudgery: papers, forms, rules, procedures, and tests.

The manifesto writers understand that information technology has the potential to reintegrate our private and public spheres by transforming the nature of work. They understand that giving people better tools to create, communicate, and collaborate can make work more like private life: intimately rewarding, participatory, creative, and less laborious.

Computers, electronic media, and networks are not just tools of business, but also, thanks to the information revolutionaries, a means of perception and self-expression. Information technology can empower us to understand and participate more fully in the workings of corporations, and economic, political, and media systems. Global networks like the World Wide Web enable people to consider and contribute worldviews not presented by the broadcast media. Computer simulations expose the causes and effects of issues such as rain forest devastation, welfare budgets, and gene cloning in political, economic, social, and personal terms. With information technology, we can become generalists as well as specialists, denizens of a global village.

The danger in losing the separation between our personal and work lives, or the local and the global, is that the harmful characteristics of one could affect the other. The global sociopolitical infrastructure may dissolve, now that the fear and hatred of a few can spread everywhere through electronic networks. Or a corporation, culture, government, or individual could take over and control us.

But the hope is that the best of both worlds can be joined, that information technologies can help people run societies in ways that are efficient and competitive, yet built on human strengths and liberties. As our technologies become more like us—complex and adaptive—our social systems can follow suit. Rigid bureaucracies and hierarchies may gradually be replaced by relationships based on merit and networks of trust. Our technologies may empower people around the world to solve problems collectively, especially in times of political upheaval, without centers of command and control. They may enable us to work in environments that better fulfill our psychological needs, empowering us to understand and participate more fully in the "big picture." They may help us replace monopolies with business environments that thrive on open collaboration and transparent intention.

In short, the goal of the information revolutionaries is to create new systems—technological, social, political, and economic—that adapt to people instead of the other way around.

Technomanifestos is the story of computer scientists, engineers, mathematicians, and other visionaries who raised profound questions of how technology relates to human beings, redefining who and what we are and where we are going. It presents a broad history of computer technology in the last fifty years through profiles of the revolutionaries and the highlights of their writings. Each of this book's four parts—"Frontier," "Revolution," "Power," and "Symbiosis"—represents a stage in the Information Revolution.

As discussed in Part I, the frontier of the Information Revolution appears in the 1940s with the dawn of cybernetics, the science that studies flexible, humanlike systems. Mathematician **Norbert Wiener** found this science of communications and control, realizing the power of adaptability and interactivity in technology that acts like biology. Cybernetics describes how regulatory feedback allows both human bodies and machines to respond to unexpected changes in the environment and correct for them. After World War II, Wiener and others apply the concept to social systems, history, and politics.

Engineer **Vannevar Bush** embraces the idea that mechanical entities can be modeled on human beings when he proposes a theoretical machine that would link the world's information in the same associative way as the mind. Mathematicians **Alan Turing** and **John von Neumann** construct the logical framework for the modern digital computer, using the language of mathematics to model the adaptive human brain and its memory. Human nervous systems, computer systems, social systems, and economic systems come to be thought of as resembling one another.

The revolution gains momentum in the 1960s and 1970s, when the established institutions of the Industrial Revolution begin to be dismantled by the seminal technologies of the Information Revolution. As discussed in Part II, **J. C. R. Licklider** and his "intergalactic network" of researchers conceive, build, and propagate ARPAnet, the forerunner to the Internet. Licklider writes about a "man-computer symbiosis" that fosters the strengths of both, implemented in this system of distributed computer networks. Artificial intelligence researcher **Marvin Minsky** and mathematician/psychologist **Seymour Papert** learn how the mind works by studying how children learn—and using computers to test their ideas. They construct a theory that the human mind works by dint of a complex society of mindless agents—that intelligence, like civilization, is a phenomenon of interaction. Minsky attempts to model computer intelligence accordingly, constructing electronic societies of mind. Papert designs ways computers can help children learn, not by training them but by giving them a world to manipulate and explore.

At the same time, engineer **Doug Engelbart** builds the Augmentation Research Center—a bootstrap project designed to augment the human capacity for collective problem solving through computer technology. Engelbart and his group devise the tools that make computers adaptable for human beings: interface features such as the mouse, windowed displays, and a working hypertext system that can link information associatively. Computer scientist **Alan C. Kay** and his team at the Xerox Palo

Alto Research Center build on the work of earlier revolutionaries to devise the "personal computer," on the principle that simple things should be easy enough for children, and everything, no matter how complex, should be possible.

Fueling these revolutionaries is the conviction that computers are tools for communication, creativity, and community, not just computation and capitalism.

Part III shows how from the 1970s on, the power of these developing technologies is unleashed and the battle for the future begins. The revolutionaries recognize that corporations and governments are institutions that will wield electronic technologies not to build communities but to control them. Media theorist **Marshall McLuhan** reveals how electronic media make the world into a "global village" that fully connects all humanity—perhaps too closely, and with power in the hands of perhaps too few. Activist **Abbie Hoffman** argues in word and action that the information age can bring with it a free society, based not on competition but on cooperation.

Visionary **Ted Nelson** conceives of a global hypertext system in which information is linked associatively and nonlinearly and is disseminated through personal computers worldwide. He imagines it neither censored nor controlled by any government or corporation. In the early 1990s physicist **Tim Berners-Lee** creates the World Wide Web, designed from the start as an open, free network. Meanwhile, hackers **Richard M. Stallman** and **Larry Wall** create "free software," or "opensource" code, to save, and then foster the spirit of collaboration among programmers that is threatened by software companies. Their alternative is to keep programming code open and available for the entire programming community to develop, modify, and use. Anyone with a personal computer can tap in and contribute to a repository of information. This becomes a new paradigm for the creation and distribution of knowledge in the twenty-first century.

Commerce encroaches on the Web, and in the mid-1990s the largest corporations are those that control electronic media and software. The threat of authoritarian governmental regulation looms over the personal freedoms that the technologies enable. Software activist **Eric S. Raymond** and legal scholar **Lawrence Lessig** explore the reasons for hope and fear as the information architecture becomes as important to society as laws and roads. There can be a society that thrives on the competition, not control, of ideas, but wrong-minded corporate and governmental regulation could make information technologies even more controlling than the machines in industrial mills. Without intelligent regulation to keep the information architecture open and interactive, technology could become the means of oppression instead of empowerment.

At the beginning of the twenty-first century, humans have reached symbiosis with their information technologies. As discussed in Part IV, the Information Revolution is in many ways an invisible revolution, because we have adapted to our technologies so readily and so well. Increasingly, computers, media, and networks infiltrate each person's awareness, connecting everyone in a global consciousness. They facilitate our political revolutions and our personal revelations. Scientists such as **K. Eric Drexler** predict that our information technologies will transform everything from manufacturing to medicine when we build computers and machines the size of molecules. Nanotechnology epitomizes the double-edged nature of our cybernetic technologies, which promise to raise the standard of human life, or threaten to grind it into dust, depending on who has power over them. Or perhaps, as computer scientist **Bill Joy** fears, they may become so complex and adaptable that they evolve by themselves, evading human control. Technologist **Jaron Lanier** emphasizes that we must remember the value at the heart of the Information Revolution: humanism.

The spirit of humanism underlies the convictions of the information revolutionaries. Humanism values the practice of compassion along with the pursuit of knowledge. It comprises a commitment to civil liberties, human rights, and participatory democracies in government, workplace, and education. It embraces the concept of a global consciousness and the collective effort to solve social problems. Most of all, humanism is the belief in free will: that each of us is ultimately responsible for the kind of world we live in now and in the future. Informed, we can choose our fate.

The visionaries featured in this book are certainly not the only information revolutionaries, but they are the best propagators of ideas central to the Information Revolution. They recognize the power of technologies to communicate ideas and have effectively amplified their own visions throughout the system. Through their writings and mastery of information technologies, they assume a position on the front lines. Many other people, from anthropologists to educators to biologists to linguists to psychologists, are an integral part of the web, and are mentioned in context. Regrettably, there are many more people who could not be included. A book is limited by its form; the world is not.

This book reveals where the Information Revolution has come from and where it may go, serving as a starting point for investigation in how information technology affects society. The ethical, political, and economic decisions that thinking people must now face are some of the most difficult, especially as these technologies become ubiquitous around the globe. The future depends upon regulatory feedback, the basis of cybernetics. Feedback enables all systems—individual, political, mechanical, economic, social—to adapt with changes in the environment and learn from past actions. These technomanifestos are part of that process.

PART I

FRONTIER

• Norbert Wiener • Vannevar Bush • Alan Turing •
• John von Neumann •

In the rubble of World War II, the information revolutionaries forge a new frontier. The principles of cybernetics, or the science of communications and control, guide them to a new understanding of the similarities between biological organisms and mechanical technologies. Applying cybernetic principles, they conceive and build machines that are responsive and adaptive because they take in information from their environment. These machines have communication and control capabilities like those of human bodies.

One revolutionary applies cybernetics to society, concluding that information needs to circulate freely. Another envisions a machine, the "memex," that will lay trails between ideas and so become a communal brain. Another imagines a machine that will trick a human being into thinking it's human, and, along with others, creates the first generation of digital computers. Together, the revolutionaries contemplate a strange future of tools that mirror our minds and consider whether that future will be terrible or bright.

By the end of the postwar era, the frontier is cleared for developments in the fields of artificial intelligence, computer science, communications science, information theory, human interface design, and education.

THE CIRCLE OF FEEDBACK

NORBERT WIENER

Revolution is not something fixed in ideology, nor is it
something fashioned to a particular decade. It is a per-
petual process embedded in the human spirit.
—Abbie Hoffman

IN 1948 NORBERT WIENER, professor of mathematics at
the Massachusetts Institute of Technology, had two fears, seemingly unrelated, concerning the future of the human race. One
was the use and misuse of nuclear weapons. The military was
hoarding information that could bring about World War III or
at least prevent world peace. He believed that the concentration
of power in government laboratories could literally backfire on
the rest of the planet.

Wiener's other fear concerned the specialization of the
human brain. Looking back at the development of *Homo sapiens*, he began to think that the human brain is much too large
to distribute information efficiently. Certain parts of it seem to
govern certain activities completely. Any other beast could lose
a chunk of its brain and still function reasonably well. In the
human brain, language and memory and color recognition all
seem to reside only in their own circumscribed areas. The brain
is associative, but not enough. As with the bomb, power is con-
centrated in certain regions. Wouldn't we be less vulnerable if

all this information and know-how were more evenly distributed? Were this the case for the bomb, maybe no one would use it. As for the brain, it might mean that people would use it more.

In fact, Wiener's concerns were intimately related: Both the atomic and anatomical, in their current states, could lead to human extinction.

Wiener had a reputation for making bold connections between seemingly unrelated things. Around campus, he was known for being an impertinent and paranoid genius. His head was perfectly egg shaped, and on it he sported heavy tortoiseshell glasses and a goatee. He often spoke in an endless stream of consciousness, drawing on a cigar, one idea drifting to the next. He taught math, but, detesting specialization, would ramble on about microbes or politics. Certain colleagues, using the "Wiener early warning system," would hide in bathroom stalls when a lookout man saw Wiener's rotund figure rounding the corner. Among his students, a litany of absentminded professor jokes circulated:

> Wiener and his family moved, so his wife pinned a note in his jacket with their new and old addresses. Wiener went for a walk, forgot about the reminder, and returned to the old house. Finding it empty, he addressed a little girl waiting on the stoop. "Little girl," he asked, "do you know where the Wieners went?"
>
> "Let me show you," she said. "This way, Daddy."

> Wiener stopped to talk to someone in the hall. When it was time to move on he asked what direction he had come from. "That way," he was told.
>
> "Good," Wiener said. "That means I just had lunch."

Wiener was the quintessential intellect, his mind on the universal, the transcendent, the worldly. His peers considered him a dismal "finisher" and a merely adequate professor, but they knew he was an excellent catalyst. It was only a matter of time before one—or the whole daisy chain—of the professor's ideas would spontaneously bloom. When they did, they assumed the form of two of the founding technomanifestos of the information age, *Cybernetics: or, Control and Communication in the Animal and the Machine* (1948) and *The Human Use of Human Beings: Cybernetics and Society* (1950).

INFORMATION

The seeds of cybernetics were sown in the two world wars. Radar, secret codes, and computing machines inspired Wiener to view the world as *information*, which he understood in terms of communications and control. When he thought about how information is controlled due to the structure of the brain or the making of the bomb, he became paranoid. Information, he concluded, should circulate. This simple concept had extraordinary implications. The distribution of information would drive the technological revolution that would follow World War II.

With *Cybernetics*, and *The Human Use of Human Beings*, which described a new science of communication and control, Wiener fired one of the first shots of the Information Revolution. At its core, cybernetics is the mathematical science of how adaptive systems, biological or mechanical, function. It describes all aspects of communication, or the transmission and exchange of information.

> Information is the name for the content of what is exchanged with the outer world as we adjust to it, and make our adjustment felt upon it. The process of receiving and using information is the process of our adjusting to the contingencies of the outer environment, and of our living effectively within that environment.[1] —*The Human Use of Human Beings*

In cybernetic terms, something is said to carry information if it *reduces uncertainty, restricts choice,* or *controls something else.* A textbook carries information in that it conveys something not already known. The dealing of cards in poker contains information as it restricts the possible play. A chromosome may be said to store genetic information to the degree it controls the development of an organism.

Information, as the stuff of communication, is a way of explaining everything from human interactions to brain functions to machine intelligence to the psychology of the cold war. Wiener revealed how the term information, in this context, encompasses human languages, machine code, signals in a phone line, body language, and atoms in the air. Every action involves information. Every object contains information. And everything can't help but interact—exchange information—with the world around it, whether through a single photon or through total immersion.

Noise is the introduction of random error in the transmission of information. It is static in a phone line, tremors in a nerve fiber, or ambiguity in a conversation. Noise destroys meaning and frustrates intent.

The struggle to communicate amid noise is like steering a ship on tossing seas. In fact, cybernetics is derived from the Greek word κυβερνετεσ, meaning *steersman*, the same word that gave us *governor*.

Proteus, the shape-changing son of the sea god Poseidon, could have been the god of cybernetics, for information assumes so many forms. Instead, Wiener chose a patron saint: Gottfried Wilhelm Leibniz, the socially conscious mathematician and philosopher of the seventeenth century. Leibniz straddled worlds both abstract and concrete: When he wasn't creating peace between the Holy Roman Empire and its neighbors, he channeled his energy into math, technology, and the practical use of his calculating machine, the calculus ratiocinator. In *Cybernetics*, Wiener credits his role model for laying the foundation of cybernetics by applying mathematical principles to human reasoning.

> Through the abacus and the desk computing machine to the ultra rapid computing machines of the present day, so the *calculus ratiocinator* of Leibniz contains the germs of the *machina ratiocinatrix*, the reasoning machine. It is therefore not the least surprising that the same intellectual impulse which has led to the development of mathematical logic has at the same time led to the idea of actual mechanization of processes of thought.[2]

In the tradition of Leibniz, Wiener would reveal how the lingua franca of mathematics can explain the behavior of both organisms and machines. He'd reveal how both process information alike, through the phenomenon of feedback.

FEEDBACK

Feedback is the process of connecting the output of a system to its input and may be positive or negative. Positive feedback amplifies errors; negative feedback corrects and controls them.

> Feedback [is] the property of being able to adjust future conduct by past performance. Feedback may be as simple as that of the common reflex, or it may be a higher order feedback, in which past experience is used not only to regulate specific movements, but also whole policies of behavior.[3]
>
> —*The Human Use of Human Beings*

This idea of feedback hearkens back to the Industrial Revolution as a way to describe the regulatory mechanisms, the "governors," of complex machinery. The governor that moderates steam engines was invented by James Watt in 1784 and described mathematically by the physicist James Clerk Maxwell in 1868. Its job was to regulate the steam engine by opposing what the system is doing if the system runs too fast, performing negative feedback.

Wiener's application of feedback is limited to that which is purposeful. He introduced the cybernetic concept of purposeful feedback in 1942 in an article in *Philosophy of Science* titled "Behavior, Purpose and Teleology," which he wrote with his longtime cohorts, Dr. Arturo Rosenblueth and Julian Bigelow. Purposeful behavior (teleological behavior) depends on negative feedback, which controls errors. Negative feedback is how people and things "learn." Cybernetic, purposeful feedback can be as simple as a mechanical counterweight or as complex as the customs of a society.

In the most general sense, cybernetics tells us that feedback is like karma: What goes around, comes around. In the stricter sense, feedback control is the basic self-correcting mechanism by which systems maintain their equilibrium, or homeostasis. A system uses feedback to interact with its environment and adjust itself accordingly. A simple example of a feedback mechanism is a thermostat, which in response to the temperature in the environment, fires up the boiler—heating the cold environment—or turns on the air conditioner—cooling the hot environment. The thermostat maintains equilibrium through negative feedback.

ENTROPY

A third key principle of cybernetics is *entropy*. Entropy is a measure of the probable, and noise, disorder, chaos, and sameness are more probable than organization, differentiation, and form. Entropy in the form of noise breaks down the signal of communication.

> As entropy increases, the universe, and all closed systems in the universe, tend naturally to deteriorate and lose their distinctiveness, to move from the least to the most probable state, from a state of organization and differentiation in which distinctions and forms exist, to a state of chaos and sameness.[4]
> —*The Human Use of Human Beings*

In its original, thermodynamic sense, entropy is a statistical measure of the disorder in a system.* The random interactions of uncountable molecules manifest on the human scale as waste, disorder, and decay. Living creatures die. Machines overheat and break down. The sun is spewing energy, converting the energy locked in molecules into randomly directed heat and light, moving toward an entropic "heat death," all of its complexity and order spent as heat. Hot things cool until they reach the temperature of their environment. These are all irreversible processes from less probable to more probable states; from low to maximal entropy.

In the long run, entropy will overrun any closed system—such as the entire universe—until it reaches maximal entropy in a state of homogeneity and disorder. In the nineteenth century, Maxwell envisioned a tiny demon that fights entropy by imposing order on systems one atom at a time. Careful study has shown that Maxwell's demon must suffer the price for its efforts: The more order it imposes, the more likely it will be destroyed. There can be no stable Maxwell's demon, but there can be demons that last for a prolonged amount of time, "metastable" demons.

---

*The related nineteenth-century sciences of thermodynamics and statistical mechanics describe mathematically how the complex behavior of the natural world arises from the constant interaction of infinitesimal, featureless particles. This realization that communication allows the simple to give rise to the complex is central to the Information Revolution.

> We may well regard enzymes and living organisms as metastable
> Maxwell's demons. Certainly the enzyme and the living organ-
> ism are alike metastable: the stable state of an enzyme is to be
> deconditioned, and the stable state of a living organism is to be
> dead.[5]   —*Cybernetics*

For Wiener, life is defined by the ability to challenge entropy. No system can defeat it forever and everywhere, but some systems can defeat it locally for a while. Enzymes and living organisms meet those criteria. Although living creatures lose vast amounts of energy in heat and waste matter every moment they breathe, they exist as highly ordered systems that can create even more order through toil and inspiration. Humans have the greatest capacity for creating ordered systems, having developed the ability to think, plan, and communicate with each other. Our ability to think is in service to the local, temporary defeat of chaos and disorder.

Wiener also places entropy in a broader context: It is the enemy of information. For example, the temperature of an object is a result of the random motion of its constituent molecules. If a scientist could know exactly how every molecule moved, she could say the object had no entropy. But measuring the temperature gives her only so much information about the molecular motion. The more motion, the greater the entropy. Entropy is the measure of what we don't know.

> Just as entropy tends to increase spontaneously in a closed
> system, so information tends to decrease; just as entropy is a
> measure of disorder, so information is a measure of order.
> Information and entropy are not conserved, and are equally
> unsuited to being commodities.[6]
> —*The Human Use of Human Beings*

Wiener used the word entropy to mean much more than its strict scientific definition. He saw entropy as the dark, vengeful side of information—its inevitable decay. It is the measurement of all that destroys meaning in this world. However, the tendency toward randomness and disorganization is also that which renews the world. Entropy guarantees that all order is ephemeral, whether such order is "good" (living beings and solar systems) or "bad" (nuclear secrets and dictatorships). No active system will forever remain in homeostasis. Entropy determines both the limits on life and the purpose of life.

> In control and communication we are always fighting nature's tendency to degrade the organized and to destroy the meaningful; the tendency . . . for entropy to increase.[7]
>
> —*The Human Use of Human Beings*

PUTTING IT TOGETHER

The wartime research that led Wiener to these observations about information, feedback, and entropy was the development of antiaircraft radar devices. Along with engineer Julian Bigelow, Wiener designed a device that, coupled with a human user, could predict the location of a moving target. In the past, a soldier had to track and shoot at an airplane by approximating where it would be by the time the missile could reach it. Wiener and Bigelow's prediction apparatus could do the same thing, but more accurately, by tracking a plane's irregular dips and curves and constantly updating its course. It relied on continuous feedback generated by radar. The information recorded was called *memory*. The machine *learned* when it could make adjustments based on that information, using negative (purposeful) feedback.

The behavior of the antiaircraft radar device was key to the formation of cybernetics. The machine trembled wildly when its feedback mechanism was overloaded. Each time the feedback mechanism tried to bring the device back into equilibrium, it would overshoot; then it would overshoot in the other direction, until the negative feedback became positive feedback, the errors amplifying. Then it would break down.

From this, Wiener and Bigelow constructed a theory: Communication in humans and machines functions (or breaks down) in the same way. The human nervous system runs on innumerable feedback loops between brain, limbs, nerves, etc., in active communication internally and with the outside world. They suspected that the body, like the radar device, regulates itself by negative feedback and would break down if the self-correcting feedback mechanisms fail.

They presented this idea to their colleague, Dr. Arturo Rosenblueth at Harvard Medical School. Rosenblueth declared that the machine's odd behavior corresponded to a well-known human pathological condition known as intention tremor. A patient with such a tremor could try to pick up a glass, miss, try again, miss, with her arm swinging more and more wildly until she couldn't swing it any more. As with the machine, the intention tremor causes the body's feedback mechanism to go from negative to positive, amplifying rather than correcting errors. In the absence of negative feedback, small errors, processed over and over again, have the potential to manifest and affect the entire system. Negative feedback corrects these errors and allows a person's brain to control her movements and successfully grab a glass. Purposeful feedback fights entropy, disorder, and chaos.

> It is my thesis that the physical functioning of the living individual and the operation of some of the newer communication machines are precisely parallel in their analogous attempts to control entropy through feedback. Both of them have sensory receptors as one stage in their cycle of operation: that is, in both of them there exists a special apparatus for collecting information from the outside world at low energy levels, and for making it available in the operation of the individual or the machine....The information is then turned into a new form available for the further stages of performance.[8]
>
> —*The Human Use of Human Beings*

The great insight of cybernetics is that all communication, all interaction—heat, impact, sound, taste, or language—is governed by the same statistical principles. Suddenly, it was legitimate to think of mechanical devices in biological terms and biological organisms in engineering terms. All machines, bodies, and even societies have systems of internal and external communication that can use regulatory feedback to learn, achieve, adapt, and evolve. Guided by feedback, organic, mechanical, or social bodies create pockets of order, strong signals in an entropic sea of noise.

FOUNDATIONS

Although Wiener and his colleagues laid the ideological groundwork for the Information Revolution, wartime research and development constituted its technological underpinnings. Federal funding flooded the coffers of research centers at the Massachusetts Institute of Technology, Princeton University, the California Institute of Technology, the University of California at Berkeley, and Columbia University. Corps of technologists built bombs, formulated nuclear technologies, and constructed computing machines designed to make and break code. By necessity, the process of collecting, storing, processing and transmitting information developed rapidly. First there were vacuum tubes; then cheap, reliable, readily available transistors; then rotating magnetic drum and disk storage, photoelectric cells, and magnetic core memory. Shortly after the war, the American Telephone and Telegraph Company (AT&T) built its infrastructure for nationwide dialing and began developing electronic switching systems (saving, Wiener quipped, the entire population of female high school graduates from careers as switchboard operators).

These wartime technologies, like the science of cybernetics, are rooted in the concepts of thermodynamics, statistics, and entropy conceived during the Industrial Revolution. Wiener and his colleagues built on those foundations at a series of ten two-day meetings sponsored by the Josiah Macy Foundation. Defying the trend toward specialization in the sciences and social sciences, the foundation encouraged science—and all fields— to be interdisciplinary and cooperative.

The Macy meetings, which began in 1944 and continued until 1955, became the primordial soup in which cybernetics evolved from a mathematical theory to something more, much more. Mathematicians, biologists, engineers, social scientists, and economists huddled together to find common denominators among neurons, languages, wires, waves. At first they called the meetings the "Conference for Circular Cause and Feedback Mechanisms in Biological and Social Systems." By the time *Cybernetics* was published in 1948, everyone agreed that the conference should be renamed "Cybernetics." Wiener was so overwhelmed by this unmistakable sign of support that he tearfully had to excuse himself from the room. Among his supporters, the first generation of "cyberneticists," were engineer Claude Shannon, neurophysiologists Warren McCulloch and Arturo Rosenblueth, mathematicians Walter Pitts and John von Neumann, and anthropologists Margaret Mead and Gregory Bateson.

Although Claude Shannon was a graduate student at MIT in the 1930s, Wiener didn't develop a working relationship with him until the Macy conferences. In 1948, the year Wiener published *Cybernetics,* Shannon wrote a related manifesto titled "A Mathematical Theory of Communication," in which he laid the groundwork of a field that would become known as *information theory.* He introduced a new and revolutionary way to measure signal transmission quantitatively, in units of what he called, for lack of a better word, "information."* The smallest possible unit of information is the *bit* (for *bi*nary digi*t*, coined by computer scientist John Tukey), which represents a single decision: yes or no, on or off, heads or tails, 0 or 1. This allowed Shannon to establish in statistical language precise mathematical definitions of signal, noise, and success of communication. He thus defined *informational entropy*, which measures the amount of confusion or ambiguity in a communication system. Just as the interaction of physical systems increases thermodynamic entropy, so does the accumulation of messages increase informational entropy. He also proved that with digital encoding, successful signal transmission is always possible, no matter how much noise there is in the channel. Years later, Wiener would dub Shannon one of the major spirits behind the age of the electronic computer and the automatic factory.

Warren McCulloch and Walter Pitts paved the way for relating cybernetic feedback machines to the human brain. McCulloch, a neurophysiologist at the Medical School of the University of Illinois, already knew Wiener and Rosenblueth, and was interested in the organization of the cortex. Pitts was a mathematical logician who had been a student of the famous logician

---

*Shannon did not mean to imply that his mathematics described knowledge or meaning, the traditional definitions of information. But, as with cybernetics, Shannon's colleagues quickly began applying information theory to just about everything in fuzzy metaphors. The process began with Warren Weaver's introduction to the 1949 publication, in which he argued that the boundary between mechanical signal transmission and human comprehension is not firm.

Rudolf Carnap before working with McCulloch. Pitts and McCulloch pioneered a theory that compared neural networks to computing machines, an important step in the development of the digital computer.

The Macy meetings also brought Wiener together with his political apotheosis, the hawkish atom-bomb-building mathematician John von Neumann, with whom Wiener jointly led one of the earlier meetings. Von Neumann, who was pioneering the first digital computers, elegantly described their construction, and Wiener exuberantly rambled on about how the principles of information and feedback apply to their operation. Both men found many ways to relate machines to organisms. Although they often benefited from this professional synergy, the sophisticated von Neumann and the socially challenged Wiener succumbed to personal and political friction. Macy meetings were often punctuated by Wiener's snoring during von Neumann's talks and the rustlings of von Neumann's newspaper during Wiener's. As the cold war progressed, the two men stood on opposite poles regarding the H-bomb and the role of the ethical scientist in society.

Meanwhile, social scientists Margaret Mead and Gregory Bateson developed a close relationship with Wiener, in whom they found the quintessential "humane scientist." Wiener had an unusual, holistic vision of the world, due in part to his travels and teachings in China, Japan, Mexico, and India. He was warmhearted, blind to class and race, and a strict vegetarian. His karmic principle of communications, the notion that what goes around, comes around, is universally relevant. Mead and Bateson applied Wiener's cybernetic vision to the social sciences as follows: If intercultural and international understanding is a foundation for human freedoms, then what better way to study civilizations and promote these ideals than by revealing feedback loops among societies and peoples? Here, at last, was a science that could help explain how civilizations worked by positioning them in terms of information and the way it circulates.*

---

*Mead and Bateson encouraged Wiener to write a book on the application of cybernetics to society. Wiener initially resisted, claiming that he had political persuasions related to his science but that societies couldn't be expressed by statistics. The anthropologists persisted and won, resulting in the publication of *The Human Use of Human Beings*. In it, he expounded on his ideas of information, feedback, and entropy and their relation to democracy and humanism.

MELDING HUMAN AND MACHINE

Despite their varied backgrounds, the Macy members agreed that the behavior of biological and mechanical systems can be defined in the same terms of information, feedback, and entropy, or communication and control. They also concluded that feedback occurs not only within but also *between* biological or mechanical systems.

In *The Human Use of Human Beings* Wiener brings the reader back to the American frontier to illustrate how feedback between humans and machines works. In 1950, when the book was published, remote settlements still dominated pioneer country. These homestead communities were too small to warrant their own electricity supply yet too large to rely on wood and kerosene. To solve the problem, engineers constructed local "self-maintaining" power stations that could supply power to inaccessible regions. The machinery had to function autonomously yet communicate with humans and adapt to their needs. In Wiener's day, a load dispatcher gave orders to the station over telephone and telegraph lines (or another carrier system) in the form of coded signals. The message the dispatcher sent to the power station contained information. The information was in the form of a code or pattern understandable to both the human and the machine. The terminal equipment translated this information into the operations of switches, valves, generators, turbines, and sluices; which, Wiener writes, "may be regarded as language in itself."

· ·

> In a certain sense, all communication systems terminate in machines, but the ordinary language systems terminate in a special sort of machine known as a human being. . . . For ordinary spoken language, the human level consists of the ear, and of that part of the cerebral mechanism which is in the permanent and rigid connection with the inner ear. The apparatus, when joined to the apparatus of sound vibrations in the air, or their equivalent in electric circuits, represent the machine concerned with the phonetic aspect of language, with sound itself.[9]
>
> —*The Human Use of Human Beings*

· ·

Wiener's description of human parts as "apparatus," "mechanism," and "terminal" indicates a literal, textual melding of human and machine. Both send and receive information, and can adapt through feedback, or "learn," accordingly. This information, whether from biological or mechanical systems, consists of patterns. In humans, the hormonal information sent and received by the endocrine system follows a pattern. Language abides by patterns of speech. Human and animal behavior follows predictable patterns. Machines, too, follow patterns. "How else," Wiener asks, "do we employ our radio than to transmit the patterns of sound, and our television set than to transmit patterns of light?" Years before the discovery of DNA or the development of computer networks, Wiener interpreted all biological and mechanical beings as patterns of information.

> We are but whirlpools in a river of ever-flowing water. We are not stuff that abides, but patterns that perpetuate themselves[10]   —*The Human Use of Human Beings*

This line of thought brought Wiener to consider the *ultimate* expression of human as a pattern of information. What if, he mused, we could simply telegraph a person from one location to another? Convert him or her to pure pattern, information transmissible by wire and interpretable by machine? He believed it would eventually be possible to determine the amount of significant information contained within a germ cell, estimating that it must convey "at least as much information as a set of the *Encyclopedia Britannica*."

> It is amusing as well as instructive to consider what would happen if we were to transmit the whole pattern of the human body, of the human brain with its memories and cross-connections, so that a hypothetical receiving instrument could re-embody these messages in appropriate matter, capable of continuing the processes already in the body and the mind[11]
>   —*The Human Use of Human Beings*

In the twenty-first century, cybernetics is usually associated with the image of the compatible-interchangeable human/machine, the *cyborg*. Indeed, Wiener popularized this notion that machines could be fashioned as natural extensions of ourselves; that the physical boundary between human and machine is a fine one.* If we begin to regard ourselves cybernetically—*in terms of information*—we must ask what are our bodies anyway but interfaces for communication? What really separates us from our technology? Thinking in cybernetic terms is powerful, but where can we draw the line?

GREAT GOOD OR EVIL

Wiener believed that the similarity between people and machines ends where human values and moral responsibilities begin. He positioned the Information Revolution as a social movement, believing that technological progress must go hand in hand with progress in education and human rights. The potential of the machine for good and evil became his favorite soapbox.

There was no doubt in Wiener's mind that turmoil would occur as machine labor replaces humans in both factories and offices. By educating labor unions, heads of industry, and political leaders of his vision of the "cybernetic future," he sought to prevent the social travesties that occurred when the West first became industrialized. On one hand, humans would be freed from the more menial aspects of labor, whether on a shop floor or in front of a filing cabinet. On the other hand, many people could become unemployed by the transition. Wealthy countries may benefit from new technologies and developing countries may suffer if the wealth is not shared. Machines could help humankind in the field of medicine, aiding us in the discovery of healing of ourselves. They could also destroy our way of living and lead to ever more gruesome ways to kill. All people, he concluded, must be educated to understand the good and bad implications of the new technologies.

In *The Human Use of Human Beings,* Wiener noted the ease with which Americans adopted new technologies in the years after World War II.

---

*Wiener emphasized the use of machines as body parts, including prosthetic limbs, eyes, and ears. For humanitarian as well as professional purposes, he was drawn to Jerome Wiesner's work on prosthetic devices for the blind or physically impaired. In the late 1940s he and Wiesner collaborated on the development of a glove that would convert speech into tactile sensations for deaf users. The glove wasn't successful, but Wiener's work on prosthetics set forth an enduring vision of how technology could fuse with biology in the creation of such devices, and so is considered seminal in the field.

Machines were not yet extensions of actual human bodies, but they were fast becoming expressions of collective cultural and material aspirations. New department stores sold mass quantities of electronic appliances—vacuum cleaners, washing machines, and cameras. Communications technologies such as the telephone and television proliferated. Politics became televised: Politicians like Ike Eisenhower were positioned in terms not much different from those used in reference to toothpaste, tonics, and deodorant. In fact, everything—the political process, Levittown houses, Chevys, and even McDonald's hamburgers—reflected a society eager to embrace the benefits of technology wedded to capitalism.

Wiener was particularly concerned about the social effects of the new media technologies. To him, it was clear that radio, television, and film were transforming the distribution of information. One sender could reach ten thousand receivers. These large producers—broadcasters—suddenly gained control over what the majority of the people watch, listen, think about. Wiener was dismayed. This was good for commercialism and totalitarianism, but not for content. He found broadcast media in the United States to be a product that, like Wonder Bread (or the new McDonald's hamburgers), was made for its selling properties rather than its inherent value.

. . . .

More and more we must accept a standardized inoffensive product which, like the white bread of the bakeries, is made rather for its keeping and selling properties than for its food value.[12]   —The Human Use of Human Beings

. . . .

Broadcast media resemble the top-down hierarchy of the military. Wouldn't it be better if the flow of information were distributed so that people could communicate with one another on a many-to-many basis? In the past, great ideas had developed by word of mouth—the *Epic of Gilgamesh, Beowulf,* and the Bible are testaments to the power of interpersonal interchanges. If information were distributed cybernetically, it would be at the personal level but unbounded by geography or politics. With many electronic connections, information could circulate between individuals but still manifest in larger spheres. One person's ideas could reach 100,000 receivers, but it would still be through (innumerable) local interactions. More people would get to exercise free speech, add their input, interact. Unfortunately for Wiener no many-to-many media technology yet existed. There were no World Wide Web or email then.

Wiener feared the potential for inhuman power and intelligence in the new information technologies. Their capabilities, especially with the advent of the electronic age, are nearly magical. There were two popular anecdotes Wiener told whenever he had the occasion. One was the well-known story of the sorcerer's apprentice who loses control of his tools when he invests them with too much autonomy. The other was the story of the monkey's paw, in which a man gets three wishes. Each wish is granted literally, without concern for the man's intentions, to devastating effect. The lesson: Human desires are tempered by human capabilities and morals. When we place power in machines, there is no such check.

> In all these stories the point is that the agencies of magic are literal-minded; and that if we ask for a boon from them, we must ask for what we really want and not for what we think we want. The new and real agencies of the learning machine are also literal-minded.[13]   —*Cybernetics*

In the end, however, Wiener resorted to the conviction that humans have free will and therefore will exercise control over their technologies. This, however, prompted his contingent fear that the robots, computers, and televisions, "though helpless by themselves, may be used by a human being or a block of human beings to increase their control over the rest of the human race."[14] It could be a corporation, a broadcaster, a government, an army—anyone or anything that aims to reduce human beings to parts of a machine.

> When human atoms are knit into an organization in which they are used, not in their full right as responsible human beings, but as cogs and levers and rods, it matters little that their raw material is flesh and blood.[15]   —*The Human Use of Human Beings*

Wiener's directive: Developing new, cybernetic technologies would only be advantageous if accompanied by a social conscience. How we use technology is entirely social and political. The way society responds to technology isn't predetermined. As humans, we have the free will to either place human rights and virtues—better distribution of wealth, free speech, human rights—in lockstep with technological advances or else suffer the consequences. Wiener believed that machines and media technologies have a place in our future, and we mustn't be Luddites. But we must value the human race enough to ensure that their power is well distributed.

INFORMATION WANTS TO BE FREE

Ensuring that power is well distributed is the same as ensuring that information is well distributed. Wiener wrote about the importance of free information in the context of the nuclear bomb. In a 1951 article titled "Communication and Secrecy in the Modern World," he disdainfully reported that the average American citizen believed military information could and should be kept secret. He was disgusted that "they think use of information by any other nationalities not only may be the result of treason, but intrinsically partakes of the nature of theft."[16] It infuriated him that most Americans thought it possible to actually *own* information, *store* it, and keep it *secret*.

Wiener detested the hoarding of information for two reasons: one was personal, the other cybernetic. The first involved a family secret. Just as young Norbert was becoming conscious of social inequities and anti-Semitism, he discovered that he was Jewish. Already socially inept, (in part because he entered college at age eleven), he was traumatized by the idea of belonging to an undervalued religious and social group. He wrote in his memoir that had he known all along he was Jewish, he wouldn't have been at all distraught. Eventually, he overcame his self-prejudice and, in turn, developed a humanitarian's hatred of discrimination.* The abiding lesson: Don't keep secrets. Don't inhibit communication.

· ·

> The dissemination of any scientific secret whatsoever is merely a matter of time, that in this game a decade is a long time, and that in the long run, there is no distinction between arming ourselves and arming our enemies.... Barring a new awareness on the part

---

*When Wiener discovered he was a Jew, he was also told that he was descended from Maimonides, the medieval Jewish philosopher, scholar, and physician (of the Muslim vizier). Although the genealogy was unconfirmed, the idea of this ancestor pleased Wiener immensely. Maimonedes had been a great bridge between cultures and disciplines.

of our leaders, this is bound to go on and on, until the entire intellectual potential of the land is drained from any possible constructive application to the manifold needs of the race, old and
new. The effect of these weapons must be to increase the entropy
of this planet, until all distinctions of hot and cold, good and bad,
man and matter have vanished in the formation of the white fur-
nace of a new star.[17]   —*The Human Use of Human Beings*

The principles of cybernetics provided Wiener with a stronger reason to
share information. It had to do with entropy—nature's tendency toward
disorder through the exchange of information. The military is a tightly organized system. Entropically, that creation of internal order and knowledge
must come at the greater expense of something else, just as an air conditioner works by heating the external environment more than it cools a
room. The military's pursuit of low entropy causes disorder and confusion
in the external world. Wiener also knew that no system could act without
exchanging information with its environment. Knowledge will leak out of
the system one way or another anyway; such is the nature of information.

Wiener applied the laws of entropy to tell us that information also loses
its value while it's contained. Just as nuclear science does not serve humanity
when it's confined to military laboratories, intellectual property such as
music, books, and movies loses its value if it is not circulated in the context of other information. Its value cannot truly and lastingly be stored or
fixed by any means, legal or physical. Furthermore, Wiener claimed that
information has no real owner, because the idea of copyright depends on
the false concept of singular authorship. There is no such thing as "genuine
originality," Wiener writes, because all ideas are derived from other ideas
through feedback and circulation of information. No knowledge can be
truly independent; the most valuable works are those that are cumulative.

The idea that information can be stored in a changing world
without an overwhelming depreciation in its value is false.[18]
—*The Human Use of Human Beings*

With his emphasis on the exchange of information, Wiener contributes
to the Information Revolution a spin on the word *revolution*—empha-

sizing the word in its original sense, as in "circulation," "rotation," and "cycle." The struggle to communicate necessitates interaction, which, on the level of social systems, means distribution. Information will decrease in value if it doesn't revolve within the system, be it one person's brain, a neighborhood, or a nation. In this is the message that became a clarion call for the Revolution: Information wants to be free.

THE CIRCLE OF "WE"

The principles of cybernetics can—and have been—universally applied. Wiener's political beliefs are deeply interconnected with the way cybernetics was interpreted by his friends and skeptics alike. As a result, some critics argue that the view that humans and machines are simply patterns of information undermines Wiener's conviction that people have volition and purpose. They maintain that cybernetics is actually another "science" of society, like Marxism and race theory, that reduces people to predetermined cogs.

Wiener spent a great deal of his later life opposing this fatalistic and over-reaching interpretation of cybernetics. He saw the truths of cybernetics to be instead a challenge and warning: Humans are different from machines because we choose to be so, not because of chemistry or God. We can create machine systems out of metal or out of other people; to pretend otherwise is to be a fool or, worse, a liar. He believed that humans are uniquely responsible for their actions and must protect the best interests of one another. We are endowed with values, morals, dignity. The solar system and all its inhabitants may be doomed to die in an entropic heat death, but humanity, conscious of its fate, can maintain its honor and self-respect to the end.

> In a very real sense we are shipwrecked passengers on a doomed planet. Yet even in a shipwreck, human decencies and human values do not necessarily vanquish, and we must make the most of them. We shall go down, but let it be in a manner to which we may look forward as worthy of our dignity.[19]
> —*The Human Use of Human Beings*

Regarding the world as a system of information, feedback, and entropy lends itself to a belief that everything in the universe is marvelously interconnected. Humankind is a part of all wondrous creation. Cybernetics leads to an understanding of how complex systems interact with one another: humans with machines, machines with machines, people with people, cells with bodies, self with society, civilization with environment, and so on. Everything contributes to the general order and disorder of the universe. Everything follows the same laws of cause and effect; every action elicits a reaction.

The circle of "we" begins with ourselves and extends outward to societies, animals, computers, and the environment. We can apply the principles of feedback to understand why we must protect fellow humans, animals, and the environment in order to protect ourselves, for we're all part of the same system. The more conscious we are of this feedback loop between ourselves and the world at large, the more effectively we can sustain democracies, protect natural resources, understand one another, and strive toward ideals of fairness and equality.

> We, as human beings, are not isolated systems. We take in food, which generates energy, from the outside, and are, as a result, parts of that larger world which contains those sources of our vitality. But even more important is the fact that we take in information through our sense organs, and we act on information received.[20] —*The Human Use of Human Beings*

The next step for humankind is to become more conscious and conscientious about how we as individuals, communities, and civilizations communicate. To do so, we must think about how to organize, use, and circulate information for future use. Like machines, we must, through purposeful feedback, develop our ability to *learn* and *adapt*.

AFTERWARD

Wiener was among the first popular science writers, although renown may have come at the expense of repute. The moment cybernetics left the domain of machines and their biological counterparts, it lost a certain legitimacy in the academic world. Critics in academe questioned its premise: What is cybernetics, really, but a loose metaphor stolen from math and engineering and applied grossly to the world at large?

It bears repeating that although Wiener penned *The Human Use of Human Beings* and applied it to his political and social convictions, he objected to cybernetics as reductive social science. But he couldn't prevent the noisy misappropriation of the concept by others who couldn't be bothered to actually understand the mathematics and science on which he based his sweeping statements. In the decades that followed, cybernetics spun into "sociocybernetics," propagated by social scientists such as Erwin Laszlo and Jay Forrester who were heavily criticized for—ironically contrary to Wiener's worldview—advocating a "totalitarian" and "technocratic" systems approach to society. Others, like Walter Buckey and Karl Deutsch, gained some respect by expanding and transforming cybernetics within existing social science and behavioral theory. Cybernetics stayed closer to its mathematical roots in Europe and Russia (which embraced it because, like Marxism, it provided a bridge between physical science and social science). In Europe "cybernetics" departments exist in universities to this day.

The idea from cybernetics that has particularly endured is feedback. Feedback enables all systems—biological, mechanical, environmental, economic, social—to adapt with changes in the environment and correct for them. It empowers these systems with the ability to be complex and to learn. It allows human-machine interaction. Feedback applies to everything from radar devices, weather patterns, and financial markets to human brains and computer interfaces. The complex systems theories that have arisen since the 1980s, including artificial life, chaos theory, bionomics, and genetic algorithms, are all rooted in cybernetic feedback.

The concept of feedback also informs the discussion of how information should circulate, particularly in reference to issues about intellectual property and open-source works. Wiener's belief that information should be shared, not concealed, encourages an Information Revolution that is defined by social progress as well as technological development.

Just as feedback would make its rounds in years to come, so would the prefix *cyber*. Wiener died on March 18, 1964, four years after the word *cyborg* entered the English language, meaning an integrated human–machine organism. In 1983 the science fiction writer Bruce Bethke wrote "Cyberpunk," a short story about computer hackers in a dystopian world. The following year William Gibson, in his cult classic *Neuromancer,* described a nervous system–like computer network called "cyberspace." Gibson's portrayal of this cybernetic world predicts an ultimate human–machine symbiosis, the extension of Leibniz's *calculus ratiocinator,* a plane on which human, machine, and mathematics meet sometime in the future:

> Cyberspace. A consensual hallucination experienced daily by billions of legitimate operators, in every nation, by children being taught mathematical concepts. . . . A graphical representation of data abstracted from the banks of every computer in the human system. Unthinkable complexity. . . . [21]

AS WE SHOULD THINK

VANNEVAR BUSH

We need to substitute for the book a device that will
make it easy to transmit information without trans-
porting material, and that will not only present information to people but also process it for them. . . . To
provide those services, a meld of library and computer is evidently required.

—J. C. R. Licklider

ON APRIL 12, 1945, just as America was emerging vic-
torious from World War II, President Franklin D. Roosevelt
died of a massive cerebral hemorrhage. On August 5, the
A-bomb exploded over Hiroshima, authorized under the new
leadership of Harry Truman. Four days later, the Americans
dropped another A-bomb on Nagasaki. Japan's sun set, and
the cold war soon began.

The link between Roosevelt's brain and the A-bomb is
Vannevar Bush. As head of the wartime Office for Scientific Research and Development (OSRD), Bush was the
president's scientific advisor, his "brain trust." The OSRD
was a war technology think tank of approximately six
thousand civilian scientists, including those who worked
on the Manhattan Project. After the bomb was dropped,
the *New York Times* ran a headline story featuring Bush as
the man who guided the war to its grand finale. Not long

afterward, Metro-Goldwyn-Meyer produced a film, *The Beginning or the End,* which depicted Bush advising an infirm Roosevelt to support the Manhattan Project. To Bush, the A-bomb was the lesser of wartime evils. He believed it could bring peace, stating that "one does not pick up a rock in the presence of an antagonist who carries a gun."*

Vannevar Bush ("Vannevar" rhymes with "believer"—people invariably got it wrong, so he went by "Van") was well dressed and of pedigreed Yankee stock. He even spoke with a pure baritone New England accent. His reputation for bullying and bluntness, tempered by good sportsmanship, was summed up in his favorite phrase, "to carry away the ball" (exaggerating the "ah"). Tall and loose-jointed, Van looked downright athletic in contrast to Wiener's barrel-chested stoutness. A famous photograph of Bush taken by Yousuf Karsh shows him in a tailored suit with his back against a stone wall. Behind thin wire glasses, his right eye is wide and alert and his left eye is slightly squinted, skeptical. He is elegant and enigmatic. In his left hand he holds his trademark hand-wrought pipe, a plume of smoke spiraling upward in a film-noir haze.

Before becoming a movie icon of wartime civil leadership, Bush was vice president and dean at the Massachusetts Institute of Technology, where he had a reputation as a gadget-making whiz. Before World War II he and mathematics professor Norbert Wiener collaborated on many projects, including the construction of an optical computing machine for harmonic analysis. Humble Wiener, who often acknowledged his own clumsiness, deemed Bush "the greatest of apparatus men that America has ever seen, who thinks with his hands as well as with his brain."[1]

Wiener's high opinion of this friend's capabilities didn't apply to Bush's work at the OSRD. Wiener wrote that a heavy wartime administration resembles the organization of a machine, and that such bureaucracies (though not Bush himself) tend to treat people like

---

*Bush, however, opposed the H-bomb and sided with Oppenheimer in voicing that the United States ought to open talks with the Soviet Union. He was on the panel to advise the government on arms control. Truman, unlike Roosevelt, didn't listen to Bush and went ahead with the tests.

machines. His diatribe intimates that Bush's two great strengths, building machines and building human organizations, are rooted in a love of predictability:

> Those who work almost exclusively with gadgets tend to develop a love for them, since they lack the unpredictable factors which affect the operation of the human being. Gadgeteering very easily becomes a sort of religion. . . . There remain many people who have not been as directly confronted as Bush with the disadvantages as well as advantages of machines, and these people follow the tendency to favor the big laboratory and the big administration.[2]

Despite their differences, Bush and his erstwhile friend Wiener shared an enduring passion: to see if machines could process information as people do. This interest encompassed a social agenda: Bureaucracies and factories are designed to make people act like machines; to be in lockstep, rigid, inflexible. What if machines could be more like humans instead of the other way around? If machines were more flexible and responsive, human organizations could change. Bush and Wiener realized that as the amount of electronic communication increases, we have a choice to either think the way machines do, or design machines that handle information and knowledge as we may think. Bush had a vision of a device that could do the latter, and he told the world about it in his manifestos, "As We May Think" (1945) and "Memex Revisited" (1967).

INFORMATION OVERLOAD

A wartime issue of MIT's *Technology Review* features a cartoon in which a cluster of unkempt, long-haired technologist types slouch to the left of a barber's chair. To the right of the chair is a line of crew-cutted military men. The barber in the middle could well be Bush; he transformed scientists into soldiers, of sorts.

Bush was responsible for making MIT the biggest academic defense contractor in the nation during World War II. The newspapers of the 1950s praised him for his organizational abilities and the breadth of his knowledge of engineering. The only other engineer-inventor to achieve such fame as a leader in government was Benjamin Franklin.

Much as Franklin's poor eyesight necessitated the invention of his trademark bifocals, Bush's immense administrative burden—the daily strain of sorting, allocating, researching, analyzing, synthesizing, crosslinking, and filing—spurred his idea for an invention that would perform this work for people. Bush popularized the idea that machines could solve the problem of *information overload*.

During the war years the problem of information overload worsened dramatically. Throughout the 1940s unprecedented amounts of money and human effort were devoted to the Manhattan Project and research in fields such as engineering, chemistry, and metallurgy. Disciplines such as mathematics and physics, once studied in American universities as simply prerequisites to engineering courses, gained importance in their own right. Science and engineering flourished like never before; subdisciplines of sciences spawned their own subdisciplines as teams of specialists developed increasingly recondite knowledge. As a result, disciplines and individuals grew ever more specialized and the connections between them lost.

In *Cybernetics,* Wiener would gripe that the increasing specialization of the human brain might lead to a declining efficiency that would, in turn, lead to human extinction. The same threat seemed to loom over civilization's collective brain. Generalists were outnumbered, overwhelmed by the specialists. And the specialists, mainly out of necessity, operated like cogs in the war machine.

Bush wondered whether all the sprigs of scientific wisdom, if not somehow preserved, would fall from the tree of knowledge. Information must be *connected* to be *relevant,* lest it become forgotten. Knowledge accumulated and stored in massive filing cabinets under lock and key would languish. An idea developed today might not be relevant until some point in the future. What happens, though, if it is forgotten? Application of all this new knowledge would require some means of keeping it available, accessible, and relevant.

. . . .

> Thus far we seem to be worse off than before—for we can
> enormously extend the record; yet even in its present bulk we
> can hardly consult it. This is a much larger matter than merely
> the extraction of data for the purposes of scientific research.
> It involves the entire process by which man profits from his in-
> heritance of acquired knowledge.[3]   — "As We May Think"

. . . .

Like Wiener, Bush saw purposeful communication and feedback as a means to fight entropy. Information that is unused and unorganized will disperse into the unknown. Bush wanted to liberate information from its byzantine card catalogs, musty libraries, and research facilities. He wanted specialists to draw connections between their work and that of others in different disciplines. He wanted them to forge new alloys in science, mixing engineering with the abstract powers of mathematics, the solutions of chemistry, the vitalism of biology. Scientists weren't the only ones suffering under the burden of specialization and information overload. So were lawyers, historians, businesspeople, and administrators. The world, this "greatest of apparatus men" proclaimed, is becoming increasingly complex.

THE MEMEX MANIFESTO

In his manifesto, "As We May Think," Bush presented an antidote to the world's chronic complexity: a mechanical aid that would act as an extension of the human brain.*

. . . .

> The world has arrived at an age of cheap complex devices of
> great reliability; and something is bound to come of it.[4]
>   —"As We May Think"

. . . .

The *Atlantic Monthly*'s educated middle-class readership was the first to read it, in June 1945. Thanks to new print technologies, the world was

---

*Bush originally wrote the article in 1939, but waited until after the war to publish it, allegedly because editors thought it wasn't of interest during the war. They were probably right.

plastered with copies of the article. The *New York Times, Time,* and *Life* popularized it, and newspapers across the United States printed excerpts of it. Headlines blared:

BUILDING TRAILS OF THOUGHT ON THE MEMEX— UNLIKE MEMORY, THEY WOULD NEVER FADE.

A TOP U.S. SCIENTIST FORESEES A POSSIBLE FUTURE IN WHICH MAN-MADE MACHINES WILL START TO THINK.

The title, "As We May Think," encapsulated the article's challenge: Bush wanted to build a machine that can think as we do, through association. He had more in mind than machines as compact, mechanical libraries; he imagined them as *extensions* of the human memory. The particular invention he had in mind would be called a *memex*: mem(ory)ex (as opposed to index). The memex would be a mechanical brain that worked and acted like an organic one.

Bush admired the work of the mathematician Walter Pitts and neurologist Warren McCulloch, active members of Wiener's cybernetics circle. In their seminal work, "A Logical Calculus of the Ideas Immanent in Nervous Activity" (1943), they propagated the cybernetic idea that the physiology of the brain resembles a circuit network. Influenced by Wiener, McCulloch and Pitts viewed neurons as devices that fire in ways similar to signals passing through a telephone wire. Incorporating the principle of feedback theory, they described a loop that exists between the brain and the muscles of the limbs, and concluded that memory is likewise derived from signals sent in a loop of neurons. Neurons firing back and forth, communicating with one another through signals, enable brains to remember things and make decisions accordingly. In the 1940s McCulloch and Pitts designed electronic replicas of such "neural nets" to simulate how neurons fire and form logical processes through association. They hoped these machines would someday track patterns and thereby learn.

Bush's idea of a mechanical aid that would work by association, like the human brain, was new to readers. Bush imagined the memex to be an "enlarged, intimate supplement" of the human memory. The user would store in the computer's memory magazines, newspapers, photographs, manuscripts, books, and letters. He or she would establish links—"trails"—between implicitly related documents. The memex philosophy:

- We should no longer organize information in classes, subclasses, and sub-subclasses.
- Information should be organized by association. When an item is selected, the device should jump to the next item, and then on to a third, and so on. These trails of association are like synapses in the brain.
- Like those of memory, the trails should bifurcate, cross other trails, and become complex.
- If items are used, such trails should be emphasized. If not used, they should fade out.
- The machine should be fast—faster and more intuitive than any existing means of information retrieval.

. . . .

[The human mind] operates by association. With one item in its grasp, it snaps instantly to the next that is suggested by the association of thoughts, in accordance with some intricate web of trails carried by the cells of the brain. It has other characteristics, of course; trails that are not frequently followed are prone to fade, items are not fully permanent, memory is transitory. Yet the speed of action, the intricacy of trails, the detail of mental pictures, is awe-inspiring beyond all else in nature.[5]   —"As We May Think"

. . . .

Bush described the memex as a robust mechanical beast with levers, wires, gears, and pulleys. It would consist of a desk over which slanted translucent screens would dominate. A keyboard would occupy the place right in front of the user, and panels of buttons and levers would be placed to the right. The user, pushing on a lever, might activate the machine to turn out link after link in rapid succession.

Bush's design for the memex followed his most famous invention: the Differential Analyzer, one of the first analog computing machines. It solved calculus equations by modeling differential operations as rotations of wheels, later as electronic signals. First built in the 1920s as an electromechanical, multiton machine, the Differential Analyzer was genuinely revolutionary and made Bush famous. It filled a large room at MIT, where graduate students waited on it hand and foot, servicing their mechanical oracle, which relied utterly on precise calibration of every part—one misalignment and every calculation would be incorrect. Gears and shafts would torturously clank and grind into action, spitting out answers. This, its admirers enthused, is a *thinking* machine. The next-generation hundred-ton $25,000 Rockefeller Differential Analyzer, which employed two thousand vacuum tubes, and Bush's other machine, the rapid selector (or Comparator), were put to great use during the war, breaking code and revealing the movements of a bomb between launch and target. Bush called the Differential Analyzer and the rapid selector the meeting of math and machine, abstraction and reality.

Bush imagined the memex to incorporate not only all the recent technological advances of the Rockefeller Differential Analyzer, but also new ones in the realm of sound and sight. One such technology was the voder, a machine that stunned crowds at the 1939 World's Fair because it created "speech" using modulated signals based on an operator's input on a keyboard. Another was its converse, the vocoder, which translated sound into text. For true multimedia input, Bush envisioned the memex user wearing a camera on his or her head, bowing industriously to photograph an image directly into the machine.

> In one end [of the desk] is stored material. The bulk of the matter is well taken care of by microfilm. Only a small part of the interior is devoted to storage; the rest to the mechanism. Yet if the user inserted 5000 pages of material a day it would take hundreds of years to fill the repository, so he can be profligate and enter material freely. [6]   —"As We May Think"

Most of the material for the memex—books, newspapers, magazines, etc.—would be prepared and purchased on microfilm. In 1945, microfilm was a marvel; at high resolution it could store the entire Bible up to fifty times on one square inch. The idea of microfilm had been around since 1853, and was used in the 1920s and 1930s in banks to record canceled checks, but the microfilm for the memex would be slightly different. Content on "memex" microfilm would arrive with ready-made associative trails to which the user could add his or her own. The rest—longhand notes, letters, memoranda, correspondence, images—could be entered directly into the system by a transparent plate, a benefit of the recent advances in dry cell photography. The user need only push down a lever for the item to be photographed onto a section of memex (microfilm) film and be made permanent. Dry photography was a monumental invention of the 1940s and Bush imagined it put to good use here.

To consult the system or the "record," the user would instruct the memex to peel through reels of microfilm using a microfilm rapid selector (another existing Bush invention), which incorporated photoelectric cell technology and stroboscopic lamps. The selector, scanning thousands of documents per second, would seek items with certain characteristics. Tapping a code on the keyboard would call up any given item. The levers, when pushed and pulled, would navigate through the text. Multiple items could be viewed in juxtaposition on the slanting translucent screens above.

To create trails, one would select a section of text, name it, and insert the name in a code book. The screens would reveal the two items to be joined. The bottom of each screen would feature blank code spaces to which the user would direct a pointer. With a single key stroke, the items would be linked. Trails could be infinitely long, concatenating thousands of documents in an intricate and unprecedented pattern. To skip from one document to another along the trail, the user would merely tap the new code into a keyboard. Whenever any one of the items was on the screen, its associated trails would appear and the corresponding documents could be called up on the adjacent screen. Bush compared the process to forming a new book.

. . . .

> The process of tying together two items is the important thing. . . .
> When numerous items have thus joined together to form a trail, they
> can be reviewed in turn, slowly or rapidly, by deflecting a lever like
> that used for turning the pages of a book. It is exactly as though
> the physical items had been gathered together from widely sep-
> arated sources and bound together to form a new book. It is
> more than this, for any item can be joined into numerous trails.[7]
> —"As We May Think"

. . . .

Bush imagined that the memex would revolutionize not only the organization of information, but its use and form. New encyclopedias and newspapers would contain built-in associative trails. Lawyers would be able to tie one case to the rest of legal history. Scientists and technologists could develop projects by building on the pieces of past projects and finding associations between different disciplines. The problem with specialization would diminish as users found links that transcended time, place, and discipline. For example, a user might draw connections between Native American arrow making and modern ballistics. Users could hop, skip, and jump along trails, finding easy, intuitive ways to draw parallels and patterns. All information could be expressed as pattern and path.

> There is a new profession of trail blazers, those who find delight in the task of establishing useful trails through the enormous mass of the common record. The inheritance of the master becomes, not only his additions to the world's record, but for his disciples the entire scaffolding by which they were erected.[8]   —"As We May Think"

In the best of worlds, the memex would empower the individual as well as the community in which the individual works. Colleagues could share trails by dint of a "reproducer" that would photograph an entire trail on microfilm, to be inserted into another memex. Of course, there was no means of sharing information with every memex out there. Each device, then, would have components that were identical to others—the same subscription microfilms, for example. Yet each station would also be unique, incorporating the user's own trails and personal documents.

The "master" of each machine, Bush wrote, could hand down a personal record, a legacy of public and personal information rendered profound over time and with use. This legacy, alive in the machine, would never die as long as it was in use. Bush believed that the information could live forever.

ANALOG VERSUS DIGITAL

The memex was never born, at least not in the incarnation Bush imagined. He meant it to be an analog machine that, like his famous Differential Analyzer, would require servile maintenance. An analog device—an *analogy machine*—translates a situation of the real world. For example, an old-fashioned wristwatch uses interlocking gears to model the cycles of the earth and sun by which we measure time. The sweep of the hour hand works analogously to the rotation of the earth to measure out a day. Telephones, radios, and stereo speakers exploit the analogy between sound waves and electromagnetic waves. In analog computers, numbers are measured as continuous quantities in moving parts or electrical signals requiring close attention to maintain precision. The brain itself is an analog machine, with neurons that transmit continuous streams of electricity and chemicals.

Digital devices, however, were the future. Electronic digital machines, unlike analog machines, *encode* information as strings of numbers. A code can represent any kind of information: an image, a calculus equation, a sound. Analog machinery would require a different system for each. The digital device does not have the same limits as the analog device. Whereas the analog device depends on precise measurement of continuous quantities, the digital device relies on the vast accumulation of simple discrete measurements. Thus digital devices require many more parts than comparable analog devices, but they are unlimited in precision, reliability, power, and speed.

For almost a decade before "As We May Think" was published, researchers at AT&T and other laboratories had been developing electric digital computing machines. Back in 1937, an engineer named George Stibitz created the first binary adder from a tobacco tin, a couple of flashlight bulbs, and the electromechanical relays from AT&T's telephone switching systems. Claude Shannon's information theory manifesto, "A Mathematical Theory of Communication" (1948), showed that through the use of digital encoding of messages (in a stream of 0s and 1s, for example) and error-checking algorithms, signals can be sent with perfect reliability even through a noisy channel. This is a feat not attainable with analog transmission.

Bush is partially responsible for the fact that government funds weren't allocated to the development of digital computers, an omission for which he was later harshly criticized. He simply didn't see much of a future in what he called those "pure logic machines" whose machinations were comparatively abstract. According to Wiener, he and Bush had a conversation about the digital computer right after the war began. He pitched a proposal to Bush, who was allocating funds through the OSRD, to support a plan to attempt to apply digital scanning technology, the "developing art of the television," to computing machines. Wiener apparently told Bush that the future of high-speed computing could not be analog machines, but rather some "enormous extension of the ordinary desk computer." In response, Bush told him that there were possibilities in the idea, but considered them irrelevant to the war and encouraged him to focus on projects of more immediate practical use.[9]

In 1945, the same year Bush published "As We May Think," mathematician John von Neumann (building directly on work by colleagues John Mauchly, J. Presper Eckert, and Arthur Burks) drafted a report describing a theoretical computer, the EDVAC (Electronic Discrete Variable Automatic Computer). Known later as the closed-storage or "von Neumann architecture," the design would become the standard on which all future computers would be based.

And it was digital.

MEMEX REVISITED

Despite Bush's shortsightedness about digital computers, he was later hailed "the father of modern computing," on account of the vision of "As We May Think." In theory, if not in practice, the memex was the closest thing to a personal computer, although it would have required a room of its very own. Bush's vision of a personal machine was exceptional, even radical, considering that, in 1943, IBM founder Thomas Watson forecasted that the world computer market would be about five computers large. Bush imagined hundreds, if not thousands, of personal memexes.

In 1967 Bush publicly, definitively, reversed his opinion about an analog memex when he wrote "Memex Revisited." By then, the idea of analog computers had largely been scrapped. The glory days of his Differential Analyzer were over. In "Memex Revisited," Bush evangelized the virtues of the digital computer.

. . . .

> [The digital computer] is often called a computer but this is a misnomer. Properly instructed it can do anything a man can

do using pencil and paper, but a million times as fast. The only
things it cannot do are those which distinguish a man from a
machine."[10]   —"Memex Revisited"

. . . .

By the time he wrote "Memex Revisited," Bush could identify the tools
that would make the Information Revolution—including the personal computer—possible. First were the advances in the tiny transistors that amplify
and modulate current or signals; then came semiconductors, photoelectric
cells, and valves, combined with resistors and capacitors. If the memex
were built in the 1960s, it might have taken advantage of magnetic tape
that could contain the informational equivalent of a seventy thousand–frame
TV broadcast. Magnetic tape could be erased, which would make the trail-
building and -erasing functions of the memex easier.* The invention of the
laser in 1958 wrought new possibilities for creating a miniature photo-
graphic document quickly, using a low-sensitivity film ideal for making al-
terations. The laser made holography possible, and Bush imagined
rotatable three-dimensional projections for the new memex. Compression
had become so cheap and effective that the film for an entire private library,
he noted, would "cost a nickel" and the written record of all civilization
could be rolled away in a wheelbarrow.

Bush's conceived the 1967 digital memex as a personal machine that
would *learn from its own experience,* that is, make its own trails. In a
cybernetic feedback loop with its user, he imagined, the machine would
identify associations between documents. If the computer could play
checkers, he reasoned, it could also build trails. His logic: Each move in
checkers requires the machine to allocate to it a value based on past experience through regulatory feedback. Likewise, the memex could assign
values to trails between documents, following the behavior of its operator. The user then could glean whatever was relevant. In future searches,
the memex would "remember" the user's patterns. Just as in checkers

---

*The impermanence of magnetic trails did open new questions: Bush feared that
people might use technology to surreptitiously alter a record without any trace, and
proposed that technologies be made to either prevent that from happening on some
forms of media or instill a code of morals against altering a record without notice.
How to deal with the malleability of digital records remains one of the great moral
and philosophical questions today.

some moves have higher ratings than others, certain trails could have higher ratings (greater relevance). There would be "main trails" and "side trails." Bush's trail-making memex was a prescient model for the search engines and agents of the future World Wide Web.

> [The memex] can build trails for its master. Say he suddenly becomes interested in the diffusion of hydrogen through steel at high temperatures, and he has no trail on it. Memex can work when he is not there. So he gives it instructions to search, furnishing the trail codes likely to have pertinent material. All night memex plods on, at ten or more pages a second. Whenever it finds the words "hydrogen" and "diffusion" in the same item, it links that item to a new trail. In the morning its master reviews the trail, discarding most of the items, and joining the new trail to a pertinent position.[11]   —"Memex Revisited"

Despite its potential as an extension to the human brain, Bush believed that no machine can be a substitute for "mature or creative thought." All the associative trails might be there, but the user would still be responsible for the process of reading, interpreting, and weeding out. The memex could help us simply to store, organize, refine, and make sense of the clutter of information out there. For better or worse, it could not make conclusions for us. It would simply eliminate some of the information overload.

In a 1963 essay titled "Man's Thinking Machines," Bush tackles the question of whether the machine will acquire consciousness or free will, and if it will usurp our own. He thinks not—the machine is a slave, a "far more useful slave than a slave ever was, that understands and obeys us, and that multiplies our thinking power, as the mighty engine multiplies the power of our muscles." Bush argues that the mechanical slave should not rattle our faith in the supremacy of humankind. Rather, it should augment our free will and "moral responsibility." We should use it as a tool for speculation. "Who knows," he writes, "in a hundred years, when some of the present turmoil has settled into form, we may yet be in a better position to contemplate the great mysteries of our existence."[12]

THE MEMEX AS DEMOCRATIZER

The *Atlantic Monthly* editor who published "As We May Think" likened Bush's essay to Ralph Waldo Emerson's 1837 oration, "The American Scholar." Delivered to the Phi Beta Kappa graduates at Harvard University, Emerson's message was that all of us should be scholars, exploring life and literature for ourselves rather than depending upon decreed authority. Self-reliant thinking, the goal of all citizens, is achieved through wide reading and, especially, critical, creative, and divergent thought. He exhorted each person, each "American scholar," to be "an university of knowledges." Such is the relationship between humankind and the sum of its knowledge:

> To the young mind, every thing is individual, stands by itself. By and by, it finds how to join two things, and see in them one nature; then three, then three thousand; and so, tyrannized over by its own unifying instinct, it goes on tying things together, diminishing anomalies, discovering roots running under ground, whereby contrary and remote things cohere, and flower out from one stem. It presently learns, that, since the dawn of history, there has been a constant accumulation and classifying of facts.[13]

Similarly, Bush's intent in "As We May Think" is to provide the tools for humankind to tie trails, diminish differences, and unearth roots. Bush was prophetic in realizing that the skill that would be most valued in the future would be to conceptualize problems and solutions by taking in the whole of a situation.

Like Emerson, his fondest wish was for humankind to absorb enough knowledge and self-knowledge to fortify itself against what Emerson called old world thinking and Bush called modern "totalitarianism." This is the word Bush used to describe what America was up against during the war and throughout the cold war era. The threat to America and to democracy, he proclaimed, could be diminished only by strengthening the country's "manifold blessings of freedom," including its access to information. Specialization, with its narrow-mindedness, furthers totalitarianism. Bush's memex would be a tool to topple the hierarchies of knowledge, liberate ideas from their rigid contexts, and, in so doing, free people from their constraints. The ideals of the American Revolution and the Information Revolution are conjoined in their goals of independent thought and expression.

> A Revolution must be wrought in the ways in which we make, store, and consult the record of accomplishment. . . . It is not just a problem for the libraries, although that is important. Rather, the problem is how creative men think, and what can be done to help them think. It is a problem for how the mass of material shall be handled so that the individual can draw from it what he needs—instantly, correctly, and with utter freedom.[1]
>
> —"Memex Revisited"

Bush understood that information is power. In a communist regime, information is controlled top-down by the state. Totalitarianism begins when the people of a land must submit to only one system. In a democracy, information is meant to be controlled by an open and fair collective of enlightened individuals. The memex would organize information into a structure that resembles a working democracy: a network of knowledge, interconnected, mostly decentralized, with a few "hubs." Used correctly, the system would prevent people from getting, as he said, "smothered in their own product"—an obvious aid to business, medicine, industry, academia, and politics in the free world. It would facilitate the cross-disciplinary innovation on which a democracy and free market thrive. It would be a *democratizer*.

Bush believed that machines that think as we may think would in turn improve the quality of our thoughts and the way we propagate them. He figured that libraries, laboratories, and corporations would be the first to be liberated from the Industrial Revolution–era bureaucracies, because they could afford to buy the memex. As a democratizer, the memex could raze existing hierarchies in the architecture of information, which in turn could lead to restructuring of organizations. The memex could provide interactivity, responsiveness, and ease never before known in creative or administrative work. Although Bush didn't say it explicitly, his vision held the promise that many workers who would otherwise sort and file could someday become knowledge workers, contributing creatively and directly to the important tasks of problem solving and building humankind's "record."

> Presumably man's spirit should be elevated if we can better re-view his shady past and analyze more completely and objectively his present problems. . . . He may perish in conflict before he learns to wield that record for his true good. Yet, in the appli-cation of science to the needs and desires of man, this would seem to be a singularly unfortunate stage at which to terminate the process, or to lose hope as to the outcome.[15]
>
> —"Memex Revisited"

Unfortunately for cold war problem solvers, Bush's vision was far ahead of the technology that could make it possible. The machine as he conceived it would simply be too expensive, problematic, and gargan-tuan for home use or even for anyone but the occasional expert. Bush's answer was that the crème de la crème, those who have risen to the top of a meritocracy, would be the primary users of the memex. In Bush's opinion, the intellectual elite would be responsible for leading the pub-lic toward humanistic goals. But would they really? Or would they hoard their knowledge?

This was the same question that Wiener tackled in his vision of the machine as a tool for great good or great evil. Yes, the technology could be a great democratizer, but it could also be a customized tool for a rul-ing class. Nothing but a personal machine, accessible and affordable to the general public, would mitigate the problem.

AFTERWARD

"Is all this a dream?" Bush asks in "Memex Revisited." He reflects, "It certainly was, two decades ago. It is still a dream, but one that is now attainable." Academics and journal writers generally agreed. In the 1960s and 1970s they revived "As We May Think," hailing its author as a computer visionary. They referred to the 1945 article as "the manifesto for information science," a new term that meant the fusion of old world library practices and new computer technologies.

> To create an actual memex will be expensive, and will demand
> initiative, ingenuity, patience and engineering skill of the highest
> order. But it can be done.[16]   —"Memex Revisited"

The memex dream was attainable—but not in Bush's lifetime, and never exactly as he planned. Indeed, he received a trickle of criticism along with the torrent of praise. Critics have called the memex a superficial and inherently self-defeating design. After all, if documents are coded by their relevance, "as the brain may think," won't the links be overspecialized, situational, and inconsistent? As knowledge evolves, aren't these links prone to change? "A personalized information system may be advantageous for an individual, but has limited usefulness for others," griped one skeptic.[17] Wiener had the same criticism, pointing out that Bush's mechanical aids could be useful, but each new user would have to pioneer his or her own associations among ideas, unless another person— "some individual with an almost Leibnizian catholicity of interest"—already made them.[18] Naturally, the more users, the more associations, the better the tool.

Decades later, Bush was also criticized for not including references to other individuals in his manifesto. The microfilm rapid selector (microfilm with an index code), a main component of the memex, is credited to Bush, but the technology was also invented by a man named Emmanuel Goldberg from Dresden, who had patented it in 1931. Only Bush's version became well-known. Other critics cite as Bush's unsung comrades now-obscure, non-American thinkers, such as Belgian Paul Otlet, who wrote *Traité de Documentation: le livre sur le livre* (1934), in which he described how material can be "tele-read" by means of a great microscope. Eleven years before "As We May Think" was published, Otlet prepared an outline of a personal information system that would convert sound into text, set up each document so that it has its own identity code and can be connected to others, perform automatic retrieval, provide the ability to make additional notes, and self-compute new combinations of recorded data according to set codes. These weren't all the ideas in "As We May Think"—some technologies, such as photoelectric cells, hadn't been invented yet—but Otlet was on the mark.

Even if a handful of European technologists beat Bush by a decade, there is no doubt that it was Bush who popularized the call for a revolution in the organization of information. Indeed, it's likely that Bush simply never heard of Goldberg, Otlet, or any of the others. Bush's manifesto was markedly different from the writings of his European peers. "As We May Think" was intended for a popular audience. Of course, Bush's wartime renown and the fact that he was an American writing for a popular audience had everything to do with successfully spreading the memex idea. "As We May Think" received attention not as a manifesto for the library sciences, but as a manifesto of democracy's and even civilization's future.

In 1974 Vannevar Bush, like his advisee Franklin D. Roosevelt, suffered from a cerebral hemorrhage and passed away. He was eighty-four and had left behind a legacy that includes, in addition to the memex idea, a system for federal funding for science and engineering that would pave the way for ARPAnet (which led to the Internet) and other government-sponsored research.* That same year the first generation of personal computers debuted, thirty-five years after Bush first penned "As We May Think" and seven years after "Memex Revisited." Personal computers solved the two major criticisms of the memex: its over customization to one user and its inability to become an ideal democratizer.

Today's combination of personal computers and the World Wide Web fulfill the memex concept—and more. Millions of networked personal computers all share Bush-style "information trails" in an ever-expanding universe of information. Bush's "trails" have come to be regarded as the first description of hypertext and the memex would be considered a forerunner to the Web itself.†

---

*This system was the National Science Foundation (NSF), the peacetime organization that replaced the OSRD. Bush's original plan for it, written in his 1945 report *The Endless Frontier,* included medical and military divisions. The plan that was finally passed reduced the power of the NSF director. It was a tepid victory for Bush.

†One advantage of the memex concept not yet shared by the Web is the ability of the user to add personal notes in the margins or the text of a document. One attempt to provide this capability on the Web is CritSuite, funded by the Foresight Institute (see Chapter 12).

The most important and lasting legacy of "As We May Think" is its impact on the numerous information revolutionaries who paved the way between the memex and today's technology. In 1945, a young radar technician named Doug Engelbart picked up the issue of *Life* that carried Bush's article in a Red Cross library in the Philippines. Fifteen years afterward, he wrote his own manifesto, "Augmenting the Human Intellect," opened a laboratory devoted to building the technology for human–computer interaction, and built the technology for the first hypertext "trails." J. C. R. Licklider, who pushed for the creation of the ARPAnet, credited Bush as the "main external influence" on his manifesto, *Libraries of the Future*. So did Ted Nelson, who coined the term hypertext.

And the chain went on and on, trails connecting each visionary to others and to the world they were shaping.

DIGITAL BRAINS

ALAN TURING AND JOHN VON NEUMANN

Digital technology could help make this a better world. But we also have got to change our way of thinking.   —Doug Engelbart

THE CYBERNETIC ANALOGY underlying Vannevar Bush's memex and the future of computing suggests that a machine can be built to resemble the brain. The idea can be traced back to the nineteenth century, when human bodies were understood in terms of levers and pulleys, engines and factories. In 1923, the word *robot* was introduced into English from the Czech *robota,* meaning "servitude, forced labor." It was just another step, then, from the indentured machines of the Industrial Revolution to the machine brains of the Information Revolution. All civilization had to do was mechanize thought as well as action.

World War II flushed Western civilization with the confidence that electronic brains could indeed be built. The triumph of the American war engine in World War II infused the 1950s with an attitude that all problems, no matter how complex, could be mastered by equally complex, but fully designed, solutions. America developed the atomic bomb, radar, and aircraft carriers. The A-bomb went from the abstruse mathematics of quantum mechanics to world destroyer in fewer than twenty years. If they could do that, the same mathematician-scientists could certainly develop intelligent computers in the next twenty years.

Alan Turing and John von Neumann did just that. They are the minds who built the computers—the digital brains—of the future. Although they are certainly not the only ones who deserve credit, their inventions and discoveries encompass all the crucial ideas that led to the modern digital computer and beyond. Of the many technical papers both wrote, only a handful of these documents can truly be called manifestos of the Information Revolution. For Turing, they are "On Computable Numbers, with an Application to the Entscheidungsproblem" (1936), *Proposed Electronic Calculator* (also called the ACE Report, 1946), and "Computing Machinery and Intelligence" (1950), one written in his early career, the other two written toward the end of his tragically short life. For von Neumann, it is *First Draft of a Report on the EDVAC* (1945), which, partly based on Turing's "Computable Numbers," outlines the progenitor of all modern computers. With these writings, the two mathematicians made the conceptual leaps that allowed the engineers to get to work. They planted the seeds of revolution.

A WORLD OF UNCERTAINTY

Ironically, the era of technological supremacy has its roots in scientific uncertainty, beginning with the breakdown of confidence in the clockwork universe and humankind's perfect knowledge of its mechanisms. In 1905 Einstein and others had shattered the confidence in physics with work on relativity, quantum theory, and statistical mechanics. In 1926, Werner Heisenberg and Erwin Schrödinger developed distinct formulations of quantum theory, opening new vistas of incomprehension. In particular, Heisenberg's uncertainty principle seemed to say that nothing in the universe really happened unless it was watched. In the following years, Wolfgang Pauli and von Neumann showed that Schrödinger's and Heisenberg's quantum theories, which seemed very different, shared the same mathematical core, and couldn't be ignored.

By Turing's era, the 1930s, Kurt Gödel had similarly destroyed the confidence in mathematics with his incompleteness theorem. At a 1928 international mathematical congress, the German logician David Hilbert formally presented three questions: Is mathematics complete, consistent, and decidable?* With the usual confidence of his age, Hilbert expected the answer to all three questions to be yes. He believed that the essential structure of mathematics did not contain paradox, though humankind had not yet discovered such structure.

At the very same congress, young Gödel introduced his proof, now known as Gödel's incompleteness theorem, that mathematics is not complete. He made the radical realization that because all mathematics is composed of symbols, the objects of mathematics (such as numbers) are inextricable from the structure of mathematics (such as truth and proofs), making paradoxes unavoidable.

Previous mathematicians and logicians showed that all mathematics can be wholly composed of statements about symbols. All the mathematics of geometry, which seem to depend on diagrams of lines and curves, can be expressed fully in a series of mathematical statements, no different from algebra or logic. Which symbols are chosen makes no difference. You can do the same math by writing $1 + 1 = 2$ or 1 gibble 1 gobble 2, as long as "gibble" and "gobble" are defined to mean the same thing as + and =, respectively.

Gödel devised a simple encoding mechanism by which any mathematical statement, such as $1 + 1 = 2$, would be encoded uniquely as a number. Every so-called Gödel number could be read either as a number or as a mathematical statement. Using Gödel numbers, he was able to essentially show that the statement "This statement is unprovable" can be constructed in any robust mathematical system.[†] Since that statement can't be proven or disproven, any mathematical system that allows it can't be complete.

---

*A mathematical theory (or system) consists of true and false statements, provable from a set of axioms; if all true statements are provable, the theory is *complete;* if it is not possible to prove a statement and its negation, the theory is *consistent;* if the theory includes a mechanism for separating all provable statements from unprovable ones, the theory is *decidable.* An inconsistent theory is trivially complete, because all statements, true or false, are provable.

†More specifically, the statement is "There is no Gödel number which encodes a proof of this statement." The statement must be either true or false. If it is false, that means a proof of the statement exists, which means that false statements in the system are provable, which we certainly don't want. So the statement must be true. Any proof must be able to be written in a finite number of steps, so all proofs are encodable as Gödel numbers. Therefore the statement isn't provable.

Gödel's proof involved a profound realization about the nature of information: In a closed, self-defined system, there is no distinction between number and symbol, object and structure, meaning and data. Only by stepping outside the system can one say that anything is true or false in any meaningful way. And if you speak only in the language of the system you are bound by its rules, the very rules that guarantee incompleteness.

As knowledge of Gödel's work spread, people began applying the incompleteness theorem in unusual ways. Some concluded human thought suffers the same limitations as mathematical logic. Some mathematicians found the theorem cause for despair; others regarded it optimistically, embracing the near-mystical uncertainty of whether or not certain theorems were indeed provable. Some asserted that it was a proof of God's existence or the magic of human intellect and consciousness. There are limitations on logic and mathematics, they said, but human emotion and thought are unbounded.

In the end, will this separate humans from machines? Alan Turing would say no.

THE TURING MACHINE

Turing followed Gödel's work with great interest when introduced to it as a graduate student at Cambridge University in the spring of 1935. Turing also met von Neumann that spring, when the famed mathematician from Princeton University gave a lecture at Cambridge.*

In April 1936, Turing presented a paper, "On Computable Numbers, with an Application to the Entscheidungsproblem," which featured a theoretical computer (later known as the Turing machine) and answered Hilbert's question about decidability, the *Entscheidungsproblem*.

In terms of logic, the decidability problem asks whether there is a definite method, an algorithm, that can determine whether any given statement is provable. Another formulation of the problem asks whether a definite

---

*Turing requested, and received, von Neumann's *Mathematische Grundlagen der Quantunmechanik* as a school prize when he was twenty years old, in October 1932. Von Neumann's physics of mathematical logic, rather than experimentation and hypothesis, appealed to Turing's way of thinking.

method can be found for the decimal expansion of any and every number. For example, there are algorithms that allow one to generate the digits of pi, or the square root of two, to any desired accuracy. People would compute these numbers using tables and formulas, often for industrial applications. These people, usually young women, who rigorously followed sets of rules to produce the desired results, were known as computers.

> The behavior of the computer at any moment is determined by the symbols which he is observing, and his "state of mind" at that moment.[1]   —"Computable Numbers"

Turing knew that if he could systematize how human computers worked, he could tackle the decidability problem. But how does one systematize a state of mind? In his paper he introduced a brilliant insight that unlocked the problem.

> We will suppose that the computer works in such a desultory manner that he never does more than one step at a sitting. The note of instructions must enable him to carry out one step and write the next note. Thus the state of progress of the computation at any stage is completely determined by the note of instructions and the symbols on the tape.[2]
>   —"Computable Numbers"

Turing's crucial realization is that the note of instructions could be more than just how to do a step of the calculation; it could also be what the next note of instructions must be. With that, the state-of-mind problem disappears, replaced by a self-contained logical system. Turing could imagine such a logical calculating machine later known as the Turing Machine. His calculator is as simple as possible, and comprises three parts:

1. A calculating machine,
2. A set of instructions,
3. An infinite tape (like a strip of paper) for input and output.

The machine reads, writes, and erases marks on the tape, governed by the instructions. The only actions possible for the machine are to write or erase a mark, move left or right, or stop. To make the calculator even simpler, the tape is broken up into separate squares. The machine can read or write only one square at a time, then it must move to an adjacent square.

What allows the machine to perform interesting calculations is its finite set of instructions. Each instruction tells the machine what to do, and then which instruction to follow next. The instructions are conditional on what the machine reads on the tape. With only four such rules, it's possible for the machine to do addition. With not many more, it can perform multiplication, subtraction, or logical calculations. In fact, it would be possible to devise a rule set to allow the machine to perform such tasks as checking spelling. It would take a very large rule set to encode an entire dictionary, but this theoretical machine has no memory limit.

Turing's system includes both the set of instructions and what's written on the tape. The set of instructions, which Turing called the *standard description,* uniquely defines the operation of the machine. A copy of the standard description could be kept on the tape.

In "Computable Numbers," Turing described a universal computing machine that could compute any computable sequence, writing down the tables of instructions in a few pages. If this universal computing machine (U) is supplied with a tape on the beginning of which is the standard description of some computing machine (M), then U would compute the same sequence as M. The universal machine could *emulate* any other computing machine. Although it seems obvious today to have a computer perform many different computations, Turing's idea was revolutionary at the time. All computers in the future would resemble the Turing machine.

The publication of "Computable Numbers" went unnoticed in 1936. About ten years later it was recognized as one of the seminal papers, the manifestos, of the computer revolution. It was not until the end of World War II that Turing would be able to begin building from his blueprint.

THE IVORY TOWER

Inspired by von Neumann's visit to Cambridge, Turing applied for and was awarded a visiting fellowship at Princeton. He arrived in the United States in September 1936, excited to attend the university that had become the lodestone of mathematicians and physicists, including Turing's heroes, Gödel, von Neumann, and Alonzo Church. Whereas Harvard and the Massachusetts Institute of Technology were the centers of American science, Princeton collected the European crème de la crème. It was the most old world of the new world schools. Steeped in money and tradition, it was the perfect refuge from the Great Depression, which then engulfed not only the United States but the entire Western world.

At Princeton, Turing had regular contact with von Neumann, who in the 1920s had been the wünderkind of mathematics in Germany. Von Neumann had come to America from Hungary in 1930 after marrying his first wife. That year he began his lifelong connection to Princeton, while still lecturing in Germany in the summers. In 1933 he became one of the original mathematics professors at the new Institute for Advanced Study, whose ranks included none other than Albert Einstein. The Institute received funding from the soap company Procter & Gamble; people soon began calling the idealistically elite academic enclave the Ivory Tower.

"Johnny" von Neumann, as everyone in America knew him, threw the most notoriously wild parties in mild-mannered Princeton. He amused his guests by dancing feverishly in the business suits he always wore, and dazzled his colleagues with the calculations he'd pull out of the air like rabbits out of hats. Norbert Wiener called him "Gentleman Johnny," in reference to his debonair ways and his mild and sophisticated European accent. Johnny relished adoration, particularly from women impressed by his wit and fame. He developed a reputation as a raconteur and libertine, and peppered his conversation with off-color jokes, of which he had an inexhaustible supply.

Von Neumann's friends noticed that he used such jokes as a defense mechanism. Whenever people tried to draw him into a disagreeable situation, he'd lighten the mood and change the subject with a titillating reference. That way, he avoided arguments with people who knew less than he did about a subject or could argue less convincingly, which was very often the case. Von Neumann was very aware of his intellectual expectations.

Although he felt he never quite lived up to his reputation as a child prodigy, others considered him the best mathematician of the century.

It is unlikely that the graduate student Alan Turing attended very many of Professor von Neumann's parties. Turing passed his time at Princeton with much less attention, as befit a bright, shy graduate student. His chief extracurricular activity was playing field hockey with other British graduate students against local girls' teams. He regularly wrote to his mother back in England, keeping her abreast of his academic progress, since there was little other news. Princeton was a strictly all-male school, and adhered to strictly all-male heterosexual stereotypes. Turing, homosexual, atheistic, found few friends at conservative Princeton and no apparent lovers. He was living an imitation game.

Turing slowly gained recognition from the famous and popular von Neumann. He designed and built an electrical binary multiplier in the fall of 1937, a first step on the path to the digital computer. Impressed, von Neumann wanted this bright student to work under him at Princeton, and offered him a research assistantship in the spring of 1938. Turing declined, opting to go back to King's College, Cambridge University. He passed his Ph. D. examination and returned to England just as war was erupting in Europe.

BUILDING THE ELECTRONIC BRAIN

Turing was not the only graduate student working on ideas crucial to the Information Revolution in the years leading to World War II. Up the coast at MIT, the lanky and dapper Claude E. Shannon, the man who would later found the field of information theory, worked on his master's thesis, "Symbolic Analysis of Relay and Switching Circuits," the first formalization of the relationship between mathematical logic and electrical engineering. Shannon wrote his thesis under the direction of Vannevar Bush, on whose Differential Analyzer Shannon worked from 1936 to 1938. His thesis was inspired by a logical apparatus he built with electromagnetic relays, similar to the binary multiplier Turing built at Princeton.

Shannon's analysis is necessary to the construction of a digital computer, because it lays down how to translate the theory Turing set forth in "Computable Numbers" into an electrical engineering reality. Engineers working on electromechanical devices, from calculators to telephone switchboards, often used devices known as "relays," which could be switched between two positions to open or close a circuit. Shannon recognized that circuits using relays followed the discrete mathematics of logic and arithmetic.

Shannon's thesis transformed relay and switching (a.k.a. digital) circuit design from an art into a science, by showing how to analyze such circuits using Boolean algebra. Boolean algebra allows the combination of propositions, which may be either true (1) or false (0), with the logical operators AND and OR and NOT. Thus, given the propositions x and y, both of which may be true or false, one can form the compound proposition x AND y, which is true only if both x and y are true.

Shannon realized that switching circuits correspond exactly to logical propositions: open circuits are "true," and closed circuits are "false." Circuits x and y connected in parallel are equivalent to compound proposition x AND y. The mathematics of switching circuits is exactly the same as the mathematics of prepositional logic. The power of computers is the binary power of duality: true/false, on/off, yes/no, 1/0. In the paper, Shannon demonstrated the power of this knowledge by devising an electric adder and an electric combination lock, and showing rigorously why they worked, without resorting to guesswork or intuition.

The idea of equating switches with logical operations is now so ingrained that Shannon's paper is nearly forgotten. We now describe digital circuits in terms of AND gates, OR gates, NOT gates, etc.—the language of Boolean algebra.

Another significant influence on the modern digital computer, as well as on Bush's memex and artificial intelligence, was a paper titled "A Logical Calculus of the Ideas Immanent in Nervous Activity," published in 1943 by the neurologist/mathematician team Warren McCulloch and Walter Pitts. Excited by Turing's "Computable Numbers," they examined the behavior of neurons, the cells that make up the brain. They reported actual observations of neuronal function, and then showed how, by making certain simplifying assumptions, one could treat a neural network (i.e., the brain) as a logical machine. Independently of Shannon, they applied Boolean algebra to the operations of a neural net.

McCulloch and Pitts described how the most complex and magical processes—ideas—arise from the accumulation, the calculus, of the simplest particles of logic. They believed that the essential nature of neurons was that they could be either quiescent or excited—the same binary duality Shannon examined. Intelligence and consciousness were just the complex interaction of simple logical switches.

To understand McCulloch and Pitts's vision, imagine a checkerboard of alternating light and dark squares. Now imagine that the squares are connected by logical rules so that flipping one square, say, from dark to light, changes the colors of other squares. Even with only the sixty-four squares of the checkerboard, the patterns that can arise are unimaginably varied. Now imagine a cloud of a billion checkerboards, all interconnected. The unfathomable structure of the cloud is illuminated by lightning flashes of the tiny light squares flickering among the dark squares. If we delve into the cloud and analyze a single checkerboard, we can follow the rules that flip dark to light, zero to one, false to true, quiescent to excited. But the behavior of the entire cloud is beyond comprehension. That is the logical calculus of the ideas immanent in nervous activity.

Any machine that, like the checkerboard cloud, calculates using discrete processes can be emulated by a Turing machine. If the human brain is a discrete calculating machine, then the brain is a computer and it should be possible to construct a computer to emulate the brain. McCulloch and Pitts were guided by this reasoning even before anyone had successfully built a digital computer.

"A Logical Calculus," inspired by Turing and Wiener, went on to inspire all the cyberneticists in the 1940s and 1950s. Scientists of every stripe were taken by the idea of the electronic brain. The science of feedback that Wiener originally applied to servomechanical devices, such as the antiaircraft radar device, now had import for the brain, for thought. Wiener's conceptions of the connections between negative feedback and thought could now be studied in terms of neuronal activity. It seemed that the great mystery of the mind was about to be unlocked. But first we needed the computer architecture that could do it.

THE ELECTRONIC DISCRETE VARIABLE AUTOMATIC COMPUTER (EDVAC)

Throughout World War II von Neumann was the top mathematician in the Manhattan Project, helping the physicists calculate the explosive nuclear forces of the atom bomb. In general, his life's work was the search for mathematical and logical order in complex chaotic systems; he wanted to know how complexity could arise out of simple order. Explosions, economics, quantum physics, the brain, life—he searched for ways of simplifying the system to its central order. Like Turing and Wiener, he was an atheist, seeing God as needlessly complicating. Appeals to religion don't explain complex systems in terms of simpler ones; they explain complex systems in terms of a more complex system.

Von Neumann's obsession with chaos and complexity stood him in good stead; he had studied the mathematics of turbulence and explosions since the mid-1930s. As early as 1937, less than a decade after he first came to America to lecture at Princeton, he began advising the U.S. military. By the end of the war, von Neumann, like Bush, was a political as well as scientific figure, pushing the United States to take a strong stance against the rising power of the Soviet Union. The fact that he was an immigrant from Hungary made him by nurture hateful of Russia, even as a wartime ally.

While working on the complex mathematical problems posed by the construction of the atomic bomb, von Neumann found great encouragement in the development of high-speed computing devices that could crunch numbers automatically. He became personally involved in the development of the ENIAC (Electronic Numerical Integrator And Computer), the first large-scale project to build the digital computer.* The ENIAC was developed to aid the war effort but wasn't fully operational until after the war ended. The ENIAC team, led by John W. Mauchly and J. Presper Eckert, attracted von Neumann's participation. They discussed what the successor to the ENIAC should be like; from those discussions arose von Neumann's computing manifesto, *First Draft of a Report on the EDVAC* (1945).†

---

*A number of machines vie for the claim of "first computer." Which machine deserves the title depends on the criteria one uses to define a computer. One can create a coherent lineage by focussing only on the machines that led directly to today's ubiquitous computers. One project that directly influenced von Neumann was Howard Aiken's Harvard Mark I, built around the same time as the ENIAC.

†The ENIAC was the Neanderthal of computing; very like the Cro-Magnon, and doomed. It was the first large-scale electronic computer, but it used parallel processing and was unprogrammable. Its development and construction lasted from glimmerings in 1941 to full operation at the end of 1945, by which time the plans for the EDVAC were already in place.

This draft, riddled with typographical errors and missing sections, changed the world. In it, von Neumann describes in detail how to build a working digital computer, incorporating his own ideas with those of Arthur Burks, Herman Goldstine, Mauchly, and Eckert. Von Neumann, more than anyone else on the team, understood that the computer was a logical machine, more than just a calculator. Nearly every computer in the world now follows his design, which became known as the *von Neumann architecture*.

Like Wiener and Bush, von Neumann was captivated by the brain-computer analogy. He recognized it would be possible to build something like a brain using electronic parts. The relay elements of a digital computer, such as vacuum tubes, which lock into particular states (for example, on or off), are much like neurons.

> It is worth mentioning, the neurons of higher animals are definitely elements in the above sense. They have all-or-none character, that is two states: Quiescent and excited.[3]
>
> —*First Draft of a Report on the EDVAC*

Von Neumann admitted that neurons are more complex than vacuum tubes, but he maintained that if the simplifying assumptions McCulloch and Pitts made in "A Logical Calculus" were used, the functions of neurons could be imitated. Von Neumann used McCulloch and Pitts's clear notation for idealized neuronal connections to describe the computing pathways of the EDVAC. With that understanding, within the framework of his own explorations in mathematics and knowledge of the Turing machine, he broke down the computer into separate "organs," analogous to the separate regions of the brain:

- A central arithmetical part;
- A logical control;
- Memory;
- Systems for input and output.

Neurologists had divided the types of neurons in the body into three classes: *Sensory neurons* detect light, pain, sound, touch, and taste; *motor neurons* drive the muscles that allow us to act; and *associative neurons* in the brain take input from the sensory neurons and direct output to the motor neurons. Von Neumann compared his input and output organs to sensory and motor neurons, and the central computing organs to associative neurons. He wasn't just describing the outline for a computer; he was describing a logical, constructable model for an *autonomous creature.*

Von Neumann recognized that technology had at last caught up with Turing's idea of a universal computing machine. Turing's machine was drastically simple, but it could perform complex tasks through the accumulation of results stored on an infinite tape. Von Neumann followed that principle: His design called for simple, one-at-a-time calculations, backed up by a huge memory. The simple arithmetical unit, as in Turing's theoretical machine, could efficiently perform binary arithmetic $(+,\times,-,\div,\sqrt{})$. The logical control, again not too large, could understand and sequence the four kinds of simple instructions:

1. arithmetical calculations;
2. orders to cause the transfer of a number from one place to another;
3. orders to transfer its own connection with the memory to a different point in memory, with the purpose of getting its next order from there;
4. orders controlling the operation of the input and output systems.

The interesting challenge was the memory. Von Neumann determined that an effective computer would need a large and consolidated memory.

. . . .

Any device which is to carry out long and complicated sequences of operations (specifically of calculations) must have a considerable memory. . . . While it appeared that various parts of this memory have to perform functions which differ somewhat in their nature and considerably in their purpose, it is nevertheless tempting to treat the entire memory as one organ, and to have its parts even as interchangeable as possible for the various functions enumerated above.[4]

—First Draft of a Report on the EDVAC

. . . .

The "tempting" idea of using the same memory to store all the memory functions, including numbers, instructions, intermediate calculations, and look-up tables, is a profound one. To a person who understands the intent of a calculation the distinction between a number and a command is obvious and essential; but to a computer, it's all the same thing. This insight reaches back to the Turing machine, which could treat its input as either a number or a command, depending on the designer's intent.

The EDVAC, unlike its predecessors, would follow the commands stored in its electronic memory, changeable in the blink of an eye, following the inspiration of Turing's universal computing machine. Previous calculating machines were designed for a particular task, like the impressive Colossus, an electronic computer designed by Turing during World War II to decrypt codes generated by a German machine. Even the ENIAC, which was not tied to a particular problem, required rewiring to perform new tasks, a process that took minutes or hours. By feeding the instructions into the electronic memory, engineers could change the operation of the EDVAC in seconds without changing the hardware.

The von Neumann architecture allows a computer to make choices. More specifically, the computer can compare the values of two different numbers to determine which instruction to follow next. Though this doesn't seem remarkable, previous computers lacked this ability.* This simple *conditional branching* is what truly makes computers cybernetic machines, able to respond, adapt, and learn. A few instructions, when run, can branch out in a myriad directions. Even without random or unpredictable input, conditional branching allows the computer's behavior to be of sufficient complexity to be unpredictable.

Conditional branching also allows the same instruction to be used over and over again, until some condition is met. A program doesn't have to have many different instructions to perform useful tasks. Turing's

---

*Other than some abortive or not widely known precursors, such as Charles Babbage's unbuilt Analytical Engine and the German Konrad Zuse's Z3, destroyed in World War II.

analogy is this: "Suppose Mother wants Tommy to call at the cobbler's every morning on his way to school to see if her shoes are done, she can ask him afresh every morning. Alternatively, she can stick up a notice once and for all in the hall which he will see when he leaves for school and which tells him to call for the shoes, and also to destroy the notice when he comes back if he has the shoes with him."[5]

Von Neumann's design relied only on simple parts—a whole lot of them (the memory would require thousands upon thousands of units). The simple calculating engine would chug through one little calculation at a time. This design went against the principles of industrial age machinery, which favored complex, highly specialized instruments. The EDVAC instead exploited the speed of electronics to balance the limits of any individual calculation. Just as the brain works by interconnecting billions of simple neurons, the EDVAC was designed to work by interconnecting thousands of simple parts. A thousand calculations doesn't take long if each takes less than a millisecond. With each generation of technological advance, the computer parts grew smaller, cheaper, and faster, doubling the power of von Neumann–architecture computers every eighteen months. Today's desktop computers, by and large still following the EDVAC design, churn through billions of calculations in a second.

With von Neumann's *First Draft*, the age of analog computers, which had flourished under Vannevar Bush, was over. The EDVAC was the practical representation of the universal Turing machine. It could emulate any other computing machine, including Bush's Differential Analyzer, if properly programmed. But the digital EDVAC, unlike the analog machine, was cheaper, faster, and could be reprogrammed for an utterly different task by loading a new program.

As the mind transcends the body, the program transcends the machine. Like the Turing machine, the von Neumann architecture separated the physical calculating parts from the task. By storing commands in the electronic memory, it began to free the computer engineers from the physical constraints of the system. A new class of engineers arose: programmers. Now people could simply type out a program of instructions and feed it into the machine. Not only did the programmers not have to worry about the electromechanical operation of the machine, they didn't even have to understand how it worked. Programs could be studied, written, and improved, all distinct from the machine. Computing was hereby separated into software and hardware.*

TURING'S RISE

While von Neumann worked on the EDVAC, Turing spent World War II in Britain, developing algorithms and computing machines to break codes generated by the German Enigma machines. He transformed cryptography and cryptoanalysis (code-making and breaking) from an erudite art of secrets hidden in rhyme and ciphers into a statistical analysis of streams of numbers.

By 1941, Turing was at the center of a top-secret British division whimsically named the Government Code and Cypher School, secreted away at a mansion called Bletchley Park, formed for the new modern world of machine-generated codes and radio transmissions. Turing, at the ripe old age of twenty-nine, led the division, which churned with creative anarchy. Young mathematicians ran the roost in a hierarchy of the fittest, utterly ignoring official rank. The meritocracy could be vicious; all knew quite well who were slow and who were insightful. Bletchley Park, in sum, emulated Turing's own mode of thought: wild, energetic, and scattered, but ruthlessly logical and persistent.

They were looking at all possible information, even the seemingly uninteresting information from weather stations and cargo transports, to construct a complete model, a virtual analog, of the German war effort based entirely on paper and punch card. Successes came to Bletchley Park as the codebreakers managed to claw their way into many of the Enigma codes by piecing together all the information they collected: Their internal communication defeated with miraculous

---

*The EDVAC was actually never fully completed, since the Institute for Advanced Study remained inhospitable to pursuits that weren't entirely theoretical. However, numerous computing projects founded upon the EDVAC model sprang up around the world, reaching operation in the early 1950s and in commercial production by IBM and Sperry Rand by the late 1950s.

frequency the enemy's attempt to prevent communication. Meaning arose out of the complex coordination of individually uninteresting or meaningless pieces of knowledge, in much the same way that life springs from the coordination of simple molecules or ideas from the cross-firings of neurons.

The chaotic world didn't last forever; Bletchley Park found form and formalization and had less need of Turing's nearly mad drive. By late 1942 he was able to turn some of his attention to related crypto-logical endeavors, and went back to the United States to teach the Americans how to crack the Enigma. Early the next year, he traveled from Washington, D.C., to Bell Labs near New York City. One of the researchers at Bell Labs was Claude Shannon, who found in Turing a kindred spirit. They discussed the implications of "Computable Num-bers," namely, that it should be possible to build a machine to emu-late the brain. Their teatime conversations in the Bell Labs cafeteria greatly stimulated both men, who discussed the new world of electronic information and communication. Turing once exclaimed, in his high-pitched voice, "Shannon wants to feed not just *data* to a Brain, but *cultural* things! He wants to play *music* to it!"

Shannon found his British colleague to be "beyond Good and Evil," like Nietzsche, with intellectual and emotional passion, but little under-standing of society's rules. Indeed, Turing had wretched manners and lit-tle respect for rule makers and bureaucrats, whether they came from politics or academia.

OF HUMANS AND MACHINES

As the war in Europe ended, Turing, like von Neumann, turned his attention to creating the digital computer. By 1946, he had published his first draft of *Proposed Electronic Calculator,* also known as the ACE Report, for the construction of the Automatic Computing Engine—a dig-ital computer—at the National Physical Laboratory.

Like von Neumann, Turing noted that a programmable computer can have a fixed set of hardware, with new tasks being added through input; that a useful computer requires a large, fast memory; and that the hardware should be simple. After all, it was he who had revealed that the very simple universal machine could properly emulate any more complex computer.

> [Digital computing machines] are in fact practical versions of the universal machine. There is a certain central pool of electronic equipment, and a large memory. When any particular problem has to be handled the appropriate instructions for the computing process involved are stored in the memory of the ACE and it is then "set up" for carrying out that process.[6]
>
> —*Proposed Electronic Calculator*

Instead of "set up" we now say "programmed." Turing noted that the actual workings of a computer should have minimal impact on interface. Though the ACE used binary arithmetic, there was no reason its results and instructions couldn't be in decimal form, since the computer could easily carry out decimal to binary conversion through additional programming, rather than additional hardware.

> There are many fussy little details which have to be taken care of, and which according to normal engineering practice would require special circuits. We are able to deal with these points without modification of the machine itself, by pure paperwork, eventually resulting in feeding in appropriate instructions.[7]
>
> —*Proposed Electronic Calculator*

Turing explicated the idea of having programs be made up of hierarchies of subroutines. He described the possibility of remote terminals. He also specified potential uses for the ACE, including producing military ballistics tables and other arithmetical calculations, solving electrical circuit problems, solving a jigsaw puzzle, and playing "very good chess."

Although computers by definition have their behavior predetermined by a set of rules, Turing explained, the rules can allow for self-modification. Therefore, predetermination does not mean predictability. It's possible to program a computer to have the capacity to learn.

Turing had written down an essential plan in *Proposed Electronic Calculator*, but he couldn't perform the necessary social maneuvering to make it happen. With the war over, the various governmental, academic, and business concerns organized to construct the ACE squabbled and developed competing projects. The end result found Turing working on a less ambitious computer at Manchester University dubbed the Mark I or "Manchester Baby," which was in the first stages of operation before he joined the project, in 1948. Meanwhile, the ACE project commenced under new individuals, who rewrote history to minimize Turing's invention.

THE TURING TEST

While Turing worked on the Mark I, tackling both theoretical and technical problems, he pondered the potential of the computer in the years ahead. He was aware of the predictions and expectations of the American cyberneticists; after all, he helped spur them with the Turing machine he proposed in "Computable Numbers." He loved the possibility of teaching a computer, since he believed that the mind was no more (or less) magical than the arms or legs. Humanity, to him, lay not in brilliance, but in love and wonder. Brainwise, humans and computers could be the very same, as far as he was concerned.

The ideas percolating in Turing's mind coalesced in his remarkable manifesto, "Computing Machinery and Intelligence," first published in the philosophy journal *Mind* in 1950, the same year Norbert Wiener published *The Human Use of Human Beings*.

> I propose to consider the question, "Can machines think?" This should begin with definitions of the meaning of the terms *machine* and *think*.[8] —"Computing Machinery and Intelligence"

Turing maintains that the question of computer intelligence is poorly framed, since no clear definition of intelligence or thought can be formed. Rather, he argues, we should test whether a computer, in a controlled conversation, could convince a person that it, too, is human. If it can, then we should consider it to be, in some real sense, capable of thought. This test is now known as the *Turing Test*.

The Turing Test is based on a parlor game known as the "imitation game," wherein an interrogator tries to guess which of two people, both claiming to be female, is the woman and which is the man. The interrogator communicates with the people only through written or typewritten messages.

It's not too great a supposition that Turing was having fun at being able to publish in an entirely serious manner a scenario in which a man plays at being a woman. As a homosexual living in a heterosexual world, Turing had to play his own version of the imitation game at all times. He was able to turn the tables in this thought experiment. Imagine one of Turing's humorless bureaucratic nemeses writing, "My hair is shingled, and the longest strands, are about nine inches long."

He then wonders what would happen if the interrogator cross-examines a computer and a person, both claiming in their typewritten messages to be human.

> Will the interrogator decide wrongly as often when the game is played like this as he does when the game is played between a man and a woman? These questions replace our original, "Can machines think?"[9]
>
> —"Computing Machinery and Intelligence"

Turing argued in the paper that a definition of intelligence that goes beyond communication is meaningless; if some entity can carry a conversation, that entity should be said to be intelligent. He considered the question of whether machines can think meaningless. What's important is how they act.

If Turing's gender imitation game is instead regarded as a sexuality game, the connection with intelligence becomes much clearer. Turing had firsthand knowledge that physical appearances did not separate heterosexuals from homosexuals. Sexuality is a matter of communication, not equipment. Turing argued that intelligence likewise did not have to be attached to a brain of neurons, but is a matter of results. The operations of the brain must in some way be computable; the difference between neurons and vacuum tubes is inconsequential. If something acts intelligent, it *is* intelligent.

WHAT IS INTELLIGENCE?

In 1950, Turing knew that the computer couldn't pass the Turing Test. But future computers would, he believed.

. . . .

> In about fifty years time it will be possible to program computers with a storage capacity of about 10^9 to make them play the imitation game so well that an average interrogator will not have more than 70 per cent chance of making the right identification after five minutes of questioning....I believe that at the end of the century the use of words and general educated opinion will have altered so much that one will be able to speak of machines thinking without expecting to be contradicted.[10]
>
> —"Computing Machinery and Intelligence"

. . . .

Is the Turing Test a reasonable test for intelligence? In embracing the similitude of humans and machines, Turing sidesteps the belief of cyberneticists, that feedback and communication are both intangible (information, speech, knowledge) and tangible (action, effect, change). To speak of thought and intention meaningfully, we must look at the change in the physical world and then the effects of that physical change on thought and intention. Turing doesn't argue against discussing sensory devices and the like, but he largely avoids the issue. The Turing Test does not require the computer to be able to manipulate media as effectively as humans in general; all it must master is the typed word.

Incidentally, Turing didn't place much weight on the intelligence of a single human. Like other visionaries who would follow him, he was much more impressed by the collective intelligence of humanity. His humanism was rooted in the compounded achievements of humankind. He believed that intelligence is an evolutionary tool that allows humankind to search for new abilities. In a confidential document that prefigured "Computing Machinery and Intelligence," Turing wrote:

> As I have mentioned, the isolated man does not develop any intellectual power. It is necessary for him to be immersed in an environment of other men, whose techniques he absorbs during the first twenty years of his life. He may then perhaps

do a little research of his own and make a very few discoveries which are passed on to other men. From this point of view the search for new techniques must be regarded as carried out by the human community as a whole, rather than by individuals.[11]

DEVIL'S ADVOCATE

The idea that collective human intelligence is formidable doesn't detract from the unsettling notion that computer intelligence will usurp the primacy of humankind. The Turing Test challenges the notion that human thought—and therefore humankind—is intrinsically unique. In "Computing Machinery and Intelligence," Turing presented the objections he anticipated to the question "Can machines think?" and responded to each in turn. What is interesting about these objections of fifty years ago is that they are the same ones raised today. In large part, they are the objections that have always been made against technology and machines. Turing classified the contrarian opinions into nine canonical objections.[12]

1. *The Theological Objection.* Because thinking is a function of an immortal soul, and God gives souls only to people, machines cannot think. *Turing's response*: "It appears to me that the argument quoted above implies a serious restriction of the omnipotence of the Almighty." More seriously, he wrote that such an objection was grounded in prejudices of the unscientific past:

> In the time of Galileo it was argued that the texts, "And the sun stood still . . . and hasted not to go down about a whole day" (Joshua x. 13) and "He laid the foundations of the earth, that it should not move at any time" (Psalm cv. 5) were an adequate refutation of the Copernican theory. With our present knowledge such an argument appears futile. When that knowledge was not available it made a quite different impression.

2. The Heads in the Sand Objection. People who fear the day that machines think may put their heads in the sand and say that day can never come. This fear is grounded in humankind's conviction that it is the superior race and no other creation can surmount it.

Turing's response: Turing acknowledged that the desire to maintain our dominion is a strong one.

> It is likely to be quite strong in intellectual people, since they value the power of thinking more highly than others, and are more inclined to base their belief in the superiority of Man on this power.

3. The Mathematical Objection. This objection rests on Gödel's incompleteness theorem and the Church–Turing thesis, which stipulate that mathematics and computers are necessarily limited. The mathematical objectors assert that those limitations must be exactly those that human thought transcends.

Turing's response:

> The short answer to this argument is that although it is established that there are limitations to the powers of any particular machine, it has only been stated, without any sort of proof, that no such limitations apply to the human intellect.

No human correctly answers every question put to him; why should a machine? Gödel's and Turing's work simply proves that machines cannot be omniscient or omnipotent. We don't consider omniscience a condition of intelligence for people.

4. The Argument from Consciousness. What is consciousness? It is mysterious, mystical, magical, and uniquely human—all that computing machines are not. Certainly, one cannot say a machine can think if it does not have consciousness.

Turing's response:

I do not wish to give the impression that I think there is no mystery about consciousness. There is, for instance, something of a paradox connected with any attempt to localize it. But I do not think these mysteries necessarily need to be solved before we can answer the question with which we are concerned in this paper.

This is Turing's weakest defense, and this objection has remained the strongest. Yet it remains strong only because consciousness, although so apparent, is ineffable and incommunicable. We know in our hearts that we are conscious, yet there is no way we can prove it to someone else.

5. *Arguments from Various Disabilities.* Computing machines have various disabilities, such as not making mistakes and not being able to enjoy strawberries and cream. Such disabilities prevent machines from being able to think.

Turing's response: This argument, which depends on whether those disabilities are true, is based on inductive reasoning: Because the machines people have known are ugly, limited, and repetitive, so must be computers in the future. But the machines of the past do not limit the machines of the future.

A very large part of space-time must be investigated, if reliable results are to be obtained. Otherwise we may decide that everybody speaks English, and that it is silly to learn French.* By observing the results of its own behavior it can modify its own programmes so as to achieve some purpose more effectively. These are possibilities of the near future, rather than Utopian dreams.

6. *Lady Lovelace's Objection.* Turing quotes Lady Ada Lovelace, the woman who popularized Charles Babbage's work on computing machines in the early nineteenth century: "The Analytical Engine has no pre-

---

*Seymour Papert expands on this example in reference to children learning mathematics, discussed in Chapter 6.

tensions to *originate* anything. It can do *whatever we know how to order it* to perform" (emphasis hers).

Turing's response: There is mystery even in systems in which all the rules are known, from chess to computers.

> The view that machines cannot give rise to surprises is due, I believe, to a fallacy to which philosophers and mathematicians are particularly subject. This is the assumption that as soon as a fact is presented to a mind all consequences of that fact spring into the mind simultaneously with it. It is a very useful assumption under many circumstances, but one too easily forgets that it is false.

It is certainly the case that digital computers are built and programmed to the last detail. There is no true randomness in their operation, unless given some outside input over which we have no control. The ability to be original and surprising is certainly on anyone's list of signs of intelligence. Even though we have all the rules for the computer, that doesn't mean we can predict its behavior. Predetermined behavior does not exclude surprising behavior.

7. *Argument from Continuity in the Nervous System.* The brain is not a discrete-state machine, while the ACE, EDVAC, and their descendants, the computers of today, are. Neurons do not behave exactly like switches, vacuum tubes, or transistors, and the brain is composed of more than simply connected neurons. For example, the neurons are suspended in an electrochemical fluid, which transmits both electrical and hormonal signals. The nervous system behaves with continuity: messages made up of curves instead of bits.

Turing's response: The imitation game is a test of output, not internal function. A simple discrete-state machine can effectively emulate a simple continuous-signal analog computer, and it is not inconceivable that a complex digital computer could effectively emulate a complex continuous system, like the brain. (In fact, today's most powerful computers do so, modeling weather systems and nuclear explosions, systems that are extremely chaotic.)

8. *Argument from the Informality of Behavior.* The behavior of humans, this argument goes, is informal: "It is not possible to produce a set of rules purporting to describe what a man should do in every conceivable set of circumstances." This argument is the converse of Lady Lovelace's objection that because computers follow sets of rules, they therefore cannot behave like humans, and humans cannot be machines. *Turing's response:* Turing agreed that such a set of rules for humans is impossible but argued that more general laws of behavior may exist that could be applied to machines. He sidestepped the issue here, for if a computer could be made to pass the Turing Test, we would essentially have produced a set of rules for human behavior. Of course, those rules would not be universal. A much more difficult test than the Turing Test would be the imitation of a particular living person. If a computer could successfully imitate someone so well that it could replace that person, we would enter into a world in which the concept of identity would dissolve. Though designing a computer that could beat the Turing Test would be a step in that direction, it's a distant step. It's much more likely that a machine that passed the Turing Test would have a personality as idiosyncratic as every person's on this planet.

9. *Argument from Extrasensory Perception (ESP).* Computers can't exhibit ESP. This is the argument to which Turing didn't have a response. In fact, he gave this objection the most credence, because scientific reports of 1950 seemed to indicate the existence of ESP beyond the ken of a digital machine. But since then it has been shown that the evidence for ESP has been invariably influenced by the experimenters' desire for there to be such a thing as extrasensory powers. A human trait indeed.

LEARNING MACHINES

The final section of "Computing Machinery and Intelligence" concerns Turing's deepest interest in computing: learning machines. The British public schools, with their formal traditions and strict regimens, raised Turing almost single-handedly. As a child he spent as much time at schools as he did with his parents. With its rote lectures and strict rules, his schooling seemed eminently transferable to the language of machines.

Turing's idea of a teachable computer came out of this background. The cyberneticists, obsessed with the idea of machine feedback and learning, supported his theory.

Instead of trying to produce a programme to simulate the adult mind, why not rather try to produce one which simulates the child's? [13]   —"Computing Machinery and Intelligence"

Turing hoped to break the problem of machine intelligence into two parts: the child program and the educational process. He supposed that the child's brain was "something like a notebook as one buys it from the stationers. Rather little mechanism, and lots of blank sheets." Therefore the problem could be solved with a simple machine but rigorous education, which would allow for a process analogous to evolution, with the experimenter's judgment taking the place of natural selection.

In 1952, the Swiss scientist Jean Piaget visited Manchester and gave a series of philosophy lectures, which Turing attended. Piaget also wanted to learn how the mind worked and believed that understanding how children learn was crucial to finding an answer. A child prodigy himself, Piaget broke new ground by actually talking with children, rather than making philosophical assertions. He found that children think differently than adults, and children think differently at different ages. It was Piaget who recognized that children went through stages of development. He found that they were not at all like Turing's blank notebook to be filled with knowledge, but actively work to construct understanding of the world. We can only surmise how Turing would have responded to Piaget's work if he hadn't died less than two years later. "On Computing Machinery and Intelligence" was his last major paper.

LIFE?

Turing and von Neumann spent the last years of their lives pursuing the secrets of life through the world of computing. They hoped to unlock the mysteries of evolution, genetics, and the mind. Von Neumann looked to the problem of self-reproduction, while Turing explored how simple interactions could tip over into complexity, how variety could arise out of a formless void. Their work was ahead of their time: It wasn't until 1966 that DNA was discovered in the laboratory.

In 1946 von Neumann began attending Wiener's cybernetics meetings, where he and Wiener collaborated to create analogies between machines and organisms, relating each other's work. In those years von Neumann was devoted to trying to synthesize the problem of *automata,* machines of logic that could make copies of themselves. His goal was to discover the underlying theory behind the Turing machine, information theory, and cybernetics. Automata theory was von Neumann's response to cybernetics, and he drew from the work of Shannon, Wiener, and McCulloch and Pitts. He was inspired by the idea that complexity could arise from the most simple of interactions; that the symphonic cloud of a billion checkerboards could be complex, remarkable, even alive. Von Neumann believed there must be some comprehensive mathematical method of describing automata, instead of focusing on one aspect of their behavior or operation at a time. Inasmuch as the theory allows the comparison between computers and biological information-processing systems, this field of endeavor became known as *artificial life*.

Through automata theory, von Neumann sought the key to life, which was, as he saw it, the ability to reproduce. In 1948 he presented "The General and Logical Theory of Automata." A working EDVAC-type computer hadn't even been built yet, but in this paper von Neumann was already discussing how to use the computer to model living creatures. Von Neumann's conceptual automaton consisted of a computer, information store, and construction arm. The computer read instructions from the store and instructed the arm how to build a copy of the automaton. The automaton was a tour de force, reworking Turing's universal computing machine into reproducible parts. It was also a work of brute force: von Neumann's cellular automaton consisted of more than two hundred thousand cells, each of which could be in any of twenty-nine states that determined their behavior. Neumann could imagine his automata as machines made from electronic parts, or chemical molecules, or even the fabric of space—perhaps the universe itself was a great cellular automaton.

Von Neumann sometimes referred to his automata theory simply as "information theory." He expected Shannon's information theory to evolve into the "logical theory of automata," which would harness the conundrum of life, or at least emulate it, with self-reproducing automata. He fathomed that life could be understood by combining the principles of information theory with computational theory. A self-reproducing automaton communicates a message into the physical world; its computational part reads the message (how to construct a copy of the automaton) and then translates the message into action (construct a copy of the automaton). As long as the automaton exists in an environment that consists of building blocks, it can reproduce itself. Von Neumann was searching for the logical core inside the fuzzy sciences of evolutionary biology and psychology. He believed that at its core, biology is a computational science.

Von Neumann died before he could put his ideas into publishable form, and it was only in 1966 that his friend Arthur Burks completed von Neumann's idea and published it under the title "Theory of Self-Reproducing Automata." This and other von Neumann papers inspired later generations of artificial intelligence researchers and nanotechnologists.

Toward the end of his days Turing likewise sought answers about life in computation. He found mystery not just in intelligence, but also in more subtle manifestations of life's magic. He looked for the answers to questions such as "Where do spots come from?" and "Why does the Fibonacci sequence show up in nature (like sunflowers)?" This field of inquiry, called *morphogenesis*, is the study of the beginnings of shape and form. "Where do spots come from?" can be reworded as "How do smooth structures develop patterns?" Embryos start as a group of undifferentiated cells but develop into complexly differentiated creatures. Spots develop on leopards, and galaxies formed out of the featureless energy of the big bang.

Turing's first successful work on morphogenesis is his 1951 paper, "The Chemical Basis of Morphogenesis." Long overlooked, it is a founding paper of modern nonlinear dynamical theory, now better known as *chaos theory*. The conundrum was that systems that started out symmetrical and undifferentiated but ended up asymmetrical somehow change drastically without any obvious outside influence. Not satisfied with an explanation involving invisible external powers, Turing sought to discover how a symmetrical system that undergoes continuous or incremental development could manifest drastic changes, such as when leaves bud off of a growing plant.

According to Turing's hypothesis, chemicals called morphogens, when present in sufficient density, generate organs. Below a certain threshold, they have no effect. But as cells multiply or generate more morphogens, at some point the threshold crossed, and the morphogens activate the formation of organs, from leaves to lungs. Turing determined many of the mathematical equations that would govern this behavior.

AFTERWARD

It was only after the theoretical work of von Neumann, Turing, and others like them that scientists discovered the mechanisms of genetic reproduction. Through a complex interplay of DNA, RNA, proteins, amino acids, and other structures, the information encoded in genes is translated into new structures, including copies of the DNA itself. It would take biologists decades to begin to isolate the embryonic morphogens that Turing predicted. The field of artificial life has progressed slowly, without the clear blueprint that von Neumann and Turing attempted to provide. Advances have been made singly and haltingly, as researchers discover isolated phenomena: a model of the behavior of a colony of ants searching for food, or a particular self-replicating pattern. At the start of the twenty-first century the fields of nanotechnology and bioinformatics are where computer science and biology again converge—where data and DNA unite as *information*—and von Neumann's automata are taken out of the attic.

The personal lives, and the deaths, of these two men show how much more complex life is than could be modeled even by today's computers. Whereas their intellectual abilities were practically inhuman, their personal lives were perfectly human. Johnny von Neumann's atheism crumbled at his deathbed, as he found himself losing his gift and armor: his brilliance.

He finally died, after a slow debilitation, on February 8, 1957, of bone cancer caused by his exposure to the nuclear weapons he helped create and believed necessary to the survival of the free world.

Turing's brilliance didn't help during the sequence of events that led to the worst moments of his life. In the early 1950s he picked up a working-class nineteen-year-old man. Their romantic tryst led to his lover's friend inexpertly burgling Turing's home. Turing reported the theft to the police, who became interested in the homosexual affair as he tried to change his story to protect his lover's involvement, without hiding the nature of the affair. A show trial for sexual perversion and gross indecency ensued, and Turing suffered from a year of forced "organo-therapic treatment," chemical castration with hormone injections, which caused him to grow breasts. The social and physical humiliation was extreme; Turing was chewed up by the society he had defended during the war, for being human instead of a machine. He committed suicide by eating a cyanide-laden apple on June 7, 1954, two weeks before his forty-second birthday.

Turing and von Neumann's legacy, the digital computer, operates on the fine line between information and reality, performing calculations that are independent of the physical mechanism. Though the physical parts of computers—gears, vacuum tubes, transistors, circuits—have changed over time, all computers have the same potential capabilities.* The conversion of genetic code into living creatures can be viewed as a massive computation, the most complex and magical known. As biology becomes more a computational science and computational models grow more complex, the vision of von Neumann and Turing of a logical theory underlying the processes of life becomes more clear. This affords great promise and danger, as twenty-first-century visionaries such as K. Eric Drexler and Bill Joy explore the implications.

The question of artificial intelligence, intimated by the cyberneticists and asked explicitly by Turing, has followed a tortuous path since Turing

---

*Albeit at different speeds: Pocket calculators now outpace the first machines in memory and speed.

first postulated the Turing Test. Psychologists changed the way they looked at how the mind worked, and computer researchers looked at computers as logic machines instead of number crunchers—leading to advances in cognitive science by researchers such as Marvin Minsky and Seymour Papert. The idea of understanding thought in terms of computation persisted, leading inexorably to greater enthusiasm for Vannevar Bush's memex and other hypertext systems.

In the years immediately after the appearance of von Neumann's *First Draft* and Turing's "Computable Numbers," the world of the high-speed, programmable computer went from the theory of a few scientists and engineers to widespread practice, used in weather prediction, university research, military operations, and administrative information processing in corporations around the world. Yet the computer revolution lay not in the hands of the institutions; only when computers could be personal tools, linked together on a network, could they begin to change society.

PART II

REVOLUTION

• J. C. R. Licklider • Doug Engelbart • Marvin Minsky •
• Seymour Papert • Alan C. Kay •

EVERY REVOLUTION BEGINS with insights about the future. When those thoughts reach enough people, they define an era. With the frontier established in cybernetics, associative text linking, and digital computers, the next stage of the Information Revolution is the development and implementation of these technologies. The revolutionaries introduce tools that begin to unite the spheres of work and personal life.

In many ways, the Information Revolution is about dealing with the social consequences of the Industrial Revolution, such as the bureaucracy of corporations and governments; the automation of production, consumption, and education; and the divergence of the sciences and humanities. The information revolutionaries provide an alternative to this indoctrination. They recognize the machine's capacity to transform human thought, knowledge, and action. Computers can augment our collective ability to solve problems and our individual capacity to be creative and artistic and understand the "big picture." Work, including learning, can become like play.

Throughout the 1960s and 1970s, as the world undergoes social and political turmoil, the revolutionaries shape new computer technologies. They build the ARPAnet, a free and open space to share ideas. They build technologies—hypertext, the mouse, sketchpads—to allow computers to work in the ways we think. They devise programs that transform the way children learn and, in turn, help us understand how we learn. They experiment with ways the computer can reveal what it means to be human and how to augment our *humanness.*

OVER THE INTERGALACTIC NETWORK

J. C. R. LICKLIDER

> When information is generally useful, redistributing it makes humanity wealthier no matter who is distributing and no matter who is receiving.
> —Richard M. Stallman

CITIZENS OF THE UNITED STATES looked nervously to the skies after October 4, 1957, when the Soviet Union launched Sputnik, the first space satellite. Only the size of a basketball, Sputnik caught the Eisenhower administration utterly unprepared, and they dismissed its importance. Soon, however, the public reaction forced Washington to take the Russian launch seriously, very seriously. The ever-hawkish and influential physicist Edward Teller called it a "technological Pearl Harbor." *Life* published "Arguing the Case for Being Panicky." The situation worsened a month later, when the Russians launched Sputnik II, carrying the dog Laika, while the United States scurried frantically to put together a working rocket system. The truth was unavoidable: The Soviets had launched not only the first satellite, but the first living being into space.

The Sputnik launches, it turns out, were the greatest postwar boon for American scientific research, as the United States pushed hard to show who was really on top. New agencies, funded to the tune of billions of dollars, were created for the express purpose of competing in space. Vannevar Bush, a pragmatic old hand at allocating funds, called the expenditure absurd, but by capturing a nation's imagination, the space program propelled American science and technology for decades to come.

In 1958, Eisenhower obtained congressional funding to create the Advanced Research Projects Agency (ARPA) as part of the Pentagon, with a planned budget of two billion dollars. ARPA's mission was to explore advanced military science, particularly nuclear and ballistic missiles, without getting bogged down by competition between the armed services. By the end of that January, America had gotten on track in the game of catch-up, with the successful launch of the satellite Explorer. But the U.S. government was far from winning the public image war, the inevitable extension of the cold war. Congress established the civilian National Aeronautics and Space Administration (NASA) to work exclusively on the problem of space travel, getting the lion's share of ARPA's intended budget. The secretive military agency's budget was left at $150 million. That money was later well spent, not simply for military purposes, but for a technology that could facilitate the betterment of the nation and the world, thanks in large part to the efforts of a psychoacoustic engineer named Joseph Carl Robnett Licklider.

In the following decades, Licklider would quietly lay the groundwork for an open network that allowed everyone to communicate and share computing power. When the government hired him to help the United States win the space race, he looked to the frontier of thought instead of outer space. His manifestos, "Man–Computer Symbiosis" (1958 and 1960), *Libraries of the Future* (1965), and "Computer as a Communications Device," written with Bob Taylor (1968), were blueprints for ideas that became realities. Like Bush, Licklider directed government funding to university researchers, who shared ideas freely. He planted ideas in the right people's minds. Of all the scientists, businessmen, and bureaucrats working on computing (and he wore all three hats), Licklider saw the future the most clearly and explained it the best. He pioneered the way not for space travel, but for an intergalactic network.

ROUNDTABLE

Licklider, born March 11, 1915, in St. Louis, got his undergraduate and master's degrees in psychology, while also studying mathematics and physics, at Washington University. In 1942 he received his Ph.D. from the University of Rochester in the cutting-edge science of the electrical impulses of the auditory cortex. After working briefly under Wolfgang Köhler, one of the founders of Gestalt psychology,* Licklider joined the Psychoacoustic Laboratory of Harvard University. The great hotbed of ideas was there in Cambridge, Massachusetts, where Norbert Wiener held court, disseminating the science and vision of cybernetics to the Massachusetts Institute of Technology (MIT) and Harvard community. Within the halls of academia, scientists buzzed with excitement about the new realms of information science.

Every Tuesday night, the sandy-haired, six-foot-tall Licklider listened to the wild and portentous words bandied about at Wiener's cybernetics roundtables. Lick, as he asked everyone to call him, humbly claimed he could barely follow the mathematics of Claude Shannon's new information theory or Wiener's ebullient ramblings about cybernetics. He sat next to fellow psychologist Walter Rosenblith, who translated the dizzying concepts for him. On the ride back from MIT, they would discuss what they just heard.

Lick loved the foment of ideas that occurred when mathematicians, physicists, engineers, psychologists, and anthropologists met and matched their brains. Psychoacoustics, the study of physical and psychological effects of sound on the brain, is a science of communication, a particularly cybernetic and cross-disciplinary science that draws from fields as diverse as psychology, mechanical engineering, and information theory.

From Harvard Licklider went to work in the electrical engineering department at MIT and then Lincoln Laboratory and Bolt Beranek and

---

*Gestalt psychology is the forerunner to cognitive science, and deeply influential on much of artificial intelligence research, particularly that of Marvin Minsky. Köhler is famous not just for his theorizing but also his cognitive analysis of animal learning, with the storied experiment of putting chimps in a room with bananas suspended from the ceiling, along with crates and poles. The chimps exhibited remarkable and irrefutable intelligence as they figured out how to get the bananas by sharing information with each other as well as by trial and error.

Newman (BBN), both MIT spin-offs during the 1950s. Lincoln Lab began as a top-secret electrical engineering adjunct that explored military research. When the laboratory got its own site in a nearby town, Lick stayed at MIT and built up a psychology department there, while using Bush's analog computers to model brain functions. Working on the Differential Analyzer helped him understand not only the connection between brains and computers but also that the fickle and inaccurate analog computer was a dead end. Lincoln Lab was leaping forward with digital computers, so Lick made sure to spend time there and use them. He was exploring communication on all fronts: psychology, acoustics, and computing.

In 1957, BBN hired Lick as vice president of psychoacoustics, engineering psychology, and information systems. Once installed in his new role, he demanded that the company spend $25,000 on a digital computer, for purposes that he had yet to figure out. Researchers Richard Bolt and Leo Beranek, who were instrumental in bringing Licklider to MIT, founded BBN in 1948 as an acoustics consulting company. Sure that the postwar boom in construction would end, they followed Licklider's directions and made the jump to the nascent field of networked and interactive computing. The field was so new that no qualifications other than curiosity and some understanding of programming were necessary. The stunning $25,000 investment in a new computer paved BBN's way to contracts with the National Institutes of Health and ARPA, which eventually led to the ARPAnet. In 1957, the year he became vice president at BBN, Lick began penning the manifestos that reshaped the way the world communicates.

HUMAN–COMPUTER SYMBIOSIS

In August 1957, just as Krushchev announced the launch of "a super-long intercontinental multistage ballistic missile," Lick penned a paper titled "The Truly SAGE System, or, Toward a Man–Machine System for Thinking." The Semi-Automatic Ground Environment System was a computer-based defense system against Soviet bomber attack, comprising twenty-four Direction Centers and three Combat Centers, linked by telephone lines to more than one hundred radar and ballistics stations. This uniquely complex network ran on large, high-speed digital computers based on MIT research. What made the SAGE system so special, even more than its breadth and complexity, was that it delivered real-time information on display screens to the dozens of operator stations. At the time, almost all computer processing was batch processing—compose a problem or program, feed it into the computer, wait for a result. In his consulting for the Air Force, Lick saw that the real-time SAGE system was the future, allowing people to communicate and think alongside networked computers. Its applications would be useful not only for war but for peace.

Lick believed that the Soviets had the ascendancy "in strength of numbers of scientists and engineers" and were seriously challenging the U.S. lead in research and development. He looked to maintain the "qualitative superiority" of the United States through technology, particularly computers. But he was interested less in the computer's military implications than in its societal ones. Like Bush, Lick believed that computers could free creative workers from the clerical work that takes up so much of their time.

Lick codified the idea of a mutually dependent relationship between people and computers thirteen years after Bush published "As We May Think." He titled his manifesto "Man–Computer Symbiosis" and presented it as part of an oral report for the Air Force, in November 1958. Although he framed the concept of human–computer symbiosis in terms of military challenges, he was clearly speaking about problems universal to society.

> What the Air Force needs most in the next decade or two is a corresponding increase in capability of figuring things out ... of perceiving and understanding complex, rapidly changing situations and of selecting among alternative courses of action those that will produce the most favorable outcomes.[1]
>
> —"Man–Computer Symbiosis" (oral report)

In "Man–Computer Symbiosis," Lick started from the tightly defined problem of military situation analysis to explore the possibility of coupled, cybernetic human-machine systems. He succinctly expressed his core insight, that "men are best at what computers are poorest at ... and vice versa." Like Turing, Lick saw immense potential for the computer to become more and more complex. It would not only expand humankind's ability to think, communicate, and act, but also acquire complex skills of its own.

> That men and computers so supplement each other ... and that jointly they possess the capabilities to think and comprehend and to decide upon effective action ... in a way totally beyond present realization ... are the primary grounds on which we base our hope.[2] —"Man–Computer Symbiosis" (oral report)

Lick envisioned a mutually productive relationship between humans and computers, not unlike biological symbiosis, wherein two utterly different organisms are linked together in intimate association. The crucial realization is that the abilities of humans and machines are very different, but also very complementary. Lick saw the greatest gains to humanity if we joined in symbiosis with computers, in a mutual dependency of thought and data processing.

For the next two years Lick continued to develop these ideas in other papers. In 1960 he wrote them all down in one central manifesto, the conclusive version of "Man–Computer Symbiosis." This time, his audience was much larger than the Air Force.

> The hope is that, in not too many years, human brains and computing machines will be coupled together very tightly, and that the resulting partnership will think as no human brain has ever thought and process data in a way not approached by the information-handling machines we know today.[3]
>   —"Man-Computer Symbiosis"

Lick's utopian vision was tempered by his realization that the task of human–computer symbiosis would be extremely difficult. Humans and computers have very different strengths in the way they handle information. We communicate slowly and with a lot of mistakes, but our brains handle information in remarkably complex ways. Computers are the very opposite: extraordinarily fast and accurate, but also simple. Another way to think of the complementary differences between humans and machines is that people can see the big picture, but computers can fill in the details. Thus people will come up with ideas and goals for the computers to process.

> Men will set the goals and supply the motivations, of course, at least in the early years. They will formulate hypotheses. They will ask questions. They will think of mechanisms, procedures, and models.[4] —"Man–Computer Symbiosis"

In "Man–Computer Symbiosis," Lick also wrote about shared computer networks. The computers of his time were extremely expensive, and already much faster at calculations than a human could imagine. Lick knew that computers would become still faster. The idea of tying one superfast, superexpensive computer to one person was a problem not just for economic reasons but because of the basic incompatibility in the speed of thinking. It made perfect sense to him to look for ways to share the computer's power among many users.*

> It seems reasonable to envision, for a time 10 or 15 years hence, a "thinking center" that will incorporate the functions of present-day libraries together with anticipated advances in information storage and retrieval and the symbiotic functions suggested earlier in this paper. The picture readily enlarges itself into a network of such centers, connected to one another by wide-band communication lines and to individual users by leased-wire services. In such a system, the speed of the computers would be balanced, and the cost of the gigantic memories and the sophisticated programs would be divided by the number of users.[5] —"Man-Computer Symbiosis"

Lick entertained the morbid outlook that someday computers would outthink humans in every way—even replace them. Just as the modern living cell, with all its embedded subsystems, exists because it absorbed free-living symbionts into it, computers may end up becoming the

---

*The idea of time-sharing had captured the computing community's interest around 1960. Licklider credited John McCarthy with making the greatest push to get time-sharing going at BBN, where Lick was at the time.

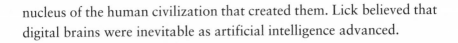

nucleus of the human civilization that created them. Lick believed that digital brains were inevitable as artificial intelligence advanced.

> It seems entirely possible that, in due course, electronic or chemical "machines" will outdo the human brain in most of the functions we now consider exclusively within that province.
> —"Man–Computer Symbiosis"

In "Man–Computer Symbiosis," he consoled the reader that at least "there will nevertheless be a fairly long interim during which the main intellectual advances will be made by men and computers working together in intimate association." That period, be it ten or five hundred years, "should be intellectually the most creative and exciting in the history of mankind."[6] In the face of the effective extinction of the human race, Lick found a silver lining.

THE DEMISE OF COMMAND AND CONTROL

The 1960s, following the trajectory of the satellite Explorer, began with the bright yet forbidding prospect of space travel. That people would walk on the moon before the decade ended seemed an impossible dream, but one that nevertheless would be realized. The frontier of space loomed as the militaries of both superpowers rushed to fill the starry void with spy satellites and intercontinental ballistic missiles. People contemplated the skies with hope, wonder, and dread, not knowing what to expect; their daily lives on Earth suddenly became awash in uncertainty, fueled by the new medium of television and new realizations about race, freedom, and society. Space beckoned with grandeur, but it would be the frontier of new forms of communication that society would rocket into.

In a 1961 report to an Air Force research panel, Lick coined the term "cerebral frontier" to describe the potential offered by the computing sciences,*

---

*Later generations have tried many a time to coin words for the cerebral frontier (each with varying inflections of meaning): Consider William Gibson's *cyberspace;* Pierre Teilhard de Chardin and Eric S. Raymond's *noösphere,* Al Gore's *information superhighway,* Neal Stephenson's *metaverse,* Jaron Lanier's *virtual reality.* All connote the opportunities of computing in terms of space and physical distance.

and compared it to the other frontier recently opened by technology: space. He wrote, "A vast cerebral frontier is open to the technologically advanced countries of the world in much the same way as the space frontier was open 15 years ago."[7]

While outer space was on the front page of newspapers in 1961, Lick saw the cerebral frontier to be much more exciting, or at least its equal in unimaginable scope. Exploration of space involves simply the ability to go greater distances in new directions. Exploration of the cerebral frontier requires the ability to create new directions. With both profundity and understatement, Lick compared the two frontiers: "The space frontier captures the imagination. The cerebral frontier *includes* the imagination. It is therefore difficult to imagine."[8]

Funding for the space frontier gave Lick the tools to tackle the cerebral frontier. Jack Ruina, the first scientist to head ARPA, hired Lick in 1962 to lead the Command and Control Research Division. Lick's vision of computing outstripped the expectations of his superiors. He wanted to do more than command and control research, which entailed constructing battle planning missions (in other words, war games); he wanted to develop interactive computing and achieve the vision of human–computer symbiosis that he had laid out in his 1958 manifesto. Lick wanted to move computing research away from batch processing, away from the idea of the computer as arithmetic engine, and toward the computer as a communication device.*

Lick had difficulty realizing his revolutionary vision, even though he had the government's pocketbook. One major problem was that the companies that controlled computer research at the time didn't want to change. They couldn't see the computer as much more than a remarkably fast calculator. Lick had a much deeper respect for pure research, the university ethos, than he did for corporations. As a result, he looked to the universities, providing the funding and computers that

---

*Lick was actually hired to head the behavioral science division, which was related to Command and Control Research. Though he didn't think he was the head of the latter, at first everyone at ARPA treated him as if he was. He creatively interpreted his official mandate and pushed exclusively for interactive computing, until people accepted it. The Command and Control Research Division was renamed the Information Processing Techniques Office to reflect Lick's broad mission.

allowed universities to set up the first computer science departments in the world.

LIBRARIES OF THE FUTURE

Another aspect of the human-computer symbiosis as Lick imagined it was that humans would live better with better information. The longer Lick worked for ARPA, the more conscious he became of the importance and difficulty of managing knowledge. He had read Bush's "As We May Think," and wrote his own vision in a book, which he dictated at a poolside in Las Vegas. Titled *Libraries of the Future,* the book is dedicated to Bush, and in the acknowledgments Lick credits Bush as the topic's "main external influence."

The relevance of *Libraries of the Future* to the Information Revolution is obvious. The national library system is part of the bedrock of democracy in the United States. The Library of Congress is a creation of the Constitution. Development of libraries is directly related to a country's socioeconomic status and should reflect societal changes. The existence of libraries tracks the concentration and disbursement of power in perhaps the most explicit demonstration that knowledge is power. From the cloistered and jealously protected libraries of the monasteries of the Middle Ages, to the great library systems of the universities, and finally to the truly public libraries that came about during the Enlightenment, library systems closely parallel the development of social equity and democratic government.

In *Libraries of the Future,* Lick wrote that libraries would become in the future "procognitive systems" wherein computers would sort, manage, and contain information that would blend the disciplines—natural sciences, computer sciences, behavioral and social sciences, library sciences, and others. Like Bush, he believed this capability would become increasingly critical to the construction and preservation of humankind's burgeoning wealth of knowledge. The library would be like a bank, holding its assets as they accrete and become more valuable over time.

. . . .

Economic criteria tend to be dominant in our society. The economic value of information and knowledge is increasing. By the

year 2000, information and knowledge may be as important as
mobility.... Thus our economic assumption is that interaction
with information and knowledge will constitute 10 or 20 per
cent of the total effort of the society, and the rational economic
(or socioeconomic) criterion is that the society be more productive with procognitive systems than without.[9]

—*Libraries of the Future*

By 2000, in fact, information, knowledge, and mobility began to be realized
in a way that combined all three, allowing "nomadic warriors" to travel
around the world, armed with cheap portable computing devices and intelligent access to the global networks. Among twenty-five criteria that he
lists for procognitive systems, many of which would have been fulfilled by
Bush's memex, Lick includes the following, later realized by the Internet:

- Be available when and where needed;
- Evidence neither the ponderousness now associated with
  overcentralization nor the confusing diversity and
  provinciality now associated with highly distributed systems;
- Essentially eliminate publication lag.[10]

Licklider called for libraries to move toward eliminating the endless cycle
of tracking, sorting, and shelving the books and the many cards—card
catalogs, library cards, due-date cards, book request cards, etc.—and
managing information with computerized systems, including bar codes
and searchable databases.

Procognitive systems require a simultaneously heightened and potentially threatening level of computer intelligence. Lick imagined such
systems to someday have the ability to become personalized and indis-
pensable symbionts of the human user and perform functions such as
translating languages, sorting through vistas of information, and solving problems for the user. Careening into the domain of artificial intelligence, Lick wrote that computers would inevitably become intelligent
enough to:

- Permit users to deal either with meta-information
  (through which they can work "at arms length"

with substantive information), or with substantive
information (directly), or with both at once;

- Reduce markedly the difficulties now caused by the
  diversity of publication languages, terminologies,
  and "symbologies;"

- Tend toward consolidation and purification of
  knowledge, instead of, or as well as, toward
  progressive growth and unresolved equivocation;

- Converse or negotiate with the user while he formulates
  a request and while responding to them;

- Adjust itself to the level of sophistication of the
  individual user;

- Display desired degree of initiative, together with good
  selectivity, in dissemination of recently acquired and
  "newly needed" knowledge;

- Handle heuristics (guidelines, strategies, tactics, and
  rules of thumb intended to expedite solution of
  problems) coded in such a way as to facilitate their
  association with situations to which they are germane.[11]

This blueprint of the library of the future is intimately related to the construction of another metalibrary: the ARPAnet.

BUILDING THE INTERGALACTIC NETWORK

The ARPAnet, the predecessor of the Internet and the World Wide Web, began as a network of human beings. In the early 1960s Lick began nurturing a constellation of university researchers who shared his vision of a networked world of information. He funded them, prodded them, and brought them together, believing that Wiener's cybernetics meetings were the right model for the new world of interactive computing. Lick had a pet name for his ARPA fundees: the "intergalactic network," a term he may have chosen in a facetious attempt to match the excitement and grandiosity of the space effort. The intergalactic network referred not just to the people but also his dream of a true intergalactic computer network, which he shared in a series of memoranda.

Licklider funded computer research groups led by principal investigators at MIT, Harvard University, the University of California at Berkeley (UC Berkeley), Stanford University, and the University of California at Los Angeles (UCLA). Each university already had some kind of a computer center, but with the ARPA funds, they began to develop full academic computer science departments, the first in the country. Before, computer science was a subsection of electrical engineering, mathematics, or specialized graduate research in a field such as artificial intelligence.

Several groups worked on developing time-sharing systems, to allow many people access to the same computer and thereby get the most use out of these extremely expensive machines. Other contracts Lick signed included work on displays, controls, and databases. Doug Engelbart at the Stanford Research Institute (SRI) worked on the organization of the computer interface. Lick was one of the first people to recognize Engelbart's genius.

At ARPA, Lick established an atmosphere that Leonard Kleinrock at UCLA described as one in which "they didn't try to control the researchers, to their great credit, but rather they gave us money, and said, do a good thing." He placed a generation of researchers in a bubble of trust and openness, in which they were assumed to do good work and pushed to communicate. As they built communication, they built community.

Lick's special skill was appreciating what others could do; in a sense, he let others do the hard work in the labs, while he simply went to all of them and watched. By seeing the different projects, he was able to understand how all the scientists could work together better than any of them could individually. Lick, notwithstanding his humble claims, could often understand the core nature of a problem more quickly than the person deeply involved with it. He brought the knowledge from being around such principal investigators as Engelbart, John McCarthy, Bob Fano, and Marvin Minsky to the rest of the intergalactic network. He also brought his principal investigators together when he could, and explained his ideas personally, in his unassuming Ozark twang.

Lick's genius is that he saw the various ARPA researchers as a community, or a potential community. He believed that individual effort is amplified by community, just as it is amplified by the computer. What made his community unusual was that it was bound not by geography but by common purpose. It was also evident that each research group relied on the others for their specialties. Lick could see that the barrier of distance, heretofore overcome only when the researchers all came together to meet, could be broken down by the networking of the computers. In a 1963 memorandum to the intergalactic network, Lick wrote:

> In the first place, it is evident that we have among us a collection of individual (personal and/or organizational) aspirations, efforts, activities, and projects. These have in common, I think, the characteristics that they are in some way connected with the advancement of the art or technology of information processing, the advancement of intellectual capability (man, man–machine, or machine), and the approach to a theory of science. The individual parts are, at least to some extent, mutually interdependent.[12]

With this, Lick subtly pushed his community of researchers to think about working together. He lit a fire under them by describing opportunities and posing problems. He understood that the most basic forms of communication create complex conditions, a process that manifests in his own field of psychoacoustics as sound generates vibrations in the ear, which ultimately can cause joy or despair, confusion or insight. There is no better way to get scientists to work than to present a challenge with a number of interesting problems, such as how to get specialized computer centers to be able to communicate with one another to form a complex network.

SEND IN THE YOUNG TURKS

Unbeknownst to Licklider at the time, the future of the intergalactic computer network would be inextricably connected with three MIT graduate students who were finishing their theses at Lincoln Lab back in 1962. One, Leonard Kleinrock, showed his analysis of information flow in networks; the next, Ivan Sutherland, demonstrated his computer-assisted design program; and the third, Lawrence Roberts, disclosed his work in image processing and character recognition. Their professors were among the likes of information theory founder Claude Shannon and artificial intelligence pioneer Marvin Minsky.

In fact, these three graduate students were central to many of the advances achieved throughout the next three decades of computing. Kleinrock's thesis, "Message Delay in Communication Nets With Storage," laid much of the theoretical groundwork. Sutherland's "Sketchpad: A Man–Machine Graphical Communications System," was the revolutionary work in computer graphics, object-oriented programming, and computer-assisted design. And Roberts, whose thesis work was later used to help astronauts send images of the moon back to Earth, would lead the construction of the ARPAnet.

In 1964 Lick decided to leave ARPA with a legacy of work in time-sharing, computer graphics, and computer language. He handed the reins of the Command and Control Research Division, by then renamed the Information Processing Techniques Office (IPTO), to Sutherland. After leaving Lincoln Lab, Sutherland had joined the army, doing computer research for the top-secret National Security Agency. Though Sutherland didn't know it, Lick had been deeply impressed by his brilliance and drive the few times they had met. He saw that Sutherland was on the same wavelength and pushed hard to make him his successor.

Sutherland continued to move the IPTO in the same directions as Licklider had in his short tenure, funding people from Engelbart to his friend Roberts. At UCLA he tried to get a networking project off the ground to connect the main computers at UCLA—medical, engineering, and administration—but the various departments had no interest in sharing control or power. Robert Taylor from NASA came on board as deputy director in 1965, and when Sutherland left to teach at Harvard, Taylor took over as director of the IPTO.

Taylor, the man who later founded the computer science lab at the Xerox Palo Alto Research Center, wanted to build a national computer network for reasons both visionary and practical. Lick had inspired Taylor with the goal of building the intergalactic network. Such a network would encourage community among the researchers, fighting digital isolationism. Taylor also became painfully aware of how redundant the independent computer centers across the country were getting. If they were connected, he figured, they would share resources, avoiding needless duplication of effort and waste of IPTO money. He knew just who he wanted to work with him to run the networking project: Kleinrock's old graduate school friend, Larry Roberts.

After earning his doctorate, Roberts had happily continued working at Lincoln Lab. Nudged by Lick, he had shifted his research from computer graphics and time-sharing to the problem of computer communications. He tackled each successive computing field with the same intensity and speed of thought that defined his personality in the minds of his admirers.

By the time Taylor asked him to join the IPTO in 1966, the twenty-nine-year-old Roberts was successfully managing the computer research at Lincoln Lab, with IPTO funding. Not only was he an expert in all matters of computing, he was a proven manager, had experience in networking, and believed in Lick's vision. Roberts was perfect for the job, but he didn't want to leave Lincoln Lab. Even after the mild but firm indication that his taking the offer would be the best thing for everyone involved, Roberts still wasn't excited about leaving the comfort and excitement of his current position for a pure management job. At the advice of Kleinrock, who was a close friend (after MIT, they had kept in touch, even at one point trying to beat roulette with concealed computers to calculate the physics of the spinning wheel), he decided to give it a shot.

Roberts started the design for the network using the networking theory Kleinrock had developed in his thesis, proposed in 1959, completed in 1962, and published in book form in 1964. Having helped do the programming for the network simulations in Kleinrock's thesis, Roberts was well aware that his friend had cracked the problem of how to envision successful information flow in large communication nets. In fact, that was the original title of this important technomanifesto which, with the choice of packet switching, became the blueprint for the ARPAnet and the Internet.*

---

*The people who developed ARPAnet now argue over who deserves credit for what, especially the idea of packet switching. Roberts and Kleinrock now say that Kleinrock was the first person to develop packet-switching theory in his thesis; Taylor, Donald Davies, and Paul Baran dispute that claim. In a paper published posthumously, Davies wrote, "The work of Kleinrock before and up to 1964 gives him no claim to have originated packet switching, the honor for which must go to Paul Baran. The passage in his book on time-sharing queue discipline, if pursued to a conclusion, might have led him to packet switching but it did not."

INFORMATION FLOW IN
LARGE COMMUNICATION NETS

To have a general understanding of Kleinrock's thesis topic, multinode communication nets, imagine a bunch of children scattered about a playground holding tin-can telephones. Each child, acting as a node, has a few of these telephones. A message sent from a child at one end of the playground to one at the other end would typically be received and retransmitted by several other children, and could follow one of many different routes. An obvious problem with such a network is that it could quickly get clogged by messages; while a child tried to shout one message, new ones would be coming in. Kleinrock studied store-and-forward communication nets, which the children could approximate if they had a tape recorder attached to each of their tin cans. If many messages came in at the same time, or new messages came in while they were sending old ones, the children would just wait until the messages finished, then play the recordings to send the messages on their way. There are clearly many issues involved in making such a system work, even if you're using computers and telephone lines instead of children and tin cans.

Kleinrock's thesis contained three core ideas: distributed control, resource sharing, and the efficiency of large networks. The ARPAnet and later the Internet show how each of those mathematical ideas has worked alongside the related social concepts. The Internet encourages open and democratic processes by its very nature. Wherein lie the technological control and resources, lies the power. Kleinrock's networks were utterly *unlike* those of the phone companies, which were as centralized as you can get, with zero resource sharing, the equivalent of one big tin-can connection run by the biggest, meanest kids, who demand that everybody else has to share in turn.

Distributed control: Each node in the network shares responsibility for knowing how to direct information and is connected to several other nodes. Instead of a single bully demanding that every message go through his tin cans, each child can send and receive messages. The smartest, quickest children get to handle the most tin cans, but they don't command the other children. Even if a child leaves, the network still functions. Messages can take any of multiple paths across the network. Distributed control shares the power among everyone. That allows the network to grow robustly—centralized control fails miserably. The best networks combine hierarchies with trust. The hierarchies maintain the trust structure, but within it everyone is a free agent. Their actions aren't totally controlled. The end is defined—get the message across the network—but not the means. Distributed control rewards intelligent collaboration.

Resource sharing: Kleinrock's network balances the needs of the many small-bandwidth messages with the few large-bandwidth messages. He recognized that every node on the network wouldn't generate the same traffic. In fact, most would communicate using relatively small amounts of information, as is typical for data communications. There would be only a few super-high-bandwidth nodes. At any one time, the same structure would be manifest: There would be a few large messages, and many small ones, going through the network. It would be easy to set up a network so that only the big messages got through, but Kleinrock saw that he could let everybody win. Everybody wins when you let the little guy go first. When choosing how to sort through a bunch of stored messages on her tape recorder, a child would ask who sent the shortest message and play that one first. But she'd play the message for only a short time, after which she would go on to the next message. If the sender had lied, and his message wasn't actually that short, the rest of his message would have to go to the back of the queue to await another turn. Well-designed resource sharing rewards honesty and punishes cheating.

The efficiency of large networks: Kleinrock discovered the remarkable fact that certain networks get more efficient as they grow to hundreds, thousands, or even millions of nodes. That efficiency allows networks with billions of bits of data coursing between millions of computers to work. This discovery is in marked contrast to common experience. A large turnpike network, for example, is no more efficient than a small one. The increase in size merely increases capacity. If you widen a turnpike, more cars can go on the road. But the time each car spends waiting for a tollbooth remains the same; the increased capacity of the turnpike is taken up by increased traffic. In certain electronic networks, Kleinrock found, it's as if larger turnpikes lead to shorter lines at the tolls, even if more cars get on the roads. On the electronic networks, the messages going over the network can be arranged, rerouted, and segmented almost instantaneously. As these networks grow they get faster and more efficient, without limit. Applying mathematical power to a large, electronic, store-and-forward communication net, one can develop a communications system that only gets more powerful as it grows. The more, the merrier. The efficiency of large networks rewards an intergalactic vision.

PACKET SWITCHING

Roberts and the IPTO researchers weren't the only ones working on the networking problem. The lads in England were also cultivating a thriving computer research scene, led by the team at the National Physical Laboratory (NPL), where Turing had written the ACE Report a decade earlier. Donald Davies, who had joined the NPL team while Turing was there, began independently developing computer network communications in 1965. In his papers, he coined the term "packet switching" to describe the method of transmitting chopped-up ("packetized") messages across the network. Messages get broken up at the initiating computer; the packets are sent out like postcards onto the network with the address of the receiving computer, which reassembles the message upon receipt of the packets. His proposals for a national packet network in Great Britain were dismissed by the institution in charge of communications, the General Post Office.

Paul Baran, a researcher at the RAND Corporation, a cold war powerhouse, also independently developed similar ideas on distributed data networks, motivated by the goal of developing a network robust enough to withstand nuclear attack, unlike the centralized telephone system controlled by AT&T. Baran spent years studying and constructing prototype data networks, only to be ignored by his superiors and scorned by AT&T. He first published his work in a series of RAND studies between 1960 and 1962 and then finally in a single eleven-volume tome, *On Distributed Communications,* in 1964. Baran worked out many of the difficulties in implementing packet switching in distributed networks, including how to handle lost packets, error checking, and addressing schemes. He later joined the informal cadre of networking experts Roberts consulted as he developed the network plans.

Packet-switching networks are an implementation of Kleinrock's distributed store-and-forward networks, having the distributed control, resource sharing, and efficiency of large networks. Packet switching ensures that all messages are created equal; the children with their tin cans now all send messages of the same size, and need only pay attention to the intended destination—the network is neutral with respect to content. This neutrality has its drawbacks: Services that require rapid, high-bandwidth transmission, such as video, break down in a neutral packet network, unless it has very high capacity. But the advantages are greater: Because there are no inbuilt preferences, the network is flexible and extensible; any use of the network that can be imagined can be implemented, by anyone. All the packet networks, from Baran's to the Internet, use this principle—though efforts are now being made to prioritize packets, which may have a chilling effect on innovation.

PUTTING IT TOGETHER

In early 1967 Roberts met with some of the principal investigators of the intergalactic network to begin determining the requirements for the network. Kleinrock wanted there to be diagnostic tools at every node, since network analysis was his metiér. The time-sharing expert at UC Berkeley, Herb Baskin, demanded a response time of no more than half a second. Another researcher emphasized the need for reliability. Roberts began sketching out possible configurations.

Armed with these preliminary ideas, Roberts presented his mandate to the principal investigators at large at a computer conference in Ann Arbor, Michigan. Most of the East Coast investigators, who were older, better funded, and more established, responded negatively to the idea of adding networking to their precious computers. No one wanted to share information. "After all," they said, "why would I need someone else's research when I have my own?" But a few were excited, including Engelbart at SRI. His own work was already based around Lickliderian ideals, and he, too, dreamed of the intergalactic network.

But it was an idea from a skeptic that kicked the network project into high gear. After the meeting, one investigator, Wes Clark, suggested to Roberts that instead of adding networking capabilities to each of the host computers at the varied sites, they could build separate dedicated computers to route information between hosts and the network. Roberts sent out a memorandum describing Clark's idea, calling the computers "interface message processors," or IMPs. This insight exploited a central principle of efficient communication, first described by Shannon in his "Mathematical Theory of Communication": Separate message transmission from message content.

All the pieces came together at a computer conference in Gatlinburg, Tennessee, later in 1967. Roberts presented a paper on his idea for an "ARPAnet" and Roger Scantlebury of NPL discussed the work done by the Davies group. It was from Scantlebury that Roberts first learned of Davies, Baran, and their independent work in packet switching. The NPL people also convinced Roberts to go with lines of higher bandwidth, based on network experiments that they began to do.* In later years this revealed to be an important decision, allowing network usage to grow freely, without the constraint of low-bandwidth lines, exploiting Kleinrock's principle of the efficiency of large networks.

In July 1968 Roberts finished the draft of the ARPAnet IMP request for proposals. This formal technical document stood as the culmination of years of work and collaborative inspiration. He had sifted through and collated all the ideas and needs of the computing community and drafted a coherent plan with which to build the network. He sent the request for proposals to 140 companies in August, and asked for a response in thirty days. IBM rejected the idea, saying it was impossible to build IMPs with anything less than extremely expensive and huge mainframe computers. Several other companies, however, replied that they could build an even faster and more responsive network than Roberts specified. Raytheon became the frontrunner, even entering final negotiations in December, but it was the small, MIT-infused company BBN, Lick's old company, that won the contract as Christmas Day approached.[†]

---

*Roberts proposed to do 9.6 kilobit per second lines; the NPL people convinced him to go for 50 kb/s lines.

[†]BBN made a furious effort to win the contract. In the month allotted, they spent $100,000 constructing a two-hundred-page document that was closer to finished blueprints and software design than to a proposal. The BBN engineer Frank Heart led the team of IMP Guys. Severo Ornstein, a close friend of Wes Clark from their days at Lincoln Lab, designed the hardware. Bob Kahn, an MIT professor whose theoretical mind-set was in every way the opposite of Heart's unyielding practicality, understood information theory innately. The software designers, including Dave Walden, Will Crowther, and Bernie Cosell, were some of the first real hackers.

1969

It all came together in 1969, the year that defined an era, the apex of conflicts and triumphs. That summer, Aldrin and Armstrong reached the Sea of Tranquility while Collins orbited overhead. The followers of Charles Manson brutally and madly murdered several people in a bizarre ritual of religious, social, and media perversion. And the Woodstock Music and Art Fair brought together a half million people, on all sides of the battles of the 1960s—Vietnam vets, antiwar protestors, Black Power, racists, feminists, pro- and antidrug rights, pro- and antigay rights, etc.—causing twenty-mile traffic jams on the roads to Woodstock, New York.

In the midst of this tumult, a handful of tie-wearing engineers steadily built the ARPAnet.

Under the guidance of engineer Frank Heart, the BBN team spent eight months translating ideas and theories into physical reality. Their manifesto took the form of a military-hardened, nine-hundred-pound Honeywell 516, which the IMP Guys had transformed into a unique masterpiece. On August 30, BBN shipped the first IMP to UCLA. Three days later, right after Labor Day, the BBN technicians and Kleinrock's grad students connected the IMP to UCLA's Sigma 7, making it the first host on the as-yet-unborn network. Since there weren't any other IMPs, messages couldn't be sent to other computers, but the Sigma 7 and the IMP began successfully communicating with each other from the very start. Both BBN and Kleinrock's team had got it right the first time.

Lick's vision was realized in October of a year filled with astounding events. BBN sent the next IMP to Engelbart's team at SRI on the first of the month. On October 29, the first message was sent over the nascent network. The researchers at UCLA tried to send the message "LOGIN" one character at a time. They successfully sent "LO" before the SRI host crashed. "LO" and behold what humankind hath wrought. Later, they fixed the bugs and set the computers happily chatting. It was this unnoticed act of decentralized democracy, born in a year of revolution, that heralded the future and defined the coming era.*

---

*In the following decades, the ARPAnet and other networks grew. Guided by the founding ARPAnet principles of simplicity, distribution and neutrality, the networking community developed the Internet, a network of networks, which supplanted the ARPAnet in the 1980s.

COMPUTER AS A COMMUNICATION DEVICE

Throughout the 1960s Lick stayed in close contact with the crew at ARPA, following the progress of his legacy there, and continued to proselytize the computer communication revolution. He managed the Information Sciences division at IBM until 1968, when he rejoined MIT as the director of its time-sharing computer center, Project MAC. That year he and Taylor published a manifesto that revisited Lick's ideas in the context of the last few years of developments, as possibilities were becoming reality.

In "Computer as a Communication Device," Lick and Taylor can't hide their enthusiasm and excitement about the future. They witnessed the nascent stages of communities with computers facilitating communication, and knew this was something new and important. They begin with a bold prediction.

> In a few years, men will be able to communicate more effectively through a machine than face to face.[13]
>
> —"Computer as a Communication Device"

They realized that computers would enhance communication deeply. Properly used, computers could add unforeseen dimensions to face-to-face conversation. Data and knowledge could be pulled up and shared at the flick of a fingertip; agreements and arguments could be recorded for later review. Computers can add effectiveness to communication by bridging the gap between the natural, ephemeral nature of conversation and the formal, permanent nature of recorded information.

Lick and Taylor also caution that when they say computers will revolutionize communication, they're not talking about computers taking over the telephone networks. That will certainly bring advantages, but the revolution will come when computers are used to provide "an interactive, cooperative modeling facility."

They go on to discuss the development of interactive multiaccess computer *communities,* a half dozen of which existed at the time. "These communities are sociotechnical pioneers, in several ways out ahead of the rest of the computer world," they wrote. Lick, Taylor, and all the other IPTO pioneers were very aware that they were living in the future.

> But now the move is on to interconnect the separate communities and thereby transform them into, let us call it, a supercommunity. The hope is that interconnection will make available to all the members of all the communities the programs and data resources of the entire supercommunity.[14]
>
> —"Computer as a Communication Device"

Like Turing, Lick and Taylor recognized that individual intelligence is of much less import than societal knowledge. When a person tries to communicate, she has to translate her internal model of an idea into an external model in some form that can be shared, such as speech or a drawing. Most ideas can't be captured fully on the chalkboard. The external model doesn't really match the internal model. The computer is a more versatile medium, allowing people to construct external models more like their internal ones, ensuring that the mental models of people who are trying to communicate more closely match. With improved communication comes increased trust; with increased trust comes increased personal power.

> When minds interact, new ideas emerge.[15]
>
> —"Computer as a Communication Device"

Lick and Taylor's estimation of the future is not unalloyed optimism, however. This communication technology has much to offer, but *how society uses it* will determine the results. They and the other members of the intergalactic network knew that their technology could facilitate democracy and make the distribution of knowledge more effective than ever before. They shared Wiener's conviction that society must take action to ensure that communications and control would be in the hands of the many. If the computer network's great advantages were controlled by only a few, computers could in fact worsen social inequality. The architecture of the ARPAnet (and later the Internet), as originally established, is essentially democratic, distributing command and control, but its advantages benefit only those who have access to it.

> For the society, the impact will be good or bad, depending mainly on the question: Will "to be on line" be a privilege or a right? If only a favored segment of the population gets a chance to enjoy the advantage of "intelligence amplification," the network may exaggerate the discontinuity in the spectrum of intellectual opportunity.[16]
> —"Computer as a Communication Device"

"Computer as a Communication Device" was written in 1968 at the height of the civil rights movement, when social turmoil was at fever pitch. Lick had begun his computing journey at the height of the cold war and now, toward the end of his career, the external conflict with the Soviet Union had become overshadowed by the internal conflict of the United States's own people. Intercommunication would be essential to the health of the nation and the world.

> On the other hand, if the network idea should prove to do for education what a few have envisioned in hope, if not in concrete detailed plan, and if all minds should prove to be responsive, surely the boon to humankind would be beyond measure.[17]
> —"Computer as a Communication Device"

AFTERWARD

The American effort to build the ARPAnet began from the same impetus that led Neil Armstrong to land on the moon in 1969. The lunar landing beat the first ARPAnet communication by three months. By the turn of the twenty-first century, we have taken humans no farther than the moon, and no one has set foot on Earth's only satellite since 1972. In contrast, we've gone further and further into the ARPAnet/Internet's ever-expanding frontier. The thirty years since 1969 have belonged to the computer and the network, not to space.

Why was Lick so important? He wasn't a great engineer, or a brilliant mathematician, or a powerful politician, or even an especially wild-eyed dreamer. Yet this unassuming man managed to be at the center of the greatest technological revolution of the last half of the twentieth century. What he had was clarity of vision, purpose, exhilaration, and communication. From his background in neurology, he understood that the brain interacts with the world by collecting thousands of bits of information through the eyes and ears and skin and processing them in the sensory cortices. Through his training in psychology, he understood that individuals interact with the world and with each other by collecting information and processing it, with language and emotion. His time in the military and business taught him that organizations and governments make decisions by the same process. And from his early days at Lincoln Lab he understood that computers were capable of facilitating this process on all levels.

In short, Lick's mind-set and experience allowed him to fully comprehend Wiener's cybernetic vision that ties together people, computers, and society: the ability to communicate and learn. He spent his whole life pushing those priorities, quietly, persistently, and convincingly. He gave people something to shoot for—the intergalactic network—while encouraging incremental progress. He understood that the visions of human–computer symbiosis and the intergalactic network were complex and idealistic. Just like any complex system, Lick's goals were composed of the near-random efforts of a hundred people, a thousand different decisions, a million tiny advances. His genius was the ability to have a grand vision but to push people to follow not his vision, but their own, with the same enthusiasm. All he did was inculcate their thinking with the big picture. Until his death in 1990 from complications of an asthma attack, Lick lived to see much of that picture actually drawn.

The basic system of trust and open communication that exemplified ARPA's relationship with its researchers, the relationship that Lick firmly established, was utterly different from the way government and businesses worked, with their layer upon layer of bureaucracy. This is not simply a coincidence; nor is it that time and again the revolutions of the information age have come out of environments without bureaucracy, including computer clubs, garages, and freewheeling university labs. The very tools these hobbyists, entrepreneurs, and students create allow them to avoid bureaucracy. In any organization managers and middlemen handle information flow and processing, but computers can do the job, often better. This reduction of bureaucracy is the basic divide between the organizations of the industrial and information ages.

Until the explosion of personal computers in the 1980s and the widespread use of the Internet, the computer industry still saw the computer more as an arithmetic engine than anything else. And only with the advent of the World Wide Web in the early 1990s did companies like IBM and Microsoft understand the value and importance of open computer networks—whereas the universities understood their value back in the first days of the intergalactic network. Today, it's still questionable whether most companies see that the computer has its greatest value as a cybernetic communication device, rather than a worker productivity or consumer-marketing tool.

Flexibility and trust are admittedly difficult to preserve as systems grow in size and complexity. The demise of the IPTO in 1974 was testament to this. The collection of projects that the IPTO funded grew ever larger, leading gradually but inevitably to the same kind of red tape and paperwork that led the government to create ARPA in the first place. Taylor had handed over the directorship of the IPTO to Roberts in September 1969. Roberts, in turn, left in 1973. Once the principal investigators could no longer meet in one place and learn fully from one another, once they broke apart into specialties, the magic of the ARPA era began to fade into the realities of managing a growing computer network amid surging personal and private interests.

The information age does not necessarily eliminate the weaknesses and injustices of the industrial age. The hierarchies based on the factory and the factorylike corporation were built as much on social groupings as on merit—the pernicious and intractable evils of racism, sexism, and classism. Computers don't eliminate social discrimination. The framework of distributed networks may be explicitly democratic, but, as Licklider and Taylor pointed out in "Computer as a Communication Device," that doesn't mean society will be, especially if all people don't have access to the technology.

What *is* possible is the establishment of systems that are more efficient at properly rewarding success and ability. The spirit of the intergalactic network revived in the 1980s with the free-software (or open-source) movement, led by such iconoclasts as Richard Stallman, Larry Wall, and Eric S. Raymond. The idea of information sharing is tied in with the concept of reputation—that you acquire power by earning the respect of your peers. The more information you share, the more you benefit. This runs contrary to proprietary information, which depends on hidden knowledge.

The most marvelous thing about the people shaping the network is that, in contrast to those heading the monoliths in the corporate and governmental world, they do not attempt to control everything. Rather, they revel in unexpected developments, with a spirit that has blossomed along with the growth of the Internet. Technology shapes culture, and culture shapes technology. No tool is more powerful for that realization than the networked computer, the intersection of a million minds on the cerebral frontier.

OF MICE AND MEN

DOUG ENGELBART

If you are interested in democracy and its future, you'd
better understand computers.   —Ted Nelson

ALMOST TWENTY YEARS BEFORE the ARPAnet went online, Doug Engelbart, a future member of J. C. R. Licklider's
intergalactic network, began to think about the state of the
world. The twenty-five-year-old World War II veteran saw
that it was getting unbelievably complex. That year, 1950,
President Harry Truman ordered work to begin on the hydrogen bomb. Senator Joseph McCarthy began his anti-Com-
munist crusade, jolting the nation when he declared that he
held a list of 205 known "Reds" working in the State Department. North Korea invaded South Korea. The rich were
getting richer and the poor poorer, the environment was under
siege by reckless industrialism, and the population was growing disproportionately. Schools were becoming overcrowded
and doomsayers grieved the future of education for the Baby
Boom generation.

Engelbart considered his own life in this context. He had recently returned from the war unscathed, got a solid job as an
electrical engineer at Ames Laboratory, and proposed to a nice
girl he met when folk dancing at the Palo Alto community center. The emerging America of brand-new appliances, prefab

houses, fast food, and steady bureaucratic jobs was all his. Engelbart was right on course for a comfortable life. He contemplated this nice long stretch of time ahead and decided that it resembled a clean, well-lit, featureless office corridor.

He didn't want it. He sought a *crusade,* a profound mission that would help ease the world of its burdens. But what? He thought about joining forces to fight malaria or boost food productivity in developing countries, but remembered stories about how such efforts sometimes backfired. Engelbart knew that in this increasingly complex world, microcosmic thinking leads to macrocosmic trauma. Killing off one pest can alter an ecosystem. Tiring the soil leaves the land and people worse off. Nevermore should specialists in any field be so ignorant of the impact of small effects on the whole system. But who really thinks about the big picture?

What the world needs, he decided, is a way for humans to work together to develop long-term solutions for long-term problems. He wanted a career that would maximize his contribution to humanity, building on his professional background as an engineer.

Engelbart had been a radar technician during the war. He recalled the training seminars in which he encountered radar that works with a screen. He knew from his background in electronics that there were computers with screens, and that if they could print or punch cards, they could draw symbols on screen. He knew that an operator could interact with the radar through a computer display terminal in real time. He imagined a station with knobs, levers, buttons, and a screen with symbols. He envisioned many such stations, with people interacting with and through their computers in real time. People could . . . *collaborate through the computer.* The machine would augment human intelligence through collective problem solving. "*Ah, I've got it,*" he said. He could use what he knew. It took him the entire decade, but he finally got it down on paper in his two manifestos, "Special Considerations of the Individual as a User, Generator, and Retriever of Information" (1960) and *Augmenting Human Intellect: A Conceptual Framework* (1962). His writings forecasted the technologies he created, including the mouse and a working hypertext system.

BEYOND CALCULATION

The only problem with Engelbart's big idea was that he didn't know very much about computers in 1950. Nor did anyone else. The average person then may have heard about them in the context of the war. A big shot mathematician named John von Neumann, after working on the A-bomb, built computers. Computers were as big as bedrooms and as heavy as buildings. They looked like generators. They didn't have screens. They were good for cracking code or crunching equations or perhaps doing something in industry.

None of the later computer visionaries had showed up on the scene yet. J. C. R. Licklider, fresh out of graduate school, was still attending Norbert Wiener's cybernetics meetings. Ivan Sutherland, Larry Roberts, Leonard Kleinrock, and Robert Taylor were still kids playing with electronics kits and crystal radios. Only a few computers existed in the world. And the closest thing to a communicating machine that many people heard about was Vannevar Bush's memex, which had been popularized in *Life* and *Time* back in 1945.

Bush's article, "As We May Think," had come into Engelbart's hands on his way home from the war that fall. When his ship stopped for a week or so on the island of Laiti in the Philippines, Engelbart grew bored and set off into the jungle, where he found a Red Cross library hut on stilts. There he read the article and became inspired by Bush's vision. He particularly liked the idea that the memex would help amplify the consciousness of a single person or a whole society of people. He also admired the idea of using the machine to make associations between ideas.

Engelbart decided to attend graduate school to learn how to build computer technology. He chose the University of California at Berkeley because they had a research contract to build a computer. Although the Berkeley computer never was finished, Engelbart received his Ph.D. in electrical engineering in 1956 (his thesis was on gas discharge devices). By then, he had married the nice girl and had three children, but still didn't know how to go about his crusade to augment human intellect through computers.

No one seemed to appreciate the idea of using computers to help humankind improve its problem-solving abilities. Engelbart turned down prospects in academia because his colleagues rolled their eyes at the idea of computer-assisted human augmentation. An elder professor, shaking his head, warned Doug if his peers didn't like his work, it wouldn't get published, he wouldn't get promoted, and he'd be an assistant professor forever. Engelbart, soft-spoken yet stubborn, also turned down a job at Hewlett-Packard after he was told that there was "not a chance" he would be developing digital technology and computers there. He encountered the same problem throughout the 1950s. For about a year he ran his own consulting company, Digital Technique, which specialized in gas discharge devices, but shut it down because he didn't want to keep up with the technology in that field. Finally, in 1957, Engelbart was offered a job developing technologies at the Stanford Research Institute (SRI) in Menlo Park, California—a friend had advised him to not talk too much about augmenting human intellect at the interview. SRI was a haven of freeform intellectualism within the larger sphere of business and industry.*

A PROTOMANIFESTO

"Crusades have many strikes against them at the outset," explained Engelbart. "In particular, they don't connect to a normal source of government or business revenue. They don't have nice organization frameworks. You can't go out on the streets and expect to find financial, production, or marketing vice presidents interested."[1] Unsurprisingly, Engelbart's colleagues at SRI were also dubious of this idea about computers augmenting human intellect. His solution: publish urgent, official articles on the topic that would attract sufficient funding from business and industry.

In 1961 Engelbart published a protomanifesto in the *Journal of American Documentation* titled "Special Considerations of the Individual as a User, Generator, and Retriever of Information." The article was aimed primarily at one small, insular community: information

---

*SRI is a not-for-profit, nonendowed corporation chartered by the State of California. SRI was founded in November 1946 by the Trustees of Stanford University at the request and with the support of a group of leading West Coast industrialists, but there is no operational connection between the university and the institute.

retrieval specialists. Engelbart assumed that the people most likely to join his movement would be those who archive and distribute newspapers, television broadcasts, and corporate data. His goal was to convince them that computing machines were the future of information—and that he wanted to build them. The secondary audience for the paper were cyberneticists.

Like most others who had studied technology at the graduate level in the 1950s, Engelbart was inspired by cybernetics. The idea of using the computer to amplify human capability was positively cybernetic. Humans working together via computers would benefit from feedback from one another and with their respective machines. In respect to information, computers would be an extension of the human brain, mimicking its storage, retrieval, and access mechanisms on a grand scale. Like the cyberneticists, Engelbart was interested in how information (in this case, text) can be packetized, transmitted, packaged, and reconstituted in and through the machine.

In "Special Considerations," Engelbart framed the problem as Bush did in "As We May Think." The uncontrollable overgrowth of knowledge could be pruned back only by effective information retrieval. With similar stateliness he wrote, "The dominant challenge of your discipline involves the problem of looking back in time to see what has been contributed by others that will be of benefit to the individual of today. But you know that to help meet this challenge tomorrow, the messages of today must be handled with care."[2] He wrote that archival systems are valuable only to the degree that they make people more effective.

People work best, Engelbart argued, when they work with small "packets" of information—bite-sized chunks of text extracted from longer sources. Engelbart discribed the job of information specialists in business and research as a necessary "cannibalizing" of raw material. The larger duty of such specialists is to provide the big picture "of the society, of its history, and its intellectual structure." In other words, specialists should also be generalists.

. . . .

The individual gains the picture only by laboriously fitting together new possibilities, generating or ferreting out new facts or

> concepts and creating this process until a view emerges that is
> compatible with the existing structure and his desires.[3]
> —"Special Considerations"

Like Bush, Engelbart lamented that humans cannot hold many concepts in their minds at the same time and that we need a tool to extend our brain capacities. That is, a machine can store information that we don't need to remember. Again like Bush, Engelbart proposed that such a tool would present information in "spatial patterns," like trails. The user should be able to link text and follow links. The important feature Engelbart added to Bush's vision is that people would be able to share information and collaborate on documents at their own terminals. Unlike the memex, the record would be common; everyone's documents and trails would be accessible. Engelbart concluded that the system should be time-shared (one powerful computer serving many workstations).

> The intellectual labors of the individual who generates a document
> are made much more effective by your seeing to it that his con-
> tribution becomes a "visible" part of society's growing structure
> of knowledge.[4]   —"Special Considerations"

Engelbart fancied himself the bridge between the age-old world of archival documentation and the new world of computers. This, he thought, would be the way to take the computer out of huge research laboratories and into public service. When he presented these ideas to an audience of information specialists at a Stanford conference, they sat quietly and listened to the sloe-eyed, long-nosed man. Afterward, four specialists invited him to step outside to the patio. "Do you realize all you're talking about is information retrieval?" they asked him.

"I said no," Engelbart recalled, "I'm also talking about how you can *create* and *manipulate* information."

"Well, that's our field and *we* know information retrieval," they said. They told him that they resented that he, an electrical engineer, was trying to tell them the future of their profession.

"You see," Engelbart laughed, "they just actually got pissed off."

THE AUGMENTATION MANIFESTO

In May 1962, Engelbart finally wrote a letter to Vannevar Bush. In it he thanked Bush for the vision of the memex and mentioned his own passion for the "promise and possibilities . . . for future improvements of our intellectual capability."*

> I re-discovered your article about three years ago, and was rather startled to realize how much I had aligned my sights along the vector you had described. I wouldn't be surprised at all if the reading of this article sixteen and a half years ago hadn't had a real influence upon the course of my thoughts and actions.[5]

Yes, even scarier

Engelbart's letter to Bush was also a request for permission to reprint excerpts from "As We May Think" in what amounted to Engelbart's own manifesto, *Augmenting Human Intellect: A Conceptual Framework*. Despite its militaristic-sounding subtitle, "Summary Report AFOSR-3223 under Contract AF 49(638)-1024, SRI Project 3578 for Air Force Office of Scientific Research," the paper was a decree for world peace through technology. Defense budgets, ironically, were the best source of funding for computer research and development at the time. In the letter Engelbart explained to Bush that he had finally persuaded the Air Force to give him some money and had turned around enough skeptics at SRI to begin working on the project almost full-time. But he needed to keep hustling for more funds and support.

. . . .

> Any possibility for improving the effective utilization of the intellectual power of society's problem solvers warrants the most serious consideration. This is because man's problem-solving capability represents the most important resource possessed by a society. . . . We spend great sums for disciplines aimed at understanding and harnessing nuclear power. Why not consider developing a discipline aimed at understanding and harnessing

---

*Engelbart regretted that he never met Bush in person. By the time Engelbart became reacquainted with the memex, Bush was in a nursing home and unavailable.

"neural power"? In the long run, the power of the human intellect is really the more important of the two.[6]

—*Augmenting Human Intellect*

. . . .

In *Augmenting Human Intellect,* Engelbart, like Bush, refers explicitly to the world's increasing *complexity* and *urgency* (words that he underlined). Because local events now have global effects, problems need to be nipped at the bud. In the context of nuclear war, pollution, and the beginning of civil rights unrest, one had the impression that the world's threshold for problems decreased and any small event could manifest itself cataclysmically.

Engelbart's conviction was that each of us within our specialty—politics, engineering, the arts, math, social sciences, design, management, etc.—can contribute to a system of collective problem solving. Because everything is interrelated, an improvement in any area, be it social, technical, economic, cultural, or scientific, can trigger a chain reaction of improvements in other areas. He believed his system-oriented approach to problem solving would also help people achieve personal intellectual effectiveness. Each user would be able to better comprehend complex, big-picture problems and realize how he or she could contribute to their solutions. One person, any person, can trigger a world of difference by participating.

. . . .

By "augmenting human intellect" we mean increasing the capability of a man to approach a complex problem situation, to gain comprehension to suit his particular needs, and to derive solutions to problems. Increased capability in this respect is taken to mean a mixture of the following: more rapid comprehension, better comprehension, the possibility of gaining a useful degree of comprehension in a situation that previously was too complex, speedier solutions, better solutions, and the possibility of finding solutions to problems that before seemed insoluble.[7]

—*Augmenting Human Intellect*

. . . .

The computer, Engelbart stressed, is the means by which people can augment their personal and collective intellect. People could work not only alone on their own machines (as Bush imagined the memex) but also *at terminals all connected to one another.* This way, people could interact in real time. The time-shared computer, first developed by John Mc-Carthy at the Massachusetts Institute of Technology around 1960, consists of one host computer connected to any number of dumb terminals or "workstations." Time-shared systems made sense because computers cost tens of thousands of dollars, process information so much faster than human brains, and can handle multiple users simultaneously. Engelbart found great inspiration in the idea of these interactive time-shared networks. Both the real-time aspect (people didn't have to wait for hours to get results) and the network idea (people never before "partnered" with their machines or through them) were completely new to the world.

In *Augmenting Human Intellect*, Engelbart supported his case by describing the extraordinary developments occurring on the East Coast. At Lincoln Laboratory Ivan Sutherland was using the display-computer facility to develop cooperative techniques to solve engineering design problems. Engelbart had read Licklider's "Man–Computer Symbiosis" (1960), which he hailed as "the most general clear case for the modern computer." Like Licklider, Engelbart believed that the relationship between the human and computer will benefit human beings. Lick called it *symbiosis*, emphasizing the mutual benefit; Engelbart dubbed it *synergism*, the "cooperative action of discrete agencies such that the total effect is greater than the sum of the two effects taken independently" (*Webster's Unabridged Dictionary*, second edition). This synergism, he hoped, would augment the human user.

> We refer to a way of life in an integrated domain where hunches, cut-and-try, intangibles, and the human "feel for a situation" usefully co-exists with powerful concepts, streamlined technology and notation, sophisticated methods, and high-powered electronic aids.[8] —*Augmenting Human Intellect*

Engelbart imagined the "augmented architect" situated at a workstation with a three-foot display screen. The user would communicate with the machine by means of a keyboard or similar device. The computer would be a "clerk," an assistant to the human problem solver. The clerk would compute the math and display information, both textually and graphically. Several people could work together to model, for example, the interior of a building. Each architect would be presented with the same information and collaborate in the same environment. The computer would manipulate and display information in real time, and people would have an opportunity to simulate various solutions to a problem. In this way, the technology fosters intuition and creativity as well as logic and reason. This, Engelbart said, is *human augmentation.*

UP THE EVOLUTIONARY LADDER

Human augmentation would be the world's new conceptual framework, Engelbart believed. Of course, the development of new frameworks, new paradigms, is nothing new to humankind. A new paradigm is created every time we develop a new tool as "an extension of the means developed and used to help man apply his native sensory, mental, and motor capabilities."[9] Engelbart wrote that the computer is a tool like the club, the plow, or the printing press, in that it will (directly or indirectly) boost human intellect and transform societies. As with earlier technologies, we must integrate this new tool into our lives, our *humanness,* for it to work for us in the best possible way.

Engelbart posits that humans have always augmented their intellect, through:

- Language ("thinking"—to parse the world into concepts that our minds use to model the world and symbols attached to those concepts);

- Artifacts (physical objects for the manipulation of materials as well as symbols);

- Methodology (methods, procedures, strategies, etc. to organize a goal-centered problem-solving activity);

- Training (conditioning required for us to attain skills in combining artifacts, language, and methodology, the point of effectiveness).

Engelbart refers to the combination of the four as the H-LAM/T system, meaning human enhanced by language, artifact, methodology, and training. He focuses attention on the LAM combination, insisting that the more adept humans are at making language, artifacts, and methods work together, the more we evolve. To illustrate how civilizations have progressed using LAM systems, Engelbart conducted a simple test he called the handwriting experiment.

The experiment consisted of writing the line AUGMENTATION IS FUNDAMENTALLY A MATTER OF ORGANIZATION with different tools and methods: a typewriter; a pencil, using cursive handwriting; and a pencil inserted through a brick. Unsurprisingly, the typewriter print was the smallest and neatest and took only seven seconds. The cursive script written with a pencil took twenty seconds. A less refined cursive script was written with the brick and pencil and took sixty-five seconds. When the experimenter tried to write quickly with the brick and pencil, the script resembled a child's uncoordinated scrawl.

How would our civilization have matured, had we never developed effective tools and methods?

> The record-keeping that enables the organization of commerce and government would probably have taken a form so different from what we know that our social structure would have definitely evolved differently. Also, the effort of doing calculations and writing down extensive and carefully reasoned arguments would dampen individual experimentation and sophisticated new concepts, to lower the rate of learning and the rate of useful output, and perhaps to discourage a good many people from even working at extending understanding.[10]
>
> —*Augmenting Human Intellect*

The lesson? The bedrock of civilization is information, which depends on language, artifacts, and methods. Our tools, even those as simple as the pencil, facilitate communication, shape our culture, and advance our species. The means determine the ends.

STEPS, SYMBOLS, AND SIGNS

Engelbart, in some ways a typical engineer, believes that we internalize the world around us through a hierarchical organization of processes. Human augmentation is a process of accretion. Every thought and action are composed of layer upon layer of subprocesses. Complex understanding emerges from learning simple concepts themselves achieved in graduated steps. An "untrained aborigine," he writes, would be able to navigate a car through traffic if taught "step by step." Such training would involve, of course, an explanation of everything from what a car is to the function of traffic signs (and how to read), to how to operate a steering wheel (and how to coordinate one's eyes and hands), to how to make good use of the horn (within the culture's strictures), and so on.

> The human mind neither learns nor acts by large leaps, but by steps organized and structured so that each one depends upon previous steps.[11]　　　　　*—Augmenting Human Intellect*

There is no point in looking for the ultimate bottom of the process hierarchies, Engelbart maintains. People reuse knowledge when they learn something new. For example, once one understands the basic motion of a wheel—*it spins*—one can conceive the basic operation of all wheels. We are inductive beings. Our learning is hierarchical yet modular, flexible yet specific. We understand complex things by understanding thousands of simple things.

We can understand things only to a certain extent, however, if we lack the ability to manipulate language and methodology, numbers and letters. A grasp of these symbols is a basic skill for living in the modern world. It is more effective to use numbers to count sheep than to remember the appearance of each one. It is more effective to write down ideas than to remember every thought. It is more effective to express a complex concept with words than with body language.

Engelbart's inspiration for these ideas was the linguist Benjamin Lee Whorf, who, in the early 1940s, hypothesized that individual and societal behavior is formed by the language—the symbols—society uses. Words shape our reality, constructed of our collective and individual thoughts and actions. Engelbart added to this his own theory, which he called the "neo-Whorfian hypothesis": A worldview is directly affected by the way a culture or an individual externally *manipulates* symbols. Getting a *computer* to externalize our symbol language could actually *transform* human thinking. Engelbart called it "automated external symbol manipulation"—which, in 1962, was quite revolutionary.

> Both the language used by a culture, and the capability for effective intellectual activity are directly affected during their evolution by the means by which individuals control the external manipulation of symbols.... Integrating the capabilities of a digital computer into the intellectual activity of human beings ... is introducing a new and extremely advanced means for externally manipulating symbols.[12]   —*Augmenting Human Intellect*

Automated external symbol manipulation meant that a person would be able to arrange and rearrange text before her very eyes. With this, Engelbart introduced the idea of a computerized "writing machine" similar to a 1960s-era electric typewriter, but boasting several extra features. The text entered into the writing machine would attach an invisible code to each word, and the text would be stored within the mechanism. The invisible code would enable the user to compose and rearrange her work an infinite number of times. She could move it from one part of a document to another, store it and recall it, and perhaps display it in three dimensions and in color. She could delete swaths of text and move single words or entire paragraphs swiftly and cleanly. The first draft of a document could be a thicket of thoughts that the user could whittle down in successive drafts. "Trails" would connect ideas within a document or between documents. With the writing machine, the user's relationship with her work would change considerably—as would her thinking process. Engelbart believed this simple symbol manipulation tool would transform worldviews.

> You can integrate your ideas more easily, and thus harness your creativity more continuously if you can quickly and flexibly change your working record....The important thing to appreciate here is that a direct new innovation in one particular capability can have far-reaching effects.[13]   —*Augmenting Human Intellect*

In addition to the pen, the plow, and the printing press would be the processor. Engelbart's writing machine would become the *word processor*.

The "trails" would become a working hypertext system, developed in Engelbart's lab at SRI in the years to follow.

BOOTSTRAPPING AFOOT

Engelbart's colleagues at SRI were surprised when *Augmenting Human Intellect* piqued widespread interest. The demand for the article became so great that SRI ran out of copies of it the summer it was published. From 1962 to 1970, it was sent out in bulk to not only potential government sponsors, but also IBM and other corporations, research scientists, engineers, and science and social science professors. The office at SRI had to lend out copies to be returned.

Licklider, by then director of his interactive computing division at ARPA, was one of the lucky early recipients. Engelbart sent the article to him knowing that Lick was doling out the new Kennedy-funded ARPA money for computer research. He told Licklider how much he admired "Man–Computer Symbiosis." Later, Engelbart joked, "There the unlucky fellow was, having advertised that 'man–computer symbiosis,' computer time-sharing and the man-computer interface were the new directions. . . . How could he in reasonable consistency turn this down?"[14] Indeed, Lick couldn't resist, and in him Engelbart found a "big brother he could talk with," who shared a vision of computers connected together in a network. Soon enough, Engelbart became a node in Lick's notorious intergalactic network—that bunch of wild-haired guys, as Engelbart called them. One of his colleagues half-jokingly told him that perhaps he should be embarrassed to receive ARPA funding—after all, "they were backing all the kooks."[15]

With his first round of ARPA cash, Engelbart had enough for his salary and some equipment, but not enough for a support staff. His other significant source of support from the beginning was The National Aeronautics and Space Administration (NASA). His patron: Bob Taylor, then working as a research administrator there. From 1964 to 1965, NASA gave Engelbart $85,000 to develop computers that would augment human intellect. After Lick left ARPA, Larry Roberts, working under Sutherland at the Information Processing Techniques Office, almost matched NASA's annual offering. Engelbart's coffers were flush with funding. The near future was secure when Roberts took over as director of the

IPTO in 1965. But commencing the project would take an immense effort to match the vision. Engelbart compared it to building an airplane for the first time. Every step of the way would be simultaneously fascinating and fraught with the peril of crashing.

The Augmented Human Intellect Research Center (later called ARC for Augmentation Research Center) was founded on the concepts of *coevolution* and *bootstrapping*.* It would promote Licklider's ideal of human–computer symbiosis. Furthermore, it would use bootstrapping to "continually evolve an ever-larger and more sophisticated system of hardware and software."[16] The verb *bootstrap,* as in "to lift oneself up by the bootstraps," had been around since 1958, meaning "to make use of existing resources or capabilities to achieve a new situation or state; to modify or improve by making use of what is already present" (*Oxford English Dictionary,* second edition). Engelbart succinctly explains it as "feeding the output of your research back into it." The first users of Engelbart's augmentation system would be its programmers, and the programmers would *use* the augmentation system to *build* the augmentation system. It would be up to the humans to train themselves and develop ways of evolving the system to suit them better. The humans and their technology would *coevolve.*

Bootstrapping is Norbert Wiener's cybernetic vision of feedback put into practice. It was Wiener who demonstrated that when a mechanism corrects the input signal using measurement of the output (whether such mechanisms are neurons, circuits, or both), humans and machines learn. Bootstrapping is a big corrective cybernetic feedback loop between human and computer for the purpose of learning and evolving the system. In *Cybernetics,* Wiener wrote:

> The principle of regeneration in physical systems is fairly well-known, where the output is reintroduced into the system in such a way as to reinforce the type of behavior that

---

*Engelbart didn't use the term "bootstrapping" in *Augmenting Human Intellect,* but the concept was in place in the manifesto.

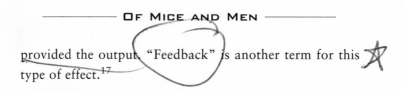

provided the output. "Feedback" is another term for this type of effect.[17]

Seen another way, bootstrapping is a feedback loop between humans, made possible by computers. In the bootstrapping project, each "problem solver" had his or her own workstation, with access to common documents. Individuals worked on the same document and the computer could merge their respective versions, identifying who made what change and when. In *Augmenting Human Intellect,* Engelbart wrote, "The whole team can join forces at a moment's notice to 'pull together' on some stubborn little problem, or to make a group decision. Most points of contention are resolved quite naturally, over a period of time, as the developing structure of the argument bears out."[18] No one can dominate the show, he added.

> Three people working together in this augmented mode seem to be more than three times as effective in solving a complex problem as is one augmented person working alone—and perhaps ten times as effective as three similar men working together without this computer-based augmentation.[19]
>
> —*Augmenting Human Intellect*

Engelbart and his partner, Bill English, and the team at SRI bootstrapped hardware and software technologies that forever changed the course of computing—and therefore communication and, indeed, society. The group (sixteen full-time people in 1968 and forty-five by 1976) devised the following tools and techniques to help augment human beings:

Chord keyset (1962): This was a five-key binary keyboard for entering letters and numbers, primarily for commands. Each alphanumeric symbol had a code, a combination of keys, that the user would enter as if playing chords on a piano. The device looks like a five-key piano and frees one hand for other activity. Once learned, it is more efficient than the traditional QWERTY keyboard, but it never gained mass appeal outside of ARC.

Mouse (1964): The mouse allows the user to point a cursor at text and select it. The original mouse was wooden, with three buttons and a tracking ball. The user forms an interactive, visual feedback loop with the computer. Researchers also experimented with a "knee mouse" and a "head mouse," the latter with a "nose pointing control" that would enable users to keep their hands on the keyboard, nodding and shaking their head to navigate the cursor. Muscles would cramp with everything but the hand-controlled mouse.

The system was designed to allow the user to coordinate the mouse and chord keyset, one under each hand, to do just about everything other than long stretches of typing, which could be done on a traditional keyboard.

By 1971 Engelbart and his team had bootstrapped their intellect augmentation system, which they called NLS (for oN-Line System), later called AUGMENT. NLS was a fully functional, time-shared personal computer network, programmed in a specially designed multilevel command language, with the following revolutionary technologies:

Structured text (including word processing): All text entered into the system was structured into a hierarchical arrangement that resembled an outline. Every sentence had two underlying tag addresses that indicated its position and place in a document. As a result, users could insert, delete, move, and copy text in anyone's documents without confusion, transcending the limitations of physical documents.

The Journal: The Journal stored all information—text and graphics—as a permanent record in an explicitly retrievable form. All users could access the record; all code was shared. Every document was uniquely and permanently identified, with a line providing the identity of the author and the date, hour, and minute of creation. It was the library of information, the central resource of the procognitive system, as

Licklider would have described it. The Journal preserved information as it adapted and evolved.

Multiple views: Users could view text in multiple ways at multiple levels in the hierarchical structure. For example, they could type commands to see only the first sentence of each paragraph, a few lines, or changes made since a particular date; they could do this for multiple documents simultaneously.

Hypertext (links):* The emphasis with NLS was on the association of information. The Journal and mail system contained an indexed library where all documents resided. The user could issue links—cross-references—between documents in the hierarchically organized system. The user followed a trail of links between documents, using the mouse to point to a line and typing or chording the code for JUMP. Engelbart also wanted documents to "back-link," which would enable the user to track all links pointed toward any given document. This technology was never fully developed. Bush is nominally credited with the idea of trails, but Engelbart made a working system to create such tags and links between words.

E-Mail: A user could submit text to other users, individually or collectively. All mail, identifiable by an identifier code, would be stored in the Journal permanently and accessed by keyword, number, or author. The NLS electronic mail system was the first one in operation.

Search capability: Users could search the NLS index using keywords.

---

*Ted Nelson introduced the term *hypertext* in 1965. With inspiration from Engelbart and the initial involvement of Nelson, Andries van Dam of Brown University built the Hypertext Editing System (HES) in 1967, which slightly preceded the NLS. In 1968, van Dam built the File Retrieval and Editing System (FRESS), a hybrid of the HES and Engelbart's NLS, and used to teach courses in English poetry. The project, which struggled for support, was dropped by the late 1970s.

---

*Windows (screen splitting):** Multiple windows on the same
screen enabled users to juxtapose information and perform
more than one activity at once. Early versions of NLS supported windows that could contain graphics or text. Later
versions were text-only, sacrificing graphics for more efficient
networking speeds.

Help system: Users could access information about a function through context-sensitive menus.

Shared screen teleconferencing: NLS enabled users to simultaneously revise a document from remote locations.

DEMONSTRATIONS OF '68

The message behind all this cutting-edge technology was that the networked, user-friendly computer would be the tool that would evolve the
human race. Human beings collaborating via computers would achieve the
most democratic means of problem solving yet. The power to manipulate
ideas on the screen and save personal and collective information would
transform the way people work. It would help people get out of their own
heads. When networked, the computer would access the legacy of humankind and make it more accessible. It would be to the Information Revolution what the steam engine was to the Industrial Revolution. It would
overthrow the outdated institutions of the past—our inflexible and restrictive bureaucracies—and replace them with a more inherently egalitarian, streamlined, participatory, and peaceful infrastructure.

If Engelbart thought the 1950s were unbearably complex, the 1960s
were outright pandemonium. He wanted to join the fray, though he was
not a hippie, just liberal. But the crusade to augment human intellect fits
nicely into the 1960s wish list of revolutionary change. The other ideological movements of the times—civil rights, environmentalist, and countercultural protests—were likewise motivated by the drive to create a

---

*These windows might more rightly be called *panes;* they split the screen, but were
not movable or overlapping, as the windows developed later at Xerox PARC.

greater good through empowerment of the people. Engelbart's long-time discontent with middle-class complacency was increasingly shared, not just by the Baby Boomers, but by all generations and creeds. Protesters identified the authorities who were supposed to protect us—our police and National Guard—with totalitarianism. The peace movement escalated into a state of violence. The assassinations of John F. Kennedy, Martin Luther King Jr., Robert F. Kennedy, and Malcolm X emphasized the darkness of the political struggle. Rioters stormed the streets of Stanford, right down the road from SRI.

The ARC itself was notorious as a counterculture think tank that guzzled deeply from the lifespring of the Bay Area attitude. Even the phrase "augmenting human intellect" intimated the countercultural trends of boosting human potential through New Age spiritualism. No doubt there is a connection between the technologically augmented human and the spiritually augmented one. (Engelbart, considering the ark-ARC analogy, even toyed with the idea of growing a biblical beard—and finally did, in 1969.)

Engelbart was partial to the holistic thinking of his friend Stewart Brand and his crew at the *Whole Earth Catalog*. They had adopted cybernetics and other modern science and spun them into an alternative and all-encompassing explanation of the world's ways. The mid-1960s Gaia theory was one example of runaway cybernetics. NASA's James Lovelock proposed that the earth is a complex single organism that, like the human body, regulates itself by dint of millions of feedback loops between countless organisms within it. Engelbart believed that *coevolution,* the cumulative and symbiotic development of humans and computers, would likewise regulate the world. Like Wiener and Licklider, he believed in forming feedback loops between ourselves and our environment, including our technologies.

Engelbart had other 1960s-era credentials as well: He participated in several Californian New Age "encounter groups" and, in 1968, hired psychologists to help ARCers communicate more effectively. Some people considered Engelbart foremost among Licklider's brilliant "kooks."

Engelbart's activism assumed the form of a demonstration executed in a white button-down shirt and tie. In December 1968, not long after the riots that year, he unveiled windows, hypertext, the mouse, and collaborative computing at the Association for Computing Machinery/Institute of Electrical and Electronic Engineers-Computer Society Fall Joint Computer Conference. This was the next phase of ARC's (co)evolution: to spread the NLS to a wider community of users.

Engelbart's partner, Bill English, had set up the system perfectly, but Doug was "nervous as hell." If the thing crashed, ARPA and NASA might pull the funding. The presentation cost about $15,000 (the equivalent of at least $70,000 in 2002). A video cast the screen onto a twenty-foot backdrop. The ARC team built special technologies for the presentation to pick up signals from Engelbart's mouse, chord keyset, and keyboard and transmit them back and forth thirty miles to the system at SRI. Video cameras, one manned by Stewart Brand, recorded Doug and the workstation, and the system at SRI; English flipped between them in real time. Between two and three thousand people watched in awe for an hour and a half as Engelbart split the computer screen into windows, linked text, unfurled menus, and wheeled around a mouse, working at the speed of thought. He collaborated online with colleagues back at ARC; the screen demonstrated how the mice-guided cursors facilitated the joint revision of a document. Jeff Rulifson, an ARC staff member, explained the NLS-structured software.

Engelbart got a standing ovation. In ensuing years, the presentation was dubbed "the mother of all demos." Technologists from Xerox Palo Alto Research Center (PARC) rushed to the stage, brimming with enthusiasm. "The demo was one of the greatest experiences in my life," gushed Alan Kay, who would later head a research group at PARC. Kay, who had seen NLS before but never with so much fanfare, *got it*. He said, "It reset the whole conception of what was reasonable to think about in personal computing. It was the romance of humanity thinking its way out of its genetic structure. The ideas invented were about superceding what our genes and mammalian brains want us to do."[20]

At the time, a significant part of computing's future rested in Engelbart's hands, suspended between government funding and future business interests. Engelbart could have capitalized on his power, selling out then and there. But he didn't believe that business alone would operate in the best interests of society. IBM, for example, had rejected the idea of the NLS at its inception. His conviction was that corporations would push for the development of new technologies without necessarily considering their long-term effects from a societal perspective. They wouldn't wait for a technology to incubate *step by step,* the only way to ensure positive social change. They would defeat the purpose of his crusade.

> Getting acceptance and application of the new techniques to the most critical problems of our society might in fact be the most critical problem of all.[21] —*Augmenting Human Intellect*

Engelbart's vision was for trainers at ARC to go forth and train other new groups of people who, like missionaries, would train others and perpetuate the crusade. Government organizations, businesses, and eventually individuals would become "augmented." Teams collaborating on networked computers would represent a new model of community in which everyone can contribute to the content, quality, and structure of information.

Engelbart argued that the process of tagging text helps one pay more attention to the overall structure of information, which in turn promotes a global worldview. Metaphorically, tagging hypertext links could help us conceive that everything is interrelated; part of an organic whole. Practically, if the system were widely used, it could help us maintain our collective record and build our government, businesses, research, and culture in the way that Bush also envisioned. It could provide the opportunity to open any issue of public discussion based on a wealth of information.

With the passion and conviction of 1960s activism, Engelbart envisioned that humankind would be able to lift itself up by its bootstraps. We have no choice. "Changes once took place so slowly that we weren't really aware of the evolutionary process," Engelbart said. "But now, with a catapulting rate of change, and the pressure to become more effective, the changes within an organization are just going to exceed the rate we know how to deal with." Little did he realize that his words would also apply to ARC itself.

He never said it, but it would be survival of the fittest on the streets and online. The activism of the sixties would dissipate and evolve into something else. The technologies developed at ARC would disperse and coevolve elsewhere. But Engelbart's values and ethics would remain hardwired into the future of the technology and become, in a sense, a lasting legacy of the 1960s push toward a collective good.

ONLINE AND OFF

ARPAnet went online in the summer of 1969. Kleinrock's lab at UCLA was the first hooked up to it. Engelbart's at SRI was the second. The ARPAnet was clearly the next evolutionary stage for human augmentation. People would no longer be tied to one time-shared computer. Information would be shareable through an unlimited number of smaller computers networked together.

Engelbart had agreed to develop and operate ARPAnet's Network Information Center as a library and online service or, to use Licklider's term, a procognitive system. He saw the newborn ARPAnet as an opportunity to spread his message and carry on the crusade. By building the library, Engelbart and the NLS would have a ready-made online community.

The Network Information Center ensured that most early users of ARPAnet became default NLS users. But NLS had been specially designed for a local-area time-shared network of computers, not the national ARPAnet. Every feature was interdependent; the NLS mail system couldn't be deployed separately from the complex Journal. The NLS required too much homogeneity for the disparate, fractious university researchers; they built each piece, from email to document sharing, one simple piece at a time, rather than reconfigure their systems and lives to the NLS way. Although Engelbart's vision of bootstrapping had worked by amplifying its users' successes, it suffered from the dangers of positive feedback: Without regulatory feedback from the outside, idiosyncrasies amplified, and NLS grew baroque, beautiful, and doomed.

When Roberts left ARPA, support for Engelbart waned. To make matters worse, the Mansfield Amendment in 1970 required ARPA to fund only projects with obvious defense applications—it could no longer be Licklider's merry intergalactic network. Soon, ARPA assumed sole responsibility for the Network Information Center, leaving Engelbart and ARC a loose skein. In late 1973 the new ARPA director sent Engelbart a letter informing him that they were going to cut his funding in three months, at ARC's anniversary in 1974.*

Around the same time, members of Engelbart's own team started to lose faith in the mission. "They started to want to do different things," Engelbart explained. "I thought that if they came to work for us they would buy into the picture." Some staff members and trainees criticized the software and the organization for its inflexible structure. Engelbart had devised a system that helped people develop ideas, organize them, associate them with other ideas, view them in multiple ways, and access them later. But they had to fit everything into the structure. The hard-coded guidelines of the software forced users to write in a certain way, prefiguring PowerPoint and other software that inhibits creativity by limiting the ways to organize ideas and information to only those the software designers believe are best. And people who weren't caught up in Engelbart's grand scheme, who were excited, say, by the prospect of making stuff that was simply *cool,* frustrated Engelbart. Schisms developed between those in the pursuit of grand schemes, some of whom also got caught up in local self-help cults, and pragmatists admired Engelbart's zeal but really just wanted to make things that worked.

SRI dismantled ARC in 1977 and sold the NLS to a time-share company already in the business of having multiple computers in their network. The aircraft manufacturer McDonnell Douglas purchased the system later. Engelbart went with it, although he was immensely frustrated when, for example, he tried to convince them to network the computers together in an early form of an intranet. Upper management refused because the big corporations like IBM and Hewlett-Packard weren't doing it.

AFTERWARD

User friendliness became the main challenge of the generation of computer technologies that followed the NLS. Engelbart positioned the computer as a tool—an artifact—with which the person would coevolve. To

---

*Although ARPA ceased to support the augmentation project after 1974, it continued to support Engelbart's development of other applications until 1977.

coevolve, the person needed to be trained in how to use the tool. Nobody really argued with the first part of Engelbart's H-LAM/T philosophy: It was true that humans have evolved through language, artifact, and methodology. The computer would help people evolve even more. But it was the T—training—that caused controversy. To many, the training at ARC was as strange and recondite as Aramaic or medieval Latin. What bizarre and complicated codes for text! The NLS had 512 separate keystroke commands. The team was using the mouse and five-fingered chord keyset in conjunction—barely touching the full keyboard. It all seemed odd and difficult to the outsider.

A foreshadowing of the problem began early when Engelbart realized that his vision wasn't exactly the same as Licklider's. Lick came to do a site visit as a consultant and reacted aversely when Engelbart told him about the training process. "What's the matter, Lick?" Engelbart asked.

"You just told me your system was no damn good," Lick said. "If it were any damn good it wouldn't take people to train people. The systems would do it."

Licklider's *Libraries of the Future* indicates the source of conflict. Lick envisaged an AI-supported computer conversing or negotiating with the user and adjusting itself to the level of the user's sophistication. His enthusiasm was for human–computer symbiosis as *a step* on the path of building computers that, in the end, exceed human beings. In contrast, Engelbart believed in coevolution, that people need to develop new skills in step with the advance of technology.

> Changes from the expected would [at first] be small, people would change their ways of doing things a little at a time, and only gradually would their accumulated changes create markets for more radical versions of the equipment. [22]
>
> —*Augmenting Human Intellect*

When ARC fell on hard times in the 1970s Bill English, Engelbart's right-hand man, went to open arms at nearby Xerox PARC and brought with him fourteen members of Engelbart's crusade. PARC benefited immeasurably from their "augmented" knowledge and training.

Key people involved in building PARC's personal computer, the Interim Dynabook/Alto, were from ARC. By the 1980s, ARC's ideas had flowed to commercial realization at Apple and Microsoft.

Engelbart and English received the patent on the mouse; most of the NLS innovations, however, were not widely recognized. For a long time Engelbart was referred to only as the inventor of the mouse; but he invented an entire system, based on his philosophy of designing computers around people's needs and capabilities. The NLS, more than anything else of its time, is unmistakably the precursor and future ideal of today's world of networked personal computers, allowing collaboration, communication, and creativity. Engelbart played a pivotal role in making computers human friendly and interactive by setting up the first computer research center founded on these principles. Word processing, the mouse, hypertext, windows, spreadsheets, graphics, computer games, and the World Wide Web all owe a great debt to Engelbart's NLS. Engelbart, however, considers today's magic-box systems inferior to what once was or what could be. "Using Windows is like getting off a motorcycle to ride a motor scooter. There are fancy things, but they have to start giving you a lot more power."

Engelbart maintains his skepticism about research and development conducted by corporations. Unlike many of his colleagues who went to the "other side" to PARC and lucrative software companies, Engelbart stuck with his vision. Technology manufacturers, he believes, don't have the best interests of the people in mind because they're fixated on profit. "Look, it's *coevolution* that we have to pay attention to—not just let the technology developers and vendors steer us along."[23] Social progress requires consideration of the big picture. To demonstrate his conviction, he has joined the board of the Foresight Institute, a nonprofit organization founded by nanotechnologist K. Eric Drexler, dedicated to preparing civilization now for the future implications of new technologies, particularly nanotechnology.

The form Engelbart's crusade has now assumed is to balance out the unabated commercial and competitive uses of technology that threaten to splinter society. In 1988 he and his daughter Christina formed the Bootstrap Institute to form strategic alliances aimed at improving organizations and society through experimental working groups on computer systems.

Engelbart's vision of human augmentation is best realized by the free-software movement that began in the 1980s—distributed collectives of programmers collaborating to create incredibly advanced and complicated software. Engelbart regards the Web and the free-software movement as the logical extension of ARC and NLS—at least in the possibilities for social change. "I think it's headed for a spiral of increasing utility and utilization," says Engelbart. "It's going to be the new social system for sure."

In 1998 more than two thousand people, including Alan Kay, Stewart Brand, Jaron Lanier, and Ted Nelson, showed up on the Stanford campus to attend an event dubbed "Engelbart's Unfinished Revolution" in honor of the thirtieth anniversary of his 1968 demonstration. The "unfinished revolution" is the *augmentation of human intellect*, the idea that computers are tools for knowledge, communication, and community, not just computation and capitalism.

Engelbart, recovering from cancer and the loss of his wife, was visibly overwhelmed at the enthusiastic display of public appreciation for his work. Jaron Lanier, virtual reality pioneer, took the microphone and spoke for Engelbart on the unfinished revolution:

> Technology can be either a finite game or an infinite game. The drive to reach others is powerful, perhaps even more than the drive to compete with each other. . . . Rather than a finite game where technology destroys us, technology has to become an infinite game, a way to reach out, to connect.

Meanwhile, the world's problems are still mounting. Engelbart asks, "How can we collectively develop an energy plan? What about the inevitable depletion of fossil fuels? Or clean water worldwide? Or the gap between rich and poor?" His answer remains: through coevolution with our computers. Through creating solutions together on the

Web and building new models to understand the long-term effects of our actions. Engelbart says, "The scale of social change inevitably evolves with technology. Even a new kind of razor can have a big effect. Television. Telephones. Computers. Huge. People are just beginning to realize how much impact they're having—and they haven't seen anything yet."

AGENTS OF CHANGE

MARVIN MINSKY AND SEYMOUR PAPERT

In a sense, artificial intelligence will be the ultimate
tool because it will help us build all possible tools.
—K. Eric Drexler

AN EXCHANGE BETWEEN Doug Engelbart and artificial intelligence pioneer Marvin Minsky has become legend:

Minsky: We're going to make machines intelligent.
We're going to make them conscious!

Engelbart: You're going to do that for the machines? What are you going to do for the people?

No one remembers Minsky's answer, but a defense of artificial
intelligence is that it leads us to a better understanding of ourselves and the functioning of our own brains. While Engelbart
assumed that computers would augment human intellect, AI researchers are interested in how it could happen. The questions
originate with John von Neumann and Alan Turing: What
about the human brain can be reproduced in the computer?
How can computers help people learn?

Turing thought of constructing a computer analogue of a
child, which would grow more intelligent as it learned. Today,
AI researchers are tackling this by studying how humans, especially children, absorb information. People learn in myriad

ways. They learn by doing, by watching others, by reading, and by making inferences. We all learn so naturally and effectively that we forget how remarkable and mysterious it is to do so. Today, engineers and computer scientists struggle to design programs that can learn as well as insects. A computer with intelligence unbounded by the physical limits of an organic brain could assimilate information in ways that would surpass the capabilities or intentions of its creators.

Minsky has led AI research from its conception. With *Perceptrons: An Introduction to Computational Geometry* (1969), he and Seymour Papert, his colleague at MIT, coaxed the research community to turn away from neural networks, a previous paradigm of AI research, and toward more generalized approaches to learning and intelligence. Minsky's later manifesto, *Society of Mind* (1985), reinvigorated a field that suffered from the high expectations it encouraged. The world of AI has always been fraught with righteousness as each group hopes that they know how to properly unlock the secrets of the mind, with neural networks, logical reasoning devices, expert systems, heuristic algorithms, robotics, or artificial life.

Papert has researched how computers and children learn to discover the nature of knowledge. He sought to unite his understanding of the brain with his understanding of computers and developed Logo, an early programming language for children, as described in his manifesto *Mindstorms: Children, Computers, and Powerful Ideas* (1980). From his early years battling apartheid in South Africa to his work in education reform, Papert has devoted his life to rehumanizing institutions.

Minsky and Papert follow the epistemological vein of the first cyberneticists, believing that knowledge and the ability to learn must be actively constructed by each individual. We are born not as blank slates to be filled, but as complex systems with many tools to develop, organize, and seek out new knowledge.

Every AI researcher has had to tackle Gödel's theorem, which declares that no knowledge representation system can be complete or perfect. Accordingly, it's impossible to know fully what comprises a system, such as the human brain, unless one steps completely outside of it, which no human can do. Despite the AI researchers' intrepid investigations, despite the work of those homesteaders out on the vast plains, the human brain remains only partially explored.

TRAILHEADS

Papert and Minsky share the same goals and interests, but they began their lives on divergent paths and, later in their careers, separated again.

Papert has led a synthesis of AI research and psychological experiment. Born right before the Depression, he was first introduced to the world of science by his father, an entomologist, who would take him on trips to study insect life the wilds of their home country of South Africa. He received his first Ph.D. from the University of Witwatersrand in Johannesburg. He and his first wife then went on to Cambridge University, where he received his second Ph.D., in mathematics. He worked at the National Physical Laboratory, then did research in cognitive psychology with Jean Piaget at the University of Geneva, Switzerland, before accepting a position at the new Artificial Intelligence Laboratory at MIT in 1963.

While young Seymour was collecting bugs, Marvin Lee Minsky was growing up in New York City, reading the inventive writings of science fiction writers such as H.G. Wells and Jules Verne. In the pages of *The War of the Worlds* and *From the Earth to the Moon,* Minsky first explored the frontiers of technology.

After World War II, Minsky studied mathematics and psychology as an undergraduate at Harvard University. There he met J. C. R. Licklider, whom he befriended and with whom he became entranced by cybernetics. Minsky admired the work of Warren McCulloch and Nicholas Rashevsky, who were developing the first learning logical systems, the precursors to computer AI.

As a graduate student at Princeton University in the early 1950s, Minsky built one of the first neural network learning machines, the SNARC (stochastic neural-analog reinforcement computer), named after the mysterious creature in Lewis Carroll's nonsense epic poem "The Hunting of the Snark." At Princeton he continued his work in mathematics and was influenced by new ways of thinking from John von Neumann. He also benefited from his fellow students, one of whom was John McCarthy, who invented LISP, developed the model of computer time-sharing, and coined the term "artificial intelligence."*

---

*McCarthy, Minsky, Shannon, and Nathan Rochester of IBM organized the first ever AI conference at Dartmouth College the summer of 1956. McCarthy's 1955 *Proposal for the Dartmouth Summer Research Project on Artificial Intelligence* defines the "artificial intelligence problem" as "making a machine behave in ways that would be called intelligent if a human were so behaving."

As a junior fellow at Harvard, he explored early directions in AI research and grew close to the mathematician Oliver Selfridge and his hero, McCulloch. In 1958 Minsky became a professor of mathematics at MIT, where he would later join forces with Papert.

THE MIT ARTIFICIAL INTELLIGENCE LAB

In 1959, Minsky and his former classmate McCarthy founded the MIT Artificial Intelligence Group, which later became the AI Lab.* Minsky and McCarthy were interested in the question of common sense: what it is, and how people use it to reason. While McCarthy looked for logical, mathematical foundations, Minsky was more interested in practical pattern recognition and analogy, as he explained in "Steps Toward Artificial Intelligence," a paper published in 1961 that established his reputation as a young firebrand. The AI Lab quickly became the focal point for advanced computer research, from novel computing methods to robotics. Presaging the Silicon Valley boom, McCarthy left MIT in 1962 to found the AI Lab at Stanford University. In 1963 Papert, at the instigation of Warren McCulloch, came to MIT, where he and Minsky soon began a rewarding friendship and professional collaboration.

Minsky and Papert set up shop on the eighth floor of the main computing building. On the fifth floor was Project MAC (later known as the Laboratory of Computer Science), which Licklider funded to research networked computing. As Project MAC and the AI Lab expanded, they shared the ninth floor to house their computers and teams of hackers, but ran a wall through the middle, separating the chaos of the AI lab hackers from the regimented order of the Project MAC time-shared computers.

Minsky impressed his growing population of graduate students with the attitude that everything that came before was of little interest. At the

---

*The MIT Lab was the second center for AI research in the world; Allen Newell and Herbert Simon had founded one at Carnegie-Mellon University just a few years before. Newell and Simon, who were great influences on the younger Minsky and Papert, built a formal theory for problem solving. The theory was powerful but unlike how people actually solve problems—it was not the end of a path, but the beginning.

time, in 1963, it seemed as if Boston were the center of the universe: The hometown hero, John F. Kennedy, was in the White House. The Speaker of the House was also from Boston. The Boston Strangler was on the loose, choking thirteen women in three years. The Boston Celtics were in the middle of an unbelievable eight-year string of NBA championships. And the kids in the lab believed that they were the real news, for they were building the future.

Favoring turtlenecks, his wide mouth set in an amused grin, Minsky managed to look something like a very hip turtle, a balding beatnik mathematician, coolly leading his charges. Papert, for his part, looked like a hippie with long hair and baggy bright shirts. The professors, students, and hackers of the 1960s created the AI Lab universe from the ground up, building computing tools as they needed them, or just for fun. Minsky, Papert, and everyone else believed that it was very difficult to discern the uselessly fascinating from the importantly fascinating.

The participants captured the ethos of the AI Lab in what they called "AI koans," after the tales of Zen Buddhism that blur the line between profundity and absurdity. One koan describes an interaction between Minsky and one of his brilliant students, Jerry Sussman:

> In the days when Sussman was a novice, Minsky once came to him as he sat hacking at the PDP-6.
>
> "What are you doing?" asked Minsky.
>
> "I am training a randomly wired neural net to play tic-tac-toe," Sussman replied.
>
> "Why is the net wired randomly?" asked Minsky.
>
> "I do not want it to have any preconceptions about how to play," Sussman said.
>
> Minsky then shut his eyes.
>
> "Why do you close your eyes?" Sussman asked his teacher.
>
> "So that the room will be empty."
>
> At that moment, Sussman was enlightened.

In these early days of AI research, there were several camps, but none more divergent than the symbolists and the connectionists. The connectionists, represented by Herbert Simon and Allen Newell, the first great team of AI researchers, were interested in the hardware of the brain. They believed the answer to artificial intelligence lay in copying nature's approach with electronic parts. They tried to develop systems to tackle single problems, such as playing chess. Like Norbert Wiener and Vannevar Bush, Minsky admired generalists a lot more than specialists, and he thought the idea of specialist computer programs was misguided. The only intelligence that excited symbolists like him was general intelligence. Instead of worrying about how the brain worked, Minsky tried to figure out practical, general approaches to tackling such problems: Write the code, build the robots, and test the problems.

The connectionists tackled AI by trying to build electronic brains one neuron at a time, inspired by McCulloch and Pitts's seminal work on the logical nature of neurons. They built devices known as *perceptrons,* which consisted of a network of self-adjusting circuits modeled after neurons, hooked up to a photoreceptor for input and a crude monitor for output. When the device was turned on, there was no relation between the input and output. But it was possible to get the perceptron to distinguish between, say, a square and a triangle, by adjusting the "neurons" in a regulatory feedback loop. The researchers didn't even have to understand how the network worked—the device "learned" on its own through feedback. It seemed as if a cybernetic McCulloch and Pitts electronic brain was imminent. Minsky and Papert were dubious.

In 1969, Minsky and Papert published *Perceptrons: An Introduction to Computational Geometry,* which killed the connectionists' enthusiasm cold. They explained mathematically the inherent disabilities of perceptrons, leading people to believe that the entire field was a dead end. The connectionists had to eat their words. The federal government, burned by grandiose, empty promises, angrily took away their funds. It took decades for much interest in neural networks to be revived, and when it did it was without the original expectations for superintelligent brains just around the corner.

After *Perceptrons,* people turned to broad-based, heuristic approaches to problem solving. Money from Lick's ARPA poured into practical robotics, especially those that tackled hand–eye coordination. The AI Lab became crowded with mechanical arms and television eyes.

So much money flowed in that people there were able to come up with their own projects, such as studying language comprehension. One researcher tried to write a system to parse children's stories; another, a system to direct in plain English a robotic arm to rearrange colored blocks.

The approach taken at the AI Lab came from the world of games and physics. Games strip away the messiness of real life and leave an environment governed by just enough rules for something interesting to happen. Physicists look for the simple rules that govern the seemingly random behavior of the real world by investigating the simplest possible cases—a pendulum swinging from a massless, frictionless string, for example. To get answers that engineers can use, the physicists just add corrective terms. Likewise, at the AI Lab, researchers looked for the simple rules that govern thought and behavior, used them in computers and robots, and left the messiness of the real world for later.

The AI Lab was home to marvelous experiments in computer graphics, including the Minsky-tron: If you wire two registers to the X and Y coordinates of a display, you could make neat pictures. The first computer video game, "Space Wars," was developed there. The lab's display terminals commonly ran "Wire Forks," which is the still ubiquitous fireworks screensaver.

The hackers who worked for the AI Lab in the 1960s and 1970s developed software tools to assist the graduate students and professors in their research that would drive the computer revolution. They popularized their jargon, stories, and attitude among the ARPAnet community, creating hacker lore. Out of the MIT AI Lab came some of the first text editors and time-sharing operating systems, as well as computer languages such as LISP and LISP-based Logo.

MILLIONS OF AGENTS

During the 1970s Minsky and Papert attempted to write a book together about the accumulative knowledge gleaned from the MIT AI Lab. They wanted to explain how, in the human brain, complex actions are made up of hierarchies of simpler ones and that the higher-level processes aren't concerned with how the lower-level ones work. How can intelligence emerge from nonintelligence? How is the brain like a computer, or, rather, how can the computer be modeled like a brain? What is the relationship between information and knowledge? How do we expand our knowledge? What is our relationship with the information we absorb?

Minsky and Papert tried to write the *Society of Mind* book together in the late 1970s. Unfortunately, as Minsky put in the postscript, "it became clear that the ideas were not mature enough." With much regret, the two men ended their decades-long collaboration. Thus *Society of Mind,* published in 1985, was authored solely by Minsky. The beginning chapters of the book reflect their collaborative work over the preceding decade. Minsky went on alone to tackle further problems, such as decision making in the presence of ambiguity, the creation and use of memories, and reasoning through analogy.

Society of Mind begins with their research in the late 1960s, trying to build a robot that could play with children's building blocks with a mechanical arm and television eye coordinated by a computer. Minsky and Papert wanted to tackle what is one of the earliest abilities of all children—an activity that uses little more than common sense. They hoped there would be a simple answer. What they found was a seemingly unending supply of challenges, all intertwined.

> As each new group of skills matures, we build more layers on top of them. As time goes on, the layers below become increasingly remote until, when we try to speak of them in later life, we find ourselves with little more to say than "I don't know."[1]   —*Society of Mind*

Minsky and Papert's robot could solve properly defined subtasks, such as distinguishing a blue block from a red block or a sphere from a pyramid if each task-solving agent were kept independent from other ones. They discovered the complexity in coordinating simple tasks—decision making. There must be some way that simple agents could work together in complex ways. But how?

This is when the two researchers devised the term "society of mind." Their idea was that intelligence emerges from mindlessness. Any agent that seems to do more than one automatic, repeatable task, that exhibits complexity, must, in fact, consist of several interconnected agents.

Intelligence is the complexity that arises from the communication and coordination of simple units. Minds are collections of millions of such agents, each autonomous and mindless.

The mind employs simple agents to solve well-defined problems. In fact, it may employ several at once, solving the same problem in several different ways. The problem could be as simple as "pick up the green block" or as complicated as "find happiness." A hierarchical society of simple agents translates observation into decision making. At the top, a goal is formed and observations made. The goal is passed down to lower layers of agents, which attempt to solve the problem as they understand it. The top agents don't care how their subordinates solve the problem—the lower agents don't care why they're being told to work.

> What magical trick makes us intelligent? The trick is that there is no trick. The power of intelligence stems from our vast diversity, not from any single, perfect principle. Our species has evolved many effective although imperfect methods, and each of us individually develops more on our own. Eventually, very few of our actions and decisions come to depend on any single mechanism. Instead, they emerge from conflicts and negotiations among societies of processes that constantly challenge one another.[2]
>
> —Society of Mind

The *Society of Mind* theory explains previously incomprehensible behaviors in the development of knowledge. It explains, for example, the phenomenon known as Piagetian conservation: Young children will believe that a quantity of liquid increases after it is poured from a squat vessel into a tall, narrow one. At a certain age, however, children universally assert that the amount of liquid remains the same when it is poured into the taller, thinner container.

Minsky and Papert's theory explains the phenomenon like this: The child's mind has one agent that measures quantities by the *height* of the container and another agent that measures quantities by the *width* of the container. Height is a constant companion in the lives of growing children, and they quickly learn "higher equals more." On the other hand, the width agent is less practiced. Another that comes into play is the history agent, which "knows" that quantities stay the same over time. This agent is insufficient on its own for the child to properly reason out the conservation of liquids, for the history agent would assert "the quantity remains the same" even if more liquid were added.

The insight is not that such agents exist—they're mindless in and of themselves—but how they interact. What allows them to reason? Minsky and Papert's theory doesn't suggest that as children mature the agents become more advanced. Rather, the connections between agents change. When the height and width agents give contradictory advice ("The quantity is greater because the glass is taller" vs. "The quantity is less because the glass is narrower"), they cancel each other out. The mind is made up of many such paired agents, and each pair is governed by (or creates) a third agent that passes along the decisions of the pair.

In the example of height and width, the agent governing the pair is a "geometry agent." When the height and width agents agree, the geometry agent simply passes along their combined assertion with great authority ("The quantity is greater because the glass is taller and wider"). When they disagree, the geometry agent passes the buck ("I'm not sure what the quantity is").

The geometry and history agents form a pair governed by the "quantity agent." In the above example, the geometry agent can't supply a decision, but the history agent can, so the quantity agent passes along its assertion ("The quantity remains the same").

. . . .

Papert's Principle: Some of the most crucial steps in mental growth are based not simply on acquiring new skills, but on acquiring new administrative ways to use what one already knows.[3]   —Society of Mind

. . . .

TO BE UNSTUCK

Minsky and Papert believed that the mind matures as its society of agents grows more complex, not as the agents themselves change. Their revelation: *The interconnection* between agents is as important to learning as the agents themselves. This idea lies at the foundation of cybernetics and the entire philosophy of information theory: We are defined through communication and feedback. The act of communicating a message transforms it. Society and civilization are the product of mass intercommunication. Minsky and Papert believed that the mind is, too.

Just as Turing turned away from the definition of intelligence in his Turing Test, so does Minsky in *Society of Mind*. He instead wanted to discover how we construct all the abilities that sum together in "intelligence." In doing so, he explained that the nature of intelligence is illusory, because its mechanisms are removed from our actions.

> Each child learns, from time to time, various better ways to learn—but no one understands how this is done....The problem is that one can't observe a child's strategies for "learning how to learn"—because those strategies are twice removed from what we can see.[4]   —*Society of Mind*

We know that there are many ways to learn. But how do we develop those abilities? We don't start with all those skills at birth. Minsky believed the process by which we acquire our full knowledge-gathering tool set is what we call "intelligence." But that doesn't explain the process at all—it just hides it behind a word. Since Minsky's goal was to understand that process, he couldn't just say, "People can learn because they have intelligence!" He had to try to observe the unobservable.

Society of Mind addresses how we acquire knowledge through communication. Minsky therefore examined each knowledge-gathering device in the human toolkit. People learn in many ways, each a rich source for insight. He observed that if a person understands an idea in only one way, she really doesn't understand it at all. For example, we may believe we understand a concept, but as we talk about it with someone else, we realize that our understanding was incomplete. Only then do new insights emerge.

> If speaking involves thinking, then one must ask, *"How much of ordinary thought involves the use of words?"* Surely many of our

most effective thinking methods scarcely engage our language-agencies at all. Perhaps we turn to words only when other methods fail. But then the use of language can open entirely new worlds of thought.[5]   —*Society of Mind*

· ·

The act of speech must engage our brains differently than silent thought. By putting a concept into words, we transform it. In fact, what happens is that the words are detached from the "meaning" of the idea—we can't directly communicate the meaning, but we can communicate the words. The words themselves don't contain the idea; they hold a representation of it. Only with language can people exchange that representation with ease and accuracy.

Computers are far from having a tool kit like the brain. The mind is incredibly complex and adaptable. The interaction of our countless small agents makes it flexible, more so than any AI yet conceived. Our agents work in concert to help us from getting stuck. If a pair of agents can't agree, a third agent can usually resolve the conflict. This is why we don't usually crash but computers do. If AI researchers like Minsky ever understand exactly how these agents work, they could reproduce them in computers to make them yet more sophisticated and flexible. Then, if a computer gets stuck it would, like us, attempt an alternative approach to problem solving. Machines, for better or for worse, could become truly intelligent.

Minsky, like Turing and Licklider, doesn't mind the possibility that our computers may one day become as intelligent as we are, if not more so. In a 1984 article, "Will Robots Inherit the Earth?" he intimates that it is far more important for us to inculcate these machines, "our children," with our human values than to hold onto some delusion that human bodies are superior to mechanical ones. Cybernetics, after all, teaches us how similar the animal and mechanical are. Minsky remains a humanist in the sense that he suggests human values can and should transcend flesh.

In the meantime, visionaries like Doug Engelbart and Papert have been interested in how the computer can improve human beings and human brains. In particular, they would like to develop technology as a means to improve the ways we represent ideas in our heads—getting us "unstuck." If simply putting a concept into words transforms it, as Minsky suggests in *Society of Mind,* then being able to manipulate it with a computer might transform the idea even more—Engelbart's "neo-Whorfian" hypothesis. Our interaction with the computer can help us learn new ways to approach and solve problems, stimulating our innate ability to grasp an idea in many ways, on many levels.

MINDSTORMING

Brandishing the computer, Papert led the charge to eliminate the narrow methods of education that were established in the days of the Industrial Revolution. Driven by the Soviet Union's launch of Sputnik, the U.S. government put its weight behind transforming science education in the 1960s and 1970s, and those efforts spilled over into all fields. This new approach to education, while breaking much new ground, was still extremely centralized. Its suggestions were executed in a manner as close to an assembly line as possible. Teachers were given textbooks, learning aids, and teaching plans that dictated their actions. The curriculum may have changed, but the environment remained autocratic and hostile to freedom.

In 1980, Papert published a transformative work on education, *Mindstorms: Children, Computers, and Powerful Ideas.* In it he described his work with Logo, the computer programming language he developed, in elementary school classrooms. He also explored the theory behind his attempts to redefine education with the use of computers. The foundation for Papert's work was his training under the Swiss scientist Jean Piaget, who revolutionized our understanding of how children learn. Papert continued to develop his own beliefs from that starting point, with the intention of using computers to achieve a revolution in the stratified educational system.

> In my vision, space-age objects, in the form of small computers, will cross these cultural barriers to enter the private worlds of children everywhere. They will do so not as mere physical objects. This book is about how computers can be carriers of

powerful ideas and of the seeds of cultural change, how they can
help people form new relationships with knowledge that cut
across the traditional lines separating humanities from science
and knowledge of self from both of these.[6]   —*Mindstorms*

Piaget reminded the world how much children learn without being expressly taught. Children pick up language, common sense, motor skills,
and cultural navigation, all before entering school. Piaget was the first
person to pay attention to this phenomenon, which is now known as Piagetian learning. He found that children acquired skills and abilities in
a steady progression, without correspondence to their formal education.
He classified their development into stages, the first step in understanding
how children develop such abilities.

Papert noted his own childhood fascination with the workings of
gears. His observations of their motions and interactions gave him a
model that he later applied to understand mathematical and physical
concepts. Instead of concluding that all children should be given gear sets,
Papert realized that knowledge—the ability to learn—comes from models of thought and that each person's models are unique. The insight that
knowledge is constructed through the creation and development of intellectual structures is one of Piaget's great lessons: *The understanding
of learning must be genetic,* from the genesis of knowledge, the kernels
of comprehension.[7]

Whereas the finished structures of knowledge, about history, algebra,
grammar, politics, are similar for different people, the germinating models are very different. Papert's mental gears unlocked knowledge for himself, but they wouldn't do so for everyone.

He concluded the best learning device would be something that exists in the real world, outside the mind, but that is as flexible and mutable as the mind. Papert believed that the computer could play that
role. To him, computers had the potential to be magic clay, infusing
ideas with active shape and form, the perfect tool with which to build
intellectual structures.

The computer is the Proteus of machines. Its essence is its universality, its power to simulate. Because it can take a thousand

forms and can serve a thousand functions, it can appeal to a thousand tastes. [8]   —*Mindstorms*

. . . .

Papert recognized that whereas children learn their native language easily, they have difficulty learning foreign languages in an educational context. He believed it is possible to design computers so that learning to communicate with them can be a natural process, like learning French in France rather than in an American classroom. Communication with a computer can change other aspects of learning. Computers can change the process of learning mathematics into the more natural process of learning to speak a language; "talking mathematics" to a computer in "Mathland," is like speaking French in France.

LOGO

Throughout the 1970s Papert could often be found at various elementary schools around Boston, surrounded by children. His shaggy hair framed his face, creased by laugh lines and punctuated by a potato-like nose. He'd get down on the floor to be at the same level with the students. Also on the floor would be a machine of gears, sensors, circuits, and wheels under a hemisphere of clear plastic. It looked somewhat like a child's idea of a robotic turtle. The turtle would trace out patterns on a giant sheet of paper with a pen attached to its underside, controlled through a long cord by a computer nearby.

It wasn't Papert who would type in the program to direct the turtle to draw. It was one of the children, who had decided what she wanted to make. In directing the turtle, she would make use of principles from geometry, arithmetic, formal reasoning, art, and generalized problem solving, skills that she would never have otherwise seen integrated in one class. Papert named this programming language Logo.

Papert had designed Logo for the express purpose of encouraging children to learn. He began work on it almost as soon as he came to the AI Lab in 1963. In 1967, he and a team led by Wallace Feurzeig at Bolt Beranek and Newman, the same company that would play a large role in constructing the ARPAnet, created the first version of Logo. MIT was the primary site where Logo was developed, along with other research sites in Scotland and Australia.

. . . .

Programming a computer means nothing more or less than communicating to it in a language that it and the human user can both "understand." And learning languages is one of the things children do best. Every normal child learns to talk. Why then should a child not learn to "talk" to a computer?[9]   —*Mindstorms*

. . . .

Logo let the programmer control a "turtle," either the robotic turtle designed by Minsky or a virtual triangle on the computer screen. What made Logo revolutionary was that it was accessible to young children, ages five and up, and designed to "have a low threshold and no ceiling." A child could learn about motion, spatial relations, logic, and probability in a game-making context. Building on simple rules, they can create incredibly sophisticated simulations.

Many theories behind Logo are directly related to Papert's work at the AI Lab and the society of mind concept. For one, Papert observed that children learn language in an orderly, step-by-step fashion. First they absorb the concept of words, then how to combine words into simple sentences. It's a constructionist, or symbolist, approach: Language is complex, but children learn it gradually by learning words and the rules of linguistics. Logo (meaning "word" or "idea") is learned in the same way, by understanding properties and relationships. Children learn natural language through feedback with people who speak it; they learn Logo by interacting with the turtle through the Logo programming language.

The Logo project really represented the entire MIT AI Lab community, with direct contributions from dozens of people and influences from nearly everyone. It was infused with the playful but brilliant attitude of the Lab's hackers. It was brought to life by the people who figured out how to translate technology into a learning environment. It was transformed as educators brought their own ideas to Papert's. Numerous students helped develop Logo, which is a descendant of the AI Lab's core computer language, LISP, which McCarthy designed to allow high-level manipulation of mathematics and language. Daniel

Bobrow, Bill Gosper, and Terry Winograd, whose own work was at the forefront of AI and computer usability, were just three of the many people who contributed to the Logo project. Minsky himself, applying his mechanical brilliance, designed and built the first turtle. Cynthia Solomon shaped the methodology of the project, its very core. Solomon worked throughout with Papert to make the Logo project a reality. Sherry Turkle, a sociologist who studies the computer culture, strengthened and inspired Papert's thinking—she also happened to be his wife.

EDUCATIONAL REFORM

As Papert wrote *Mindstorms,* the personal computer entered the American landscape. The general perception of computers shifted from a vague public awareness of giant, expensive backroom machines to general excitement about the incorporation of small, usable computers into everyone's daily life. Most people who knew about computers talked about the potential applications such as playing games and doing finances. If computers were thought of as teaching machines, it was as lightning-quick didactic machines. Few considered the computer's potential to augment human intellect.

> There is a world of difference between what computers can do and what society will choose to do with them. Society has many ways to resist fundamental and threatening change. Thus, this book is about facing choices that are ultimately political. It looks at some of the forces of change and of reaction to those forces that are called into play as the computer presence begins to enter the politically charged world of education.[10]
>
> —*Mindstorms*

Despite the Sputnik-incited attempts to reform education in the 1960s, the role of computers was still squarely within the traditional educational structure. Schools used computers to drill children in rote exercises and standardized tests with tightly defined questions. No attempts were made to allow children to explore or communicate using computers. Computing in education was defined by the attitude that computers are fast calculators, not communication devices.

. . . .

> In many schools today, the phrase "computer-aided instruction" means making the computer teach the child. One might say the *computer is being used to program* the child. In my vision, *the child programs the computer* and, in doing so, both acquires a sense of mastery over a piece of the most modern and powerful technology and establishes an intimate contact with some of the deepest ideas from science, from mathematics, and from the art of intellectual model building.[11]   —*Mindstorms*

. . . .

Papert was one of the first to insist that computers can help transform education from its nineteenth-century mechanistic roots to a more flexible feedback-oriented approach. The student and the worker in the information age require skills other than the ability to memorize facts and excel at standardized tests. People need to be capable of discerning causes, consequences, and relationships between situations. They need to be able to develop solutions by gleaning meaning from masses of data. The focus of education should be on the creation, judgment, and interpretation of information—not just the transmission of facts.

Papert's struggle was the same as that of Turing, Engelbart, and Licklider. He believed in the cybernetic nature of computers: They are valuable not because they can place the intellectual realm on the assembly line, but because they can adapt with humans in a relationship built on corrective feedback. Programming a computer changes its nature; programming teaches the computer to act and respond in novel ways. At the same time, the actions of the computer teach the child. A program is the mutual, even symbiotic, combination of the child's and the computer's contributions. With Logo, Papert saw that children could have a relationship with the computer. Before, all they had was instruction and direction, learning through Pavlovian reinforcement. It is reasonable for a scientist to decide all the parameters of an experiment on canine behavior. It is a tragedy for a school to do the equivalent to a child.

How would the mechanical nature of computers shape children's thinking? The sharpest critics of computers in the classroom feared an

Orwellian system of thought control and worried that children would become immersed in computers to the neglect of social contact.

> Marshall McLuhan's dictum that "the medium is the message" might apply here: If the medium is an interactive system that takes in words and speaks back like a person, it is easy to get the message that machines are like people and that people are like machines. What this might do to the development of values and self-image in growing children is hard to assess. But it is not hard to see reasons for worry.[12]   —*Mindstorms*

Papert agreed with the critics that computers will immerse children in mechanical thinking, but he believed that this will be beneficial. Mechanical thinking underlies science and mathematics. Through immersion children would understand when mechanical thinking worked, and when it didn't. Like Minsky, Papert believed that a diverse approach to problem solving is the most important skill to learn.

> We are at a point in the history of education when radical change is possible, and the possibility for that change is directly tied to the impact of the computer. Today what is offered in the education "market" is largely determined by what is acceptable to a sluggish and conservative system.[13]   —*Mindstorms*

AFTERWARD

Although Papert moved into educational reform and Minsky stayed with AI theory, their work remains linked by their understanding of knowledge. The classroom is a society of mind, but so may be the computer. They both believe that insights drawn from teaching children can be applied to AI research. And insightful AI research tells us how our own minds work. The computer is the machine of the mind.

Notwithstanding its influence in fields as diverse as psychology and computer science, Minsky's *Society of Mind* has not escaped criticism in his own field of AI. Some claimed that it is merely the model of object-oriented programming applied to the human brain. Newell, whose work on perceptrons was dealt a death blow by Minsky and Papert's *Percep-trons*, said he doesn't consider *Society of Mind* a serious work because it's too general to apply directly to any research. The step from mind-less agents to thinking and acting humans is just too great

Now in his seventies, Marvin Minsky has been working on *The Emotion Machine*, the follow-up to *Society of Mind*. The book will focus on the agents that give rise to our wishes, desires, hopes, and goals. Minsky's work continues to be that of clarifying the functioning of the human mind so that we might someday better apply it to AI. He hopes that his work, and that of a new generation of researchers, will lead to the development of increasingly sophisticated machines that will, in a feedback loop be-tween creator and creation, lead to the development of yet more complex machines. This may someday lead to a computer that reaches or surpasses human intelligence in every meaning of the word.

Despite the failings of the entire AI field, the goal of mechanizing in-telligence has spurred creative work. When people try to tackle magically complex questions, they create a magically complex universe. The chal-lenge may be artificial intelligence, or computer learning for children, or augmentation of human intelligence. Whenever people see computers as intelligence machines, they do great things. They push the limits of com-puter hardware and software. Whereas in other fields people strive to make computers faster and more powerful, people in AI try to make computers more usable. They aim to create thinking machines, com-munication devices, machines that use language and model thought.*

As for Papert's Logo, the software was an unprecedented success in many schools around the world, although, as Papert grimly acknowledged, half of them later dropped it for more conservative uses of the computer in the classroom, such as word processing. In the 1990s, Logo evolved into new forms, such as LEGO Mindstorms (named after the book). In this version,

---

*Many current projects in AI now point to the Web as a trawling-grounds for agents to learn language and meaning. Major projects include CYC, an inference engine that contains over a million common-sense statements programmed by researchers. An-other is GAC (General Artificial Consciousness), with the objective to train a neu-ral net to mimic a human, powered by tens of thousands of online participants.

children could write programs on their personal computers that, through an infrared beam, would command their robotic LEGO creations. The first sets were sold in 1998, delighting children and adults with the experience of learning how to program something that could function in the real, physical world.

Papert now works out of the Learning Barn, his small lab in Maine, and sits on the advisory boards of interactive educational children's web sites, such as MaMaMedia. He continues to believe that putting children in control of a "microworld" realizes the full meaning of feedback and, in turn, helps children learn. Some critics have called him a romantic, pointing out that computers are still too difficult and time-consuming. They assert that the strictures of teaching twenty-five children in a forty-five minute class prevent a teacher from being able to instruct students to do anything more than type or surf the Web. Others fear that hard-pressed schools will substitute computers for human teachers. Yet others have observed that Papert undermines his effort to get schools to use computers more meaningfully by his intolerance for the current educational environment.

Despite the adoption of computers and the widespread use of Logo in classrooms since the 1980s, the trend toward specialization continues. The curriculum may have changed, but the environment in many schools has remained as autocratic and regimented as it was in the nineteenth century. The present trend in the United States is one in which the entire primary and secondary educational experience revolves around mandatory, national, standardized testing—as far as possible from a nurturing or innovative learning environment.

The traditional educational institution considers the sharing of ideas and work anathema. To grade the ability of children individually we force them to act alone. The adult world in the information age is entirely different: People are expected to work together for mutual benefit and toward a shared goal. Although individual effort is encouraged and rewarded, group effort is demanded. In the vision of Engelbart and later revolutionaries, computers can make possible group efforts that discern the contributions of each individual. In a traditional collaborative effort, only the final result is evident; the constructive process leaves few traces. With computers, the process can leave a permanent record as well

as the final result. Teachers can follow how the final result was reached, and what each child did. But this of course requires careful planning and oversight by the teacher, a Herculean effort with the giant classes and restrictive curricula of the modern school. The lesson: The transformation of education, changing minds, is a complex task.

THE MESSAGE IN THE MEDIUM

ALAN C. KAY

> Instead of trying to produce a programme to simulate the adult mind, why not rather try to produce one which simulates a child's?　　—Alan Turing

TWO MIND-ALTERING events transformed Alan Kay in late 1968.

The first was when he made the trip to the Massachusetts Institute of Technology Artificial Intelligence Laboratory to meet Seymour Papert. There he encountered children using Logo, an early programming language aimed to teach children how to use computers as well as how to teach themselves using computers. Papert's setup was interactive and immediate, and allowed the kids to exercise their creativity. Kay wrote, "That's when I was struck by the idea that the computer isn't a vehicle, which was the way I was thinking about it, but a medium."[1] Kay was inspired to come up with the vision of a personal computer, which he called the Dynabook, in the conviction that if the computer could help children learn how to think better, they could grow up to make better-informed decisions for themselves and for the world.

Kay's second reality-blowing event of that year was the ACM/IEEE–Computer Society Fall Joint Computer Conference, where he watched Doug Engelbart present the oN-Line

System (NLS), which he had seen before but never on such a grand scale. There he watched Vannevar Bush's memex come to life before a rapt audience in the form of a mouse, hypertext links, windows, word processing, and file sharing. People were interacting with their computers in ways they never had before. Kay, who likes to use cybernetic metaphors, thought of the NLS as the romance of humanity thinking out of its genetic structure. He was smitten.

Kay's life work has straddled the missions of both Papert and Engelbart. He, too, seeks to develop computers as a tool to amplify human minds. Like Papert, he has developed programming languages aimed at educating children. Like Engelbart, his focus is on developing a user interface and hardware, namely, the *personal computer,* a term he coined. He realized that the best part about Papert and Engelbart's technologies was that they were not just machines, but provisions for human creative and intellectual growth. They were models of the machine as a *medium.* The double meaning of the word applies to the way Kay began thinking about the computer: A *medium* is "an intermediate agency, means, instrument or channel . . . of mass communication" and "a pervading or enveloping substance; the substance or 'element' in which an organism lives; hence *fig.* one's environment; the conditions of life" (*Oxford English Dictionary*).

Both biologically and sociologically, culture thrives on media. Kay imagined the computer as a metamedium in which ideas could grow, thrive, and spread. His far-out vision in 1968 was for every person to have his or her very own computer, a metamedium that enriches human culture. This was the topic he addressed in five major writings: his Ph.D. thesis, "The Reactive Engine" (1969), "Personal Dynamic Media" (with Adele Goldberg, 1977), "Microelectronics and the Personal Computer" (1977), "Computer Software" (1984) and "Computers, Networks, and Education" (1991).

FLEXING

Alan Kay was the seventh person admitted into the graduate program in the ARPA–endowed computer science department at the University of Utah in 1968. He entered with a double degree in molecular biology and mathematics from the University of Colorado. Like Norbert Wiener, Kay had been a child prodigy, but, unlike Wiener, he had been a recalcitrant one. In grade school he accused his teachers of having a limited point of view; in high school he got suspended for insubordination; in college he was expelled for protesting what seemed to him to be a Jewish quota. In addition to being a bright yet unruly student, Kay has been a portrait painter, professional jazz guitarist, theatrical designer, and amateur classical pipe organist. His upbringing separated him from many of his peers: Soon after his birth in 1940 in Springfield, Massachusetts, his parents took him to Australia for a few years. His father was a scientist and his mother was an artist, and he is the fusion of the two.

The Papert and Engelbart demonstrations of 1968 tapped into Kay's conviction that computers can and should be whole-brain devices. His unconventional Ph.D. thesis, titled "The Reactive Engine" (1969), described the design of an interactive computer called the FLEX (for "flexible extendible"). His description of the FLEX included several adjectives rarely associated with computing. An *interactive* tool, the FLEX would be *simple* enough to be used by a nonexpert, *cheap* enough to be owned (like a grand piano), and *versatile* enough to take on various useful forms. Users would interact with it by means of a keyboard, cathode-ray tube monitor, and tablet. It would be able to both crunch equations and help create art. Most of all, it would be a tool for every person. A *personal* computer.

> The desire is still to design an interactive tool which can aid in the visualization and realization of provocative notions. It must be simple enough so that one does not have to become a systems programmer (one who understands the arcane rites) to use it. . . . FLEX is an *idea* debugger and, as such, it is hoped that [it] is also an idea *media*.[2]
>
> —"The Reactive Engine"

One evolutionary leap Kay wanted computerkind to make was from displays of alien green type on black to a graphic display with colors and patterns—a better *human*-computer interface. Kay's adviser, Dave Evans, had introduced him to Ivan Sutherland's 1963 Ph.D. thesis on Sketchpad, which was a working vision of an interactive physical modeling system. Sketchpad, with the first graphical user interface, allowed people to draw anything from bridges to circuits and manipulate them in real time to see how they work. In 1968 Sutherland began teaching at Utah, where he became Kay's other mentor and a member of his thesis committee.

In "The Reactive Engine," Kay wrote that it is common knowledge that if humans want to really *learn* an idea, they need to build a mental model of it. Like Engelbart, Kay draws on the lessons of linguist Benjamin Whorf, who concluded that the way people see, hear, and think about things is determined by language. Language is the ultimate medium with which we build, manipulate, and communicate our internal models of the world. For this reason Kay, again like Engelbart, reasoned that the computer could help us forge new relationships with language and thus improve the way we think. On the computer, writing and drawing would be more fluid and dynamic because the user could interact with his or her ideas by adjusting them in real time. Kay figured that a combination of something like Sketchpad along with the mouse, word processor, and other Engelbartian tools would form a complete vehicle for thinking, working, and playing.

The FLEX vision was a step beyond Engelbart's NLS in terms of empowering the individual. The latter was originally built at a time when computers were so expensive that time-sharing one central powerful computer was the best way to get more people on a system. Ultimately, the system's inability to transfer well to the decentralized ARPAnet was its failing. Kay later likened the difference between the mainframe NLS and the personal FLEX to that between a train and a car.[3] The mainframe was like a railroad, owned by an institution that decided what you could do and when you could do it. It was meant to be organized and efficient and in the best interest of all, like good government. The personal computer, on the other hand, would be like the automobile—people would be able to use it to go wherever they want, when they want, and how they want.

Kay aimed to do for the computer what Henry Ford did to transportation: Individualize it and make it affordable and practical for every-one to use. In "The Reactive Engine," he listed his basic rules for the in-expensive personal computer:

- The communications device must be as readily available (in every way) as a slide rule;

- The service must not be esoteric to use. (It must be learnable in private);

- The transactions must inspire confidence. (Kindness should be an integral part).[4]

Sutherland and Evans passed Kay's thesis in 1969. By the time Kay left the University of Utah, he had made a few advances toward bringing the FLEX to life, including writing two compilers for its operating language (also called FLEX). He experimented with several graphics display routines, character generators, and editors, but he wasn't satisfied with FLEX's clumsy language or low power. He knew he had the right spirit but not the right medium.

THE XEROX PALO ALTO RESEARCH CENTER

In 1969 the climate in computer research was undergoing a dramatic shift. Pressures from Congress and the Department of Defense were crushing ARPA's expansive funding for computer research and development. It wasn't long before Congress introduced the Mansfield Amendment, requiring that the Department of Defense support only basic research with a direct application to military function or operation. The glory days of ARPA funding for basic research without clear application were over. Funding for interactive computing and university projects like Engelbart's NLS diminished. ARPA brought back the days of command and control.*

Vannevar Bush died just after the Mansfield Amendment was passed. Its effect on him couldn't have been salutary; it went against everything he had hoped. In his plan for the National Science Foundation, Bush had emphasized that federal support of research and education is "the

---

*The IPTO shut down in 1986 as other departments subsumed it.

bulwark of democracy." He believed that the government and the military should review the operation but not interfere with it. He objected to the idea that basic and pure research be mixed up with industry and proposed that government funds not go to universities that also accept money from corporations. This would ensure that such research and development is in the best interests of the people rather than in the interests of a particular enterprise or product. Without the separation of research from commercial application, there would have been no ARPAnet, time-shared computers, or NLS—at least not as they happened. What advantage would those developments have been for corporations like IBM, which didn't stand to benefit from more efficient use of hardware? From the Mansfield Amendment forward, however, industry would take the lead on computer research and development.

Disillusioned by Vietnam and the election of Richard Nixon from working for the Pentagon, Bob Taylor left the post as director of the IPTO at ARPA in 1969, took a sabbatical at the University of Utah, and went to the Xerox Palo Alto Research Center (PARC), which had opened in July 1970. PARC swiftly became known as the premier center for research and development in the post-ARPA era. Taylor joined in September to manage its Computer Science Laboratory and recruit talent. He had met Kay while at Utah and read his thesis on FLEX. Just as he had once persuaded Larry Roberts to head the networking project at ARPA, he now sought to convince Kay to be a technical leader in a sister laboratory, the Systems Science Lab.

After his visit to Papert, Kay had been working at the Stanford Artificial Intelligence Lab designing a machine that, like Logo, would be simple enough for a child to use. Kay wanted this machine to weigh two pounds, be compact (8 x 10 x 2 inches) and much more powerful than FLEX.

Taylor offered Kay the opportunity to continue his work at PARC. Kay accepted the offer and was joined by other recruits such as Bill English, who had been the head engineer at Engelbart's Augmentation Research Center.

The ferment of Xerox PARC under Taylor influenced the development of the Internet, which reflected a global collaboration that built on the original ARPAnet concepts of simplicity, distribution, and neutrality. At this time the national networks, including those in the United States, Britain, and France, came together.

A researcher named Bob Metcalfe led the networking effort at Xerox PARC, inventing, with other researchers, Ethernet and the PARC Universal Packet (PUP), which together allowed PARC to have interlinked, high-speed computer networks. Metcalfe's packet-based Ethernet incorporated a variety of earlier concepts, notably Norm Abramson's wireless ALOHANET in Hawaii, to empower local high-speed networks. PUP was designed to interconnect different networks, separating the information necessary for creating and reassembling packets (message) from the information needed to get packets across the networks (medium), just as the ARPAnet IMPs had separated the host computers (message) from the network (medium).

By the mid-1970s, Xerox PARC had Licklider's intergalactic network, but locked behind corporate and legal walls. But Metcalfe's researchers deliberately let their ideas leak out, and PARC's work influenced the people who transformed the ARPAnet into the Internet.

The transmission control protocol (TCP), first described by Vint Cerf and Bob Kahn, former grad students of Len Kleinrock, in their 1973 paper, "A Protocol for Packet Network Intercommunication," extended the concept of packet neutrality to internetwork communication. In 1978, the network community, led by yet another Kleinrock protégé, Jon Postel, and inspired by PUP, broke TCP into two sets. The packet transmission set of protocols was dubbed the Internet protocol (IP). Over the following decade, TCP/IP networks replaced the ARPAnet and the other early national networks, forming the Internet. One significant development would bring the Internet into homes and schools around the world: the personal computer.

INVENTING THE FUTURE

"The best way to predict the future is to invent it," Kay notoriously quipped while arguing with a Xerox planner. At PARC it was his mission to convince his colleagues that personal computers were the future. Until the early 1970s, computers were whirring, churning, gargantuan devices, monolithic time-sharing mainframes used and maintained by experts.

Kay's vision of the "Dynabook" involved cheap, personal computers usable by children—everything that the computers at the time were not.

In 1971 only computer industry types knew about the projects underway at Xerox PARC. By the end of 1972 so did the readers of *Rolling Stone*, thanks to Stewart Brand. This cybernetic journalist and all-around revolutionary had been helping shape the technophile counterculture through his *Whole Earth Catalog*, a publication that defined a trend toward personal empowerment through computers:

> A realm of intimate, personal power is developing—power of the individual to conduct his own education, find his own inspiration, shape his own environment, and share his adventure with whoever is interested. Tools that aid this process are sought and promoted by the WHOLE EARTH CATALOG.[5]

In mid-1972, idle after ceasing publication of the *Whole Earth Catalog*, Brand decided to do some investigative journalism into what he called the "youthful fervor and firm dis-Establishmentarianism of the freaks who design computer science . . . the people who adapt computer nature to fit human nature." He had wielded a camera at Engelbart's 1968 demonstration and now sought to follow through on the epic of computer development at PARC. He obtained Taylor's permission to hang out in the Computer Science Lab for a few weeks, and celebrity photographer Annie Liebowitz followed with her camera, snapping pictures of beanbag chairs, unkempt hair, bicycles in the hallways, and sandaled feet.

The result was Brand's incendiary "Spacewar: Fanatic Life and Symbolic Death among the Computer Bums." The title was taken from the name of the first video game ever, developed in 1961 by the hackers at the MIT Artificial Intelligence Lab to change an oscilloscope display into a spaceship battleground. The article begins, "Ready or not, computers are coming to the people."

Brand's interaction with Kay strongly colors the piece. With and because of Kay, Brand germinated the computer hacker myth.

> They are the ones who translate human demands into code that the machines can understand and act on. They are

legion. Fanatics with a potent new toy. A mobile newfound elite, with its own apparent language and character, its own legends and humor. Those magnificent men with their fly-ing machines, scouting a leading edge of technology which has an odd softness to it; outlaw country, where rules are not decree or routine so much as the starker demands of what's possible.[6]

PARC and Kay, Brand intimated, would play no small role in the computer revolution. He thought Kay's Dynabook—the personal computer—would be key. Kay and English told Brand that the Dynabook would be a per-sonal editing, scanning, and viewing device. A person could use it to write, paint, compose music, and program, Kay said, and should be able to link to other Dynabooks. Ideally, the Dynabook would sell for less than five hundred dollars apiece—cheap enough for schools to purchase en masse. Millions will buy them when, Brand trumpeted, "computing power be-comes like telephone power."

> That is the general bent of research at Xerox, soft, away from hugeness and centrality, toward the small and the personal, toward putting maximum computer power in the hands of every individual who wants it. [7]

The Xerox management in Stamford, Connecticut, was appalled. The ar-ticle portrayed PARC's well-paid researchers as the offbeat, countercul-tural, free-thinking longhairs that most of them were.

THE ALTO, OR THE "INTERIM DYNABOOK"

In 1973 the Computer Science Lab at PARC introduced the first opera-tional computer designed to be used by only one person. It was the "In-terim Dynabook," or Alto, as Bob Taylor officially called it. Kay, who had been working on a new programming language called Smalltalk, had ad-vised and inspired the Alto's principal designers, Charles Thacker and But-ler Lampson. The Alto wasn't quite the Dynabook vision reported by Brand; it did not weigh just two pounds, and it was not exactly for public consumption. Knowing that the technology necessary for the Dynabook wouldn't be possible until the early 1980s, the researchers built the Alto to bootstrap toward the Dynabook.

That same year, Metcalfe developed Ethernet, which would influence the Internet, allowing PARC engineers to network the Altos together. Shortly thereafter, researchers Charles Simonyi, Tim Mott, and Larry Tesler created Bravo and Gypsy, programs that constituted the first user-friendly word processing system. This became one of the killer apps of the personal computer. Back in 1971, Gary Starkweather, a member of the Systems Science Lab, had invented the lucrative laser printer, which enabled the Alto and future computers to be multimedia tools for printing text and art and made Xerox a fortune. One could print out a letter or picture created on the Alto exactly as it looked on the screen, a phenomenon known as WYSIWYG (what you see is what you get).

In 1977 Kay wrote two similar papers on their work on the personal computer, which he still called the Dynabook, bringing it to the attention of the greater public. The first, "Personal Dynamic Media," was coauthored with his team member Adele Goldberg and published in the March issue of *Computer,* a magazine read mostly by members of the computer society: engineers, scientists, and technicians. The next, "Microelectronics and the Personal Computer," debuted in the September 1977 issue of *Scientific American.*

Kay held fast to the belief he had expressed in his doctoral thesis, that to manipulate ideas through the medium of the computer would transform the way one thinks. Kay and Goldberg wrote, "External media serve to materialize thought and, through feedback, to augment the actual paths the thinking follows."[8] The difference between a piece of paper and a computer, of course, is that the latter can provide more *individual feedback*. The computer should immediately extrapolate and simulate an idea, offering the user a vision of new worlds and possibilities of his or her own making.

. . . .

The ability to simulate the details of any descriptive model means that the computer viewed as a medium itself, can be *all other media* if the embedding and viewing methods are sufficiently well provided. Moreover, this new "metamedium" is interactive—it can respond to queries and experiments—so that the messages may involve the learner in a two-way conversation. This property has never been available before except through the medium of an individual teacher. We think the implications are vast and compelling.[9]

—"Personal Dynamic Media"

. . . .

The Alto incorporated many "metamedium" features inherited from Engelbart's NLS and Sketchpad, including the mouse, menus, and windows. Kay's Learning Research Group brought windows to the next level of evolution, making them overlap like sheets of paper on the screen. The user would use the mouse to click on a window to activate it and send it to the "top of the pile." Dan Ingalls, a member of Kay's team, also incorporated the mouse to activate "pop-up menus." These would become the desktop paradigm for decades to come. As for the other features of the NLS—the bootstrapped operating system with its rococo links and hierarchies—the researchers at PARC left them in the scrap pile.

Kay's group was focused on children, and children needed a very different interface from the NLS. Kay believed that Engelbart was trying to make a violin—and it's difficult for kids to learn the violin. He shared Engelbart's conviction that a computer should be able to become a violin, for expert users, but believed the metamedium should be rich, colorful, and easily interactive for beginners.

. . . .

If the computer is to be truly "personal," adult and child users must be able to get it to perform useful activities without resorting to the services of an expert. Simple tasks must be simple, and complex ones must be possible.[10]

—"Microelectronics and the Personal Computer"

. . . .

PROGRAMMING IN VITRO

Kay pioneered three areas of computing: the vision of the personal computer, a programming language for it, and the instruction of how best to use it. He believed the architecture, interface, and programming language should evolve together, just as flesh evolves with genes. The medium (the hardware) and the message (the code), in this case, are inextricable.

Kay had read media theorist Marshall McLuhan, whose claim that "the medium is the message" struck a chord. Content is shaped by context. McLuhan believed that TV, for example, has a profound impact on children not because of what is on TV, but because of what TV *is*. Children prefer it to books, he said, because it's an engrossing aural and visual experience. The TV's mosaic of dots, its lack of detail, its motion and sound, he said, are far more interactive than reading.

Kay thought the computer should be able to integrate touch, sound, images, and symbols. His team worked to develop a message, a "communications system," that would extend the relatively passive but literate reading culture to an interactive computer–using culture of math, science, and simulation, as Papert had envisioned. Knowing how to program is essential to using the computer to its fullest extent, and Kay wanted that task to be as easy as possible.

> Our experience, and that of others who teach programming, is that a first computer language's particular style and its main concepts not only have a strong influence on what a new programmer can accomplish but also leave an impression about programming that can last for years.[11]
> —"Microelectronics and the Personal Computer"

Kay's teammates dared him to write an entire programming language in just one page of code. The challenge was to make it so that it would be simple and easy to access, as well as an improvement on expert-level programming. Kay did, and called it Smalltalk. His humor is understated: The name defies the godlike appellations (like "Thor") often granted to languages. If Smalltalk did big things, people would be happily surprised. The moniker is also in reference to its intended programmers: children.

The problem with common 1970s-era programming languages like BASIC and FORTRAN is that they were too difficult for anyone but an expert to program. Kay even thought that Papert's Logo wasn't adequate for six-year-olds to create and express themselves. Most programming languages were sequential, meaning that any change in the code necessitates changing the rest of the code, so the programmer must be excruciatingly careful. The more complex the program, Kay explained, it is geometrically more difficult to get the system to work.

Kay's insight about programming is that, like natural language, it is a means to "shape the invisible." To use a cybernetic metaphor is to say that code is the DNA of the computer. DNA is composed of just four base units, and Kay sought similar austerity in software. Like DNA, software should be designed to create the very complex from the very simple. The fusion of elegance and practicality is what Kay calls *beauty*. It's technology that resembles nature.

> Complexity can be safely handled because the language severely limits the kinds of interactions between activities, allowing only those that are appropriate, much as a hormone is allowed to interact only with a few specifically responsive target cells. SMALLTALK, the programming language of our personal computer, was the first computer language to be based entirely on the structural concepts of messages and activities.[12]
>
> —"Microelectronics and the Personal Computer"

Smalltalk is guided by the same cybernetic concept that underlies biology, artificial intelligence, and some branches of psychology: Repeated interactions or feedback between basic things manifest in the complex. Kay's Smalltalk is simple and organic and consists of mobile units of code.* Kay likens the transition from the old sequential programming languages to Smalltalk to the evolution of floating molecular chains in the primordial sea to complex life forms with cells and cell membranes. Instead of naming them "cells," Kay called these units of code "objects." Just as cells constitute tissues and organs, so objects make possible robust, malleable programs.

In "Microelectronics and the Personal Computer," Kay describes how objects can perform specific acts such as drawing, making sound, or adding numbers. An object—for example, "brush symbols"—could share, send,

---

*Smalltalk was influenced by FLEX, Planner, Simula, LISP, Logo, and META II.

and receive different commands or "messages." Just as pressing the "open" button of a garage door opener sends the door a message to open, so in Smalltalk one can send an object a message to perform an action (such as combining with another object). Smalltalk objects, Internet servers, Marvin Minsky's agents, John von Neumann's automata—all build complexity through a society of simple communication.

Kay deemed this approach "object-oriented programming." He wasn't the first to think of a modular approach to programming—that credit goes to Norwegian researchers Ole-Johan Dahl and Kristen Nygaard. But Kay, assisted by his PARC colleagues Dan Ingalls, Adele Goldberg, Ted Kaehler, and Diana Merry, was the first to build a full-fledged, practical object-oriented programming language in Smalltalk, founded in the concept of a society of communication. This simpler, modular approach to computing enables both high-level programmers and novices (including children) to develop powerful programs to suit their own needs and abilities.

Just as Smalltalk is modeled after biological behavior, so human brains can be shaped by Smalltalk. The act of programming, Kay believed, can help people achieve higher levels of thought (what Engelbart called *coevolution*), because it requires us to create symbols and abstractions. From cave drawings onward, symbols have allowed us to make complex ideas simple by generalizing them. They allow us to make metaphors and mathematics.

Symbols also allow us to make *nonsense*. A programmer can make the computer follow arbitrary sets of rules to create magnificent simulations: sounds that no instrument has previously made, intricate patterns undiscovered in nature, visual, aural, and textual worlds where natural laws don't apply. Within a computer, a spacecraft could travel faster than the speed of light, enabling time travel to occur. Manipulating symbols on the computer allows us to create things that could or couldn't, should or shouldn't, exist. The computer is a medium for the real world and wonderlands alike.

. . . .

The range of simulations the computer can perform is bounded only by the limits of the human imagination. . . . It may seem almost sinful to discuss the simulation of nonsense, but only if we

want to believe that what we know is correct and complete.
History has not been kind to those who subscribe to this view.
It is just this realm of apparent nonsense that must be kept
open for the developing minds of the future. Although the personal computer can be guided in any direction we choose the
real sin would be to make it act like a machine.[13]

—"Microelectronics and the Personal Computer"

. . . .

Evolution on a genetic or cultural level is impossible without variations
of the norm. Kay says that *nonsense* is just another name for unprecedented change. Mutations in DNA are genetic nonsense. Art, poetry,
and the new ideas that underlie revolutions are cultural nonsense. The
symbolic nonsense of computer code changes the coder and his or her
world. The medium can help us make new messages.

THE INTERFACE IN VIVO

Kay admires the work of education activist Maria Montessori, who he
says advocated "the invention of twenty-first century toys that are fun
and deeply involved for the children, and that have big fundamental side
effects on children's heuristic approaches to thinking about the world."
Throughout the mid-1970s and early 1980s Kay was devoted to bringing these "twenty-first century toys"—namely, the Alto—out of the
PARC labs and into the little hands of children.

In 1977 Steve Jobs and Steve Wozniak started to sell the preassembled
Apple II out of their one-year-old company, Apple. Their computer was a
very different beast from what PARC had been developing. The Alto was a
truly powerful and useful tool with features like Engelbart's mouse and windows improved and enhanced by the animated capabilities of Smalltalk. The
Apple II was nearly just a box of wires by comparison, but since Woz's wiz-
ardry resulted in an affordable, usable machine, it became the PC of millions.
An Apple employee named Jef Raskin devised a vision of a computer out-
fitted with communication networks and an interactive interface. Furthermore, he had seen the developments at PARC and wanted to convince Jobs
that the Alto's graphics and other features were similar to what he and his
team were working on in their research project, code-named Macintosh.

Meanwhile, Kay's Learning Research Group opened its doors, allowing kids to play on the Alto and program in Smalltalk. As he had predicted, the heavy use of interactive graphics and animation delighted the children. Goldberg came up with the "Joe Book," a way of teaching object-oriented programming to young people. An entire culture of schoolchildren spent their free hours at PARC developing complicated Smalltalk programs of their own. One twelve-year-old girl developed a painting system. Fifteen-year-old boys wrote music score capture systems and a circuit design program.

. . . .

> The kids love it! The interactive nature of the dialogue, the fact that they are in control, the feeling that they are doing real things rather than playing with toys or working out "assigned" problems, the pictorial and auditory nature of their results, all contribute to a tremendous sense of accomplishment to their experience. Their attention spans are measured in hours rather than minutes.[14]   —"Personal Dynamic Media"

. . . .

By then, mostly everybody at PARC knew that it was only a matter of time before, one way or another, the technology would reach the mass market. The only questions were *how* and *when*. The answer came in 1979.

How elements of the Alto's graphical user interface made the crossover to the modern PC is now legendary. Xerox PARC demonstrated Smalltalk and the Alto to hundreds of people from the computing community including some at Apple. Raskin, with the help of his Apple colleague, Bill Atkinson, finally succeeded in getting Jobs to see the demonstration. In exchange for a peek under the corporate covers, Apple offered Xerox 100,000 private shares of Apple stock at $10.50 per share. At this time, the Xerox management was considering selling the PARC technology as a means to make the transition from the lab to marketplace. Perhaps, they pondered, Apple would build computers for Xerox. The decision to share the technology with Apple was extremely controversial and each member of the Learning Research Group had his or her own opinion about it. Many, such as Goldberg, wanted Smalltalk and the Alto to debut as an exclusively Xerox product. Others, such as Tesler, wanted a deal with Apple. Kay, who had been trying to get his group to "burn the disk packs" and start anew, was less protective than Goldberg and other colleagues. By 1979 he considered the Smalltalk demo "an artifact of the past." In the end, the Xerox management decided to go ahead and make the deal.*

What most impressed Jobs, who is no computer scientist, wasn't the networking or object-oriented programming, but Kay's Smalltalk-driven graphical user interface, with its pop-up menus, scroll bars, icons, and overlapping windows. What was originally designed as a kids' interface entranced Apple's mercurial founder. The Apple Lisa interface they were developing was much more static than the interactive Alto's. After watching the presentation, the Apple design team wanted to make the mouse a standard device on every Apple computer. The overlapping windows on the Alto inspired Apple's designer Bill Atkinson to devise a way to do the same. The team decided to make their computers more user friendly, like the Alto, adding features like the one-button mouse and the trash can following consistent interface principles. In 1981 IBM launched their first personal computer, but it lacked the interactive, dynamic interface of the Macs that were to come.

In 1984 the Apple Macintosh debuted and, at $2,495, blew away all the competition in the personal computer market (including the $10,000 Apple Lisa and PARC's $16,595 STAR, the doomed commercial version of the Alto). Its interface was the legacy of elements from Sutherland's Sketchpad, Engelbart's NLS, the ARPAnet, and PARC's Alto combined with the ingenuity of Apple's designers and visionaries. Indeed, it was this interface that made Apple a giant when desktop publishing software, its killer app, was developed. Microsoft Windows was later modeled after the Mac interface.

The Apple Macintosh didn't wholly fulfill the Dynabook vision: Though it came as a single unit and could be carried by its handle, it was hardly the size of a notebook. It didn't come with an object-oriented programming language. Some designers working on the Macintosh wanted to fulfill Kay and Papert's mission to make a machine that would open the world of programming to children and adults alike, but Jobs believed that to be user friendly, the machine's workings shouldn't be exposed.

---

*The decision paid off financially; the Apple stock Xerox received became worth over $17 million after Apple went public in December 1980, though it's impossible to calculate what Xerox could have made if it had led the personal computing wave.

Even today, the Dynabook idea—the marriage of a simple, powerful interface with a simple, powerful programming language in a simple, powerful machine straight out of the box—hasn't yet been fully realized.

Around the same time that the Macintosh debuted, Xerox, suffering from an identity crisis and a fatal lack of foresight, cut back funding on PC development. PARC, so close to introducing the PC, was also so far. It let a $95 billion-a-year industry slip through its fingers. It has been estimated that all of the innovations of Xerox PARC generated about $10 trillion of the U.S. gross national product from 1980 to 2000.

THE USER ILLUSION

By the time the Macintosh was introduced in 1984, Kay's career had already touched on the major developments in computer development: the PC, a programming language, and children's education. Working with kids, he'd say, is his favorite part of the "romance." His enthusiasm for education inspired him to do further work on the human–computer interface, which Kay called "the user illusion."

That year, after a brief stint at Atari, he made the exodus to Apple and wrote a *Scientific American* article titled "Computer Software," in which he declared that the user illusion was the driving force behind the personal computer. He expounded on his definition of the user illusion to mean "the simplified myth everyone builds to explain (and make guesses about) the system's actions and what should be done next." It is what is presented to our senses as the computer itself. When a user is creating a document on a computer, he or she uses the mouse and keyboard to manipulate a representation of the document that is designed to stand for the document. This is the illusion—no icon, no paper and pen, no text actually exists. The user illusion is successful when the metaphorical conception works effortlessly. Using devices like the mouse and windows (and others) to create the best user illusion became the key to popularizing the computer. They made the magic of the medium possible.

. . . .

> The objective is to amplify the user's ability to simulate. A person exerts the greatest leverage when his illusion can be

> manipulated without appeal to abstract intermediaries such as the hidden programs needed to put into action even a simple word processor.... [A] software designer's control of what is essentially a theatrical context is the key to creating an illusion and enhancing its perceived "friendliness."[15]
>
> —"Computer Software"

. . . .

The best user illusion, Kay maintains, would be software that enables the user to do something that the designer didn't foresee. The computer then would transcend the realm of a mere tool with a specific function and enter the realm of a truly intimate, protean, personalized medium.

Kay envisioned that the future of software design or the user illusion would be *personal agents*—"extensions of the user's will and purposes, shaped and embedded in the stuff of the computer."[16] In "Computer Software" Kay perpetuated the biological analogy, stating that if organic material can form complex organizations such as people, computer material likewise should produce complex bodies, even semi-intelligent ones.

He imagined the agent as a "soft robot" living inside a computer, that would execute the task of being a librarian, a pilot, or a gofer for the user. The agent would be the meeting of artificial intelligence and personal computing. The agent would become essential to the user illusion in that it would be part of the computer's interface. It would communicate with the user and ask for and give advice, and it would trawl through data retrieval systems on networks. Like Vannevar Bush thirty years earlier, Kay imagined the agent working around the clock to look for things that the user is interested in and presenting them as a personal portfolio. It'd help navigate the user through vistas of information, extracting meaning from mayhem and easing the problem of information overload.*

The idea of creating a user illusion that incorporates agents veers into artificial intelligence. Object-oriented programming, with its emphasis on the interaction of organic modularity, was already one step

---

*Kay noted in "Computer Software" that the idea of the software agent originated with John McCarthy, the founder of the artificial intelligence labs at MIT and Stanford University, in the late 1950s, and that the term was coined by McCarthy's colleague Oliver G. Selfridge.

NORBERT WIENER

Norbert Wiener (*center*), the absentminded father of cybernetics, holds a cigar stub and expounds on ideas with Julius Stratton and Claude Shannon.

Courtesy of the MIT Museum.

VANNEVAR BUSH

A young Vannevar Bush displays his Differential Analyzer, the famous analog computer that inspired his vision of the memex.

Courtesy of the MIT Museum.

JOHN VON NEUMANN

"Gentleman Johnny," sporting one of his pressed suits, stands in front of the Institute for Advanced Study computer, which was built following his vision.

Photograph by Alan Richards. Courtesy of the Archives of the Institute for Advanced Study

ALAN TURING

Alan Turing was the first to envision computers as machines of pure logic. The Turing Test remains a standard for determining whether machines are intelligent.

Courtesy of the National Portrait Gallery, London.

J. C. R. LICKLIDER

J. C. R. Licklider fostered his dream of human-computer symbiosis amongst the "intergalactic network" of researchers he supported.

Courtesy of the MIT Museum.

DOUGLAS ENGELBART

Douglas Engelbart's efforts to augment human intellect paved the way to the personal computer and the World Wide Web.

MARVIN MINSKY

Marvin Minsky poses one of the robots in MIT's famed AI Lab, the place where he developed his theories of human and artificial intelligence.

Courtesy of the MIT Museum.

SEYMOUR PAPERT

Seymour Papert, here immersed in his playful pursuit to build a world of exploration for children through computers.

Courtesy of the MIT Museum.

ALAN KAY

Alan Kay's definition of beauty is the fusion of elegance and practicality. His aim is to get programmers of all ages to realize it.

Courtesy of Owen Egan.

MARSHALL McLUHAN

McLuhan's maxim, "the medium is the message," would become a tenet of the electronic global village.

Courtesy of Horst Ehricht/National Archives of Canada/PA198674.

ABBIE HOFFMAN

Abbie (*center*), political radical, understood the power of the electronic media and harnessed it in order to make it obvious to others.

Courtesy of Corbis.

TED NELSON

Nelson dreamt up Xanadu, an information repository wherein everything is intertwingled, everyone is compensated, and nothing is forgotten.

TIM BERNERS-LEE

Berners-Lee's World Wide Web began as a tool for researchers to share information and collaborate.

Courtesy of Graham Flack and BT.

RICHARD STALLMAN

Richard Stallman has based the Free Software Foundation on the Golden Rule. Source code should be open because it harms society for it to be proprietary.

Courtesy of Sam Ogden.

LARRY WALL

In creating Perl, Wall enticed lazy, impatient, and hubristic programmers to enjoy the benefits of free software.

Courtesy of www.storyphoto.com.

ERIC S. RAYMOND

Raymond showed the computer culture why the open source Bazaar is better and more fun than the proprietary Cathedral.

Courtesy of www.storyphoto.com.

L. LAWRENCE LESSIG

Lessig believes that the Net, if left to the powers-that-be, would not fulfill the promise of freedom. Rather, it would become the perfect tool of control.

Courtesy of www.storyphoto.com.

K. ERIC DREXLER

K. Eric Drexler (*left*), nanotechnologist, talks with Doug Engelbart. Drexler believes the technologies of tomorrow will benefit the majority of humankind only if we plan ahead by using the information technologies of today.

BILL JOY

Among other technologists, Bill Joy's apocalyptic vision of humans losing control of their creations startles some, and exasperates others.

Courtesy of Greg Poschman.

JARON LANIER

Virtual reality pioneer Jaron Lanier argues for a humanistic approach to technology instead of what he deems "cybernetic totalism."

in that direction. Taking advantage of ever more sophisticated (virtually *organic*) programming, agents would be the next step toward intelligent machines.

In "Computer Software" Kay is undecided about how sophisticated these entities should become. He acknowledged that designers of artificial intelligence had gone only so far as to create machines that mimicked hardwired human behavior—that which doesn't require learning or experience (limb movement, vision, etc.). He states that the dream of constructing an agent with an adult mentality or "raising" a machine with an infant mentality is distant. The most we can expect in the near term are artificial systems that look and act *somewhat* intelligent. Whether or not they can pass the Turing Test remains to be seen.

> Agents are almost inescapably anthropomorphic, but they will not be human, nor will they be very competent for some time . . . Surely users will be disappointed if the projected illusion is that of intelligence but the reality falls far short. [17]
>
> —"Computer Software"

SOCIAL COMPLEXITY

Like other information revolutionaries, Kay is a humanist concerned about the flip side of the universal, user-friendly technology he is introducing to the world. The computer should be used as an amplifier of the user, not merely as a tool. Following McLuhan, he notes, "It is always a good question of any technology to ask: When is it an amplifier and when is it a prosthetic?" [18] When is it like a bicycle (which amplifies the body's movement), and when is it like a car (which doesn't)? We may shape the tool, but the tool also reshapes us. The challenge is to ensure that it stimulates rather than squelches our creativity, compassion, and comprehension. As sophisticated as the user illusion gets, the important transformations must take place in the minds of the users.

> If teachers do not nourish the romance of learning and expressing, any external mandate for a new "literacy" becomes as much a crushing burden as being forced to perform

Beethoven's sonatas while having no sense of their beauty. Instant access to the world's information will probably have an effect opposite to what is hoped: students will become numb instead of enlightened.[19]

—"Computers, Networks, and Education"

· ·

In 1991, Kay wrote his next major article, "Computers, Networks, and Education," which also appeared in *Scientific American*. In it, he first and foremost identifies the responsibility of the parent or teacher to provide a context and a catalyst for learning. No matter how sophisticated the technology, true knowledge develops only in a social or historical context, not a vacuum.

Given that, Kay frequently refers to the social potential of the computer as a *paradigm shift*. Engelbart tried to bring about a shift that would enable people to use computers to collaborate in the interest of solving complex social dilemmas. So is Kay. "What is great . . . in humankind's great investigations," Kay writes, "can be learned—by giving students direct contact with 'the great chain of being,' so that they can internally generate the structures needed to hold powerful ideas."[20]

The new worldview made possible by the computer, aided by the Internet, is *complexity,* which, like other paradigms of the Information Revolution, hearkens back to cybernetics. As Kay realized, the technologies that were developed to parse information in an increasingly complicated world ironically contribute to the world's complexity. Complexity increases proportionately with information, but we can apply computer simulations to help understand complexity better. Kay uses the rain forest as an example: We know that burning up parts of the rain forest provides us with arable land in the short term, but computer models reveal the deleterious long-term effects of slash-and-burn forestry. He frequently taught students at the Open School in West Hollywood, California, how to use computer models to simulate, for example, the slow formation of smog over an imaginary city. As with Papert's Logo, kids learn that activity in a microenvironment can have widespread repercussions.

Kay called these computer models "mental bricks." Layer upon layer of these bricks can contribute to the gradual realization of a new humanistic worldview that usurps the inflexible and inhumane institutions of the past.

> Many of the most valuable structures devised from our newer bricks may require considerable effort to acquire. Music, mathematics, science and human rights are just a few of the systems of thought that must be built up layer by layer and integrated. Although understanding or creating such constructions is difficult, the need for struggle must not be grounds for avoidance. Difficulty should be sought out, as a spur to delving more deeply into an interesting area.[21]
>
> — "Computers, Networks, and Education"

Kay, like other computer visionaries, realizes that the most valuable skills in the information age are no longer the piecemeal labors of the factory or the bureaucracy, but the ability to understand how parts of reality are linked together. In the past, people were spoon-fed facts to be regurgitated; in school, the study of one subject was separated from the study of another. What Papert and Kay seek to do, through computers, is to stimulate minds to think systemically. Rather than tell children the answer to a problem, the computer could help them discover the solution by understanding *why* the problem arises and *how* it relates to other problems. Unexpected solutions are born of understanding causes and consequences in the broader scheme. Systemic thinking was once the privilege of policymakers and scientists; now the tools for it are in the hands of anyone who has a computer and an Internet connection.

DIGITAL DEMOCRACY

Kay believes that engaging in this sort of experimental, skeptical, and associative thinking will make our minds—and our democracies—stronger. Just as the founders of the United States encouraged dissent through a free press, Kay encourages subversion through the use of a PC plus the Internet. These, he says, will "provide ways of learning powerful ideas outside of official processes (even outside of those that seem to be benign)."

. . . .

It is therefore the duty of a well-conceived environment for learning to be contentious and even disturbing, seek contrasts over ab-
solutes, aim for quality over quantity and acknowledge the need
for will and effort. I do not think this goes too far to say that these
requirements are at odds with the prevailing values in American
life today.[22]   —"Computers, Networks, and Education"

. . . .

Kay poses a crucial question that aims at the junction of technology,
media, and democracy: Where and how would the Federalist Papers be
published today? The essays of James Madison, Alexander Hamilton,
and John Jay that shaped the American Revolution were originally published in newspapers of the thirteen colonies. Nowadays, Kay observes,
we wouldn't publish such in-depth debate in our newspapers. Books,
with the rare exception of a *Harry Potter*, don't reach a broad readership. TV can't handle such complex content. But computers might.

The online version of the Federalist Papers, of course, wouldn't be
in the same format as the eighteenth-century version. But Kay envisions
a new online Constitution wherein users could not only run simulations
but also change assumptions to test the ideas. The model could be
hyperlinked to sources such as the constitution of Virginia so that readers might readily compare the new ideas against the old. Now the receivers could have something other than static essays. And feedback
about the proposals—again by network—could be timely and relevant.[23]

. . . .

If the personally owned book was one of the main shapers of
the Renaissance notion of the individual, then the pervasively
networked computer of the future should shape humans who
are healthy skeptics from an early age. Any argument can be
tested against the arguments of others and by appeal to simulation.[24]   —"Computers, Networks, and Education"

. . . .

Just as a good republic takes into account multiple viewpoints, so the computer
can represent them adequately, with context and complexity. Kay imagined that

certain software technologies could combat "naïve acceptance" of information by displaying instances where the alleged "fact" does not hold. Other computer technologies could combat tunnel vision by adding a serendipitous element to an Internet search. Others could re-wed fact with context by providing sequences of related ideas. A user could read about a contagious disease, an election, or a weather pattern; run a simulation of its potential long-term effects; and see it from multiple points of view, even, or especially, those that are alien to him or her. Kay says, "The more cultural diversity, the more points of view we have access to, the better off we all are.[25]

> Computers can be programmed so that "facts" retrieved in one window on a screen will automatically cause supporting and opposing arguments to be retrieved in a halo of surrounding windows. And ideas can be shown in prose, as an image, viewed from the back and the front, inside or out. Important concepts from many different sources can be collected in one place.[26]
> —"Computers, Networks, and Education"

There's a caveat, of course. The computer may provide users with the opportunity to explore complexity and make informed long-term decisions only if the individual or the society desires to use it to those ends. It's a feedback loop: Humans can use computers to perpetuate humanistic values only if they are educated to do so. And good education begins with people, with humanistic values.

AFTERWARD

Kay and Tesler, who worked together at both Xerox PARC and Apple, came up with three paradigms of the Information Revolution. The first they called the institutional stage, referring to the day of (functional and utilitarian) mainframe computers owned by big companies or the government. The second stage, the Gutenberg stage, was the first generation of bulky PCs that were semiexpensive; were available to millions, not billions; and featured clumsy interfaces. The third phase of the paradigm shift, Kay's mission, is intimate computing, and at the start of the twenty-first century it is still in flux. "Intimate computing involves billions of people, not millions," Kay says, "because it is going to incorporate pervasive networking—particularly on the telephone—and it is going to sell to everybody who now has a phone."[27] He hopes that this will include the majority of people the world over.

Kay is now credited as a major influence behind the interface that drove the third paradigm shift.* The shift has depended on the FLEX, the interim Dynabook, the Macintosh interfaces, and object-oriented programming.† The next step is to develop technologies that will help users both navigate and take advantage of the complexity of information available. Kay believes that the only way to complete the paradigm shift is to push toward true computer literacy through a user-friendly interface that may include software agents. Then the computer revolution will really begin.

He also emphasizes that in the next phase people need to learn to use computers not only to (passively) access information, but to (actively) contribute information in the form of text, music, art, and code. So far, Kay says, "The expected (and disappointing) thing has happened: That most people are only using the computer to imitate the old paper media. It will take a while for what's really important about computing to be learned and understood." His hope is that nonprogrammers become programmers, as they did in a big way with spreadsheet software, and that people use the computer as a more powerful means of representation, self-expression, and self-empowerment. After all, it was literacy that separated the rulers from the ruled in the ancient world: The illiterate masses were subject to the elite's interpretation of documents. Those in power didn't want the masses to write poetry and plot against them.

. . . .

If you like to draw, do not automate drawing, rather, program your computer to give you a new set of paints. If you like to play

---

*Kay is only one of many important visionaries of human–computer interface design, whose ranks notably include Nicholas Negroponte, Doug Engelbart, Ivan Sutherland, Gabe Groner, Tom Ellis, Dan Bricklin, Bob Frankston, Jef Raskin, Bill Atkinson, Brenda Laurel, Jakob Nielsen, Terry Winograd, and David Gelernter.

†Neither the FLEX nor the Dynabook was realized commercially. In the 1990s Java and C++, both object-oriented languages, rose to dominance in the programming field. Smalltalk never realized commercial success, which some attribute to PARC politics. Smalltalk is now available as free software.

music, do not build a "player piano"; instead, program yourself a new kind of instrument.[28]

—"Microelectronics and the Personal Computer"

Kay continues to follow his own advice. In 2001 he left Disney (where he had been since 1986) and established the Viewpoints Research Institute, a nonprofit public benefit corporation. Another Kay project that is underway is Squeak—a Smalltalk-based object-oriented programming language with the tagline "a universal IdeaLand for children of all ages." Squeak is a tool for people who want to experiment with their computers to design anything from numerical analysis, graphics, distributed computing, music synthesis, educational aids, and more. It's open source—users can view, use, and modify the source code to make anything from window gadgets to text handling. Best of all, it's designed so that a child can pick up on how to do it.

The human body fascinates Kay as the ultimate model of complexity derived from simple elements, the principle underlying object-oriented programming. In a recent speech, he said, "We as a system have a hundred trillion cells that soak up energy and reform ourselves." He is hopeful that human-made systems like the Internet will compare favorably. To think deeply about this emergent complexity in living and mechanical beings is to delight in its magic. Unity from complexity, form from chaos, is part of life's user illusion.

Which inspired Kay, at a 2001 Smalltalk conference, to tell the audience this anecdote:

> The first time I visited a Zen Buddhist monastery, the monks would always clasp their hands. After two days I asked one of them why. They said, "We believe the world of appearances is an illusion, but for reasons of efficiency, most of the time we have to pretend that it is real. Many times a day, such as before we eat and work, we clasp our hands to pause for a moment to realize that the world is much more complex than our tiny minds can deal with at any one time."

PART III

POWER

• Marshall McLuhan • Abbie Hoffman • Ted Nelson • Tim Berners-Lee •
• Richard M. Stallman • Larry Wall • Eric S. Raymond • Lawrence Lessig •

THE POWER OF COMMUNICATION, of knowledge, can be used to inspire others—or to control them. Information technologies amplify and extend that power over the entire globe. The real battle of the Information Revolution occurs as new technologies become part of society. The powers that be, grounded in the past, realize the profit in acquiring and wielding the new tools to buttress their control. Technologies developed for humanistic or democratic purposes can be co-opted and readapted to achieve repressive or unintentional ends. The revolutionaries react by attempting to push political and corporate power structures toward balanced, empowering democracy. They strive to bring power to the people, to keep information as open and accessible as possible. They aim to uphold the principles of cooperation, communication, and creativity.

The revolutionaries reveal how the architecture of global communications affects society. Beginning in the 1960s, they reveal how the media—particularly the broadcast media—mediate us all. Throughout the 1970s and 1980s, one revolutionary dedicates his life to an alternative to the established media corporations: a global electronic hypertext publishing system. In the 1990s, the power of the networked personal computer is finally realized and another revolutionary creates the World Wide Web. Governments and the most powerful corporations in the world realize the power of the Internet and Web and threaten to control innovation or institute harmful regulation. The revolutionaries leading the free software and open source movements fight for the universal freedom to run, share, study, change, and improve software. With computers everywhere, the struggle to keep software free is the struggle to keep society free.

MEDIATION FOR THE HELL OF IT

MARSHALL MCLUHAN AND ABBIE HOFFMAN

Any medium powerful enough to extend man's reach
is powerful enough to tackle the world.
—Alan Kay

BY THE 1960S AND 1970S insightful scientists and engineers understood that the information age would open new vistas of knowledge. But there is more to it than that. The Information Revolution would affect *all* of society, and to see how required either a broad, historical perspective or a position on its frontlines.

The baby boomers were the first generation to grow up in the information age. The influx of postwar technologies such as telephones and televisions empowered them with a new consciousness and the means for immediate and ubiquitous change. The broadcast media created a narrative of nationally gripping events: the race to the moon, the House Un-American Activities Committee hearings against the Red Menace, and the Cuban missile crisis. TV defined the civil rights movement, with images of black children locked out of schools, a rally of thousands in front of the nation's Capitol, and marchers blown back by fire hoses and attacked by police dogs. The Vietnam War was the first TV war. The protests were televised nightly, juxtaposed with the images of battle beamed from across the globe.

TV fueled the activism of the 1960s and 1970s as much as that activism contributed to its use. Activists realized the power of electronic communication: When technologies are decentralized, inexpensive, and easily accessible, unprecedented freedom in all aspects of life is possible. When they are under central control, or are scarce or costly, people can be restricted by them. There is a feedback loop between society and its media. We are cybernetic beings—shaped by our technologies, just as they are by us.

Media theorist Marshall McLuhan and activist Abbie Hoffman brought the issues of the Information Revolution to the forefront. In March 1967, the National Broadcasting Company aired "This is Marshall McLuhan," an hour-long show in its *Experiment in TV* series. McLuhan, a tall, cool Canadian professor, delivered one-liners in a fast-cut assemblage of pop art, bold newspaper headlines, animations, and photographs. The media theorist was processed by the very media machine he analyzed and was delivered to the masses in a deliberately confusing blur of information.

A few months later, in August, the nightly news programs featured a strange story following the stock report. That day a group of long-haired hippies led by Abbie Hoffman, an energetic young man with a wild afro, had walked up to the balcony overlooking the floor of the New York Stock Exchange and started tossing wads of dollar bills to the crush of brokers below. "Free! It's free!" they shouted. Pandemonium erupted as people grabbed the bills and the central nervous system of the world economy broke down. Refusing to talk to the press, Hoffman ran outside, burned some dollar bills in front of the television cameras and print reporters, then made off in a cab before the police arrived. This event, which exposed the fragility of inhuman global institutions, hit the TV screens, newspapers, and magazines that served as the informational sensoria of the nation.

McLuhan and Hoffman complement each other. McLuhan revealed to the world the ways in which information technologies form, inform, and transform every aspect of human existence in his manifestos, *The Gutenberg Galaxy: The Making of the Typographical Man* (1962) and

Understanding Media: The Extensions of Man (1964). Hoffman, through his street activism and manifestos, *Revolution for the Hell of It* (1968) and *Steal This Book* (1971), simultaneously revealed the power of electronic media and told the world how to rebel against the technologies under corporate control.

AN EDUCATION IN COMMUNICATIONS

In *Understanding Media,* McLuhan established a basic and essential lesson of communications: Our minds are not in direct contact with the world. All communication and interaction must occur through some medium. A naked person interacts with her environment through the media of her own body: her feet, eyes, skin. The technologies we use to interact with the world are also media. These media serve as extensions of ourselves. The foot is our natural tool for locomotion; the wheel extends that power. Our skin protects us from the elements; clothing extends that protection. In protecting and enhancing us, our technologies also reduce and replace the power of our bodies.

For example, the automobile both extended and numbed the power of the foot and, in doing so, reshaped our entire lives. When we're inside a car, we're subservient to its needs. Moreover, the existence of the car changes our overall environment in ways that erode our previous ability to get around by foot. Suburbs are designed for automobiles, not pedestrians. Houses and shops become spread apart such that visiting a neighbor or getting a carton of milk often requires use of the car. Even our architecture is transformed. The driveway and garage become the primary features of the suburban house.

The man who revealed how media both empower and disable us experienced the enormous changes of the post–World War II era as an adult. Born Herbert Marshall McLuhan in 1911, he was raised on the wide plains of Canada when the frontier had been opened by railroads but not yet conquered by the automobile. Young Marshall was a voracious reader and an overwhelming debater who favored his strong-willed, elocutionist mother more than his laidback father. He went to the University of Manitoba, trying out engineering before returning to his strengths, English and philosophy. In 1934 he graduated with a master's degree.

McLuhan continued his education in England, where he was exposed to both tradition and modernity at Cambridge University. A staunch conservative, he fit in with the student athletes known as "the hearties," competing in rowing and rugby. He disdained the other social crowd at Cambridge, the liberal aesthetes with their appreciation of beauty and acceptance of homosexuality. In fact, Alan Turing was there at the same time as part of the crowd McLuhan feared and despised. At Cambridge, McLuhan met and learned from F. R. Leavis, whose *Culture and Environment* (1933, with Denys Thompson) opened his eyes to the idea of applying literary criticism to societal phenomena.

After leaving Cambridge with his Ph.D., McLuhan began teaching at various universities in the Midwest. In his classes he dissected pop culture, scrutinizing advertisements, popular films, and comic strips to discover their foundations. In 1937 he converted to Catholicism, drawn to its complex mysteries and deep moralism. From that point on, McLuhan lived his life with one foot planted in the moral firmament of medieval times and the other in the shifting sands of modernity. He applied this dual worldview to his observations about the history and development of media technologies.

THE MEDIUM IS THE MESSAGE

Understanding the nature of media depends on understanding the history of media. In *The Gutenberg Galaxy* (1962), McLuhan explores the transition from the "typographical man" of the Gutenberg printing press to the "global village" of the electronic era. In *Understanding Media* (1964), he develops the central concept that "the medium is the message."*

Medieval media, McLuhan writes in *The Gutenberg Galaxy,* were radically different from the media that arose after the advent of the printing press. The concept of authorship was practically nonexistent. A work was a collection of bits of text from innumerable authors. Most knowledge was communicated orally through apprenticeships and guilds.

---

*McLuhan coined the phrase in 1958, using it in the keynote address he delivered at the annual meeting of the National Association of Educational Broadcasters.

Medieval scholars treated manuscripts not as distinct books, each with an individual creator, but as collections of thought. They spent most of their time copying the expensive texts, adding their own comments in the process. There was no such thing as identical copies of a text, as each was hand-rendered. Every copy reflected the influence of the copyist.

> Scribal culture could have neither authors nor publics such as were created by typography.[1] —*The Gutenberg Galaxy*

The printing press eliminated anonymity, facilitating fame for the author whose ideas are frozen on the page. The book became an economic commodity, and ideas could be considered a form of property to be protected from piracy or degradation. The concepts of originality, authenticity, and copyright arose. Different genres of literature began to grow. The typographic age distinguished story from history, fiction from fact.

McLuhan reminds us that medieval society was an oral society. The predominant form of communication was speech, which is mutable and ephemeral. Ideas communicated through oral transmission change with each telling, which promotes the explosion of rumors, superstitions, and tribal passions. The typographic age, in contrast, brought in a visual society. The phonetic alphabet, which breaks the continuous spoken language into discrete visual elements, became the primary mode of communication.

The mass distribution of ideas created both personal individuality and societal homogeneity. Along with authors, the printing press created a homogenous public of readers. The reader is a human being with an individual identity who also shares the mind-set of her fellow readers. She is able to remain in communication with others while being alone. The realization of being an individual within a society of peers leads to the belief in inherent individual rights, that all people are created equal. Nations formed as the sociopolitical racial myths that establish national identity were codified, printed, and mass distributed.

> The medium is the message.[2] —*Understanding Media*

McLuhan taught in *Understanding Media* that the nature of the medium defines the message, regardless of the content. The printed word is not the same as the spoken word. A handwritten manuscript is utterly different from a page printed with the same text. Radio, television, film—and the computer—all affect people in unique ways.

When people talk about the effects of television on society, they discuss the amount of violence or sex shown on the screen. It is certainly true that the introduction of television has caused major changes, but it is not the content that did so. It is the medium itself. It's not as if people communicate completely different ideas on television than in books or film. To understand why television is changing society one has to study the intrinsic nature of television.

. . . .

A hot medium is one that extends one single sense in "high definition."[3]   —*Understanding Media*

. . . .

McLuhan classified all forms of media as either "hot" or "cool." A hot medium, he asserted, is high definition, like the technicolor extravagance of the movies or the crystal–clear stereo sound of FM radio. Hot media overwhelm the senses and discourage active participation, A cool medium is low definition, like the pixelated small screen of television or the static signal of the telephone, and therefore high participation, because the person must compensate for the amount of information it lacks. The computer is both hot and cool as it assumes the role of all other media: the radio, the phone, the television, and much more.

THE GLOBAL VILLAGE

McLuhan believed that electric technology in the 1950s and 1960s transformed everything. Political, social, economic, and psychological truths, the foundations of society, became dependent on yet deeper foundations of mechanical technology. As these foundations shifted, so did everything else. People had to face the new reality of total interconnectedness, of total information, of total change.

. . . .

Today we live on the frontier between five centuries of mechanism and the new electronics, between the homogenous and the simultaneous.[4]   —*The Gutenberg Galaxy*

. . . .

McLuhan began lecturing on the effects of media technologies at the same time that people couldn't help but to notice the change themselves. The United States and the Soviet Union ruled the world through nuclear weaponry and modern industry. No longer were there gas lamps, telegraphs, and ships that took a month to cross the Atlantic. There were electric lights, televisions, and jet planes. The mechanical world became the electric world. Suddenly, any place on the globe could be accessible and inhabitable. The globe became a village.

This was not a matter that McLuhan took lightly. The pragmatic academic cherished quiet, nature, a calm neighborhood. Commercialism, paved roads, and noise appalled him. He preferred the local but understood that it was now inseparable from the global.

> The new electronic interdependence recreates the world in the
> image of a global village.[5] —*The Gutenberg Galaxy*

McLuhan's phrase "global village" was inspired by a sentence from his friend, Wyndham Lewis, the writer, painter, and social critic. In a 1948 work titled *America and Cosmic Man*, Lewis wrote, "the earth has become one big village, with telephones laid on from one end to the other, and air transport, both speedy and safe."[6] During World War II, McLuhan took the global village idea—his theories on how the electronic media were changing society—back to the University of Toronto. There, he disseminated and developed them by organizing discussion clubs, just as Norbert Wiener had done with his cybernetics roundtables. His house was a permanent center for intellectual activity. People could drop by at any time to engage in debate and toss around ideas. McLuhan carefully structured his discussions, choosing a topic, presenting a new concept, which would spread virally across the campus, often causing other professors to throw up their hands as they watched all their students abuzz with yet another catchy idea from McLuhan. The campus was both stage and workshop for McLuhan. His clutch of fascinated graduate students were dubbed "McLuhanatics."

> If the work of a city is the remaking or translating of man into
> a more suitable form than his nomadic ancestors achieved, then

might not our current translation of our entire lives into the
spiritual form of information seem to make of the entire globe,
and of the human family, a single consciousness?[7]

—*Understanding Media*

Before McLuhan, Pierre Teilhard de Chardin had tackled the spiritual
consequences of a global information network. Born in 1881, the Je-
suit priest and paleontologist challenged both the religious and scientific establishments with his theistic embrace of evolution. He believed
that evolution was directional, toward greater complexity and consciousness. The earth, he maintained, was developing in successive
stages of complexity: the geological earth, the biological earth, the noölogical (conscious) earth. All of nature was evolving toward an ultimate
state, the Omega Point, which was, in essence, God. While de Chardin
was firmly religious, and Wiener an avowed atheist, they shared the
same spiritual and moral appreciation for conscious life—the connection between individual evolution and the evolution of humanity. De
Chardin's writings were repressed by the Church until sometime after
his death in the mid-1950s.

McLuhan carried de Chardin's torch, envisioning the evolution
of human consciousness through technology. Like Wiener, he
equated consciousness with information. Human beings become
units of information, each contributing to this new world sentience.

In this electric age we see ourselves being translated more and
more into the form of information, moving toward the technological extension of consciousness.[8]

—*Understanding Media*

De Chardin called this informational consciousness "noölogical." He recognized that the primary mechanism of noölogical evolution was scientific research, supported by the modern communication network that
now spanned the globe:

And here I am thinking of those astonishing electronic machines (the starting-point and hope of the young science of

cybernetics), by which our mental capacity to calculate and combine is reinforced and multiplied by the process and to a degree that herald as astonishing advances in this direction as those that optical science has already produced for our power of vision.[9]

The senses of the individual are extended to every point on the globe, such that she is at once everywhere, the global electronic network her new nervous system. Just as a human central nervous system is composed of electric pulses, so the electronic media act as the central nervous system of the global village. McLuhan reveals that the electronic media extend and replace our own nervous systems, our senses.

> This externalization of our senses creates what de Chardin calls the "noösphere" or a technological brain for the world. Instead of tending toward a vast Alexandrian library the world has become a computer, an electronic brain, exactly as in an infantile piece of science fiction. And as our senses have gone outside us, Big Brother goes inside. So, unless aware of this dynamic, we shall at once move into a phase of panic terrors, exactly befitting a small world of tribal drums, total interdependence, and superimposed coexistence.... Terror is the normal state of any oral society, for in it everything affects everything all the time.[10]
>
> —*The Gutenberg Galaxy*

By the mid-1960s it was clear to people as varied as those inspired by de Chardin and the cyberneticists led by Wiener that human civilization was being transformed by electronic technology, creating new and instantaneous forms of communication. McLuhan extended this understanding by realizing that communication would reestablish the supremacy of oral society. If the globe was now in the reach of the individual, as small as a single village, the benefits and drawbacks of oral tribalism should reemerge globally.

The tribal drums began beating as the baby boomers came of age.

FREE SOCIETY

Battles erupted as physical boundaries of the global village dissolved. In late 1961, John F. Kennedy began providing American military support to South Vietnamese forces. The Congress of Racial Equality sent one thousand student volunteers, the first Freedom Riders, on bus trips across the South to test the illegal segregation of interstate facilities. In 1962, Kennedy commanded federal marshals to escort the first black student to enroll at the University of Mississippi; in the ensuing riot, two students were killed. That same year, Kennedy and his Soviet counterpart, Nikita Krushchev, took the planet to the brink of nuclear war in the Cuban missile crisis.

McLuhan predicted in *The Gutenberg Galaxy* that the electronic media would bring forth mass terror, passion and involvement as people became more interconnected. The events of the 1960s proved him right: In August 1965 alone, while McLuhan attended a festival in his honor in San Francisco, the predominantly poor, black Los Angeles neighborhood of Watts erupted into six days of rioting and police violence, leaving thirty-four people dead, about a thousand injured, and four thousand arrested; the Beatles played to fifty-six thousand fans in New York City; and thousands of volunteers for the Student Nonviolent Coordinating Committee, including Hoffman, went down to Mississippi to combat racial injustice.

By the end of 1967, just as McLuhan was reaching the height of his fame from the sexily produced handbook *The Medium Is the Massage: An Inventory of Effects,* the Yippies were born. The Yippies (the name ostensibly derived from the Youth International Party) were the perfect counterpart to McLuhan. Abbie Hoffman and the other Yippies lived and breathed McLuhan's pronouncements about how the new communication technologies were transforming the globe. Hoffman's 1968 manifesto, *Revolution for the Hell of It,* chronicled the mad run of the Yippies.

Hoffman was born on November 30, 1936, to John Hoffman, a Jewish Russian immigrant, and his young wife, Florence. He immediately started showing off, even in the cradle. As a teenager he mastered the minutiae of sex, cards, zoot suits, and the pool halls of his working-class hometown of Worcester, Massachusetts. He was brilliant, which made him dangerous. Without studying, he got top grades, went to Brandeis University, and read the prophets of the countercultural revolution— Maslow, Marcuse, and McLuhan, the first two of whom were Brandeis professors.* In the 1960s, Hoffman dropped out of graduate school at the University of California at Berkeley, grew his hair yet longer, and became a full-time activist.

As *Revolution for the Hell of It* describes, the formation of the Yippies followed a series of Abbie escapades. He frolicked with and frustrated the Diggers, who had opened the first Free Store in San Francisco in their artistic pursuit of a free society; he soon dominated New York City activism with stunts like the stock exchange event, which mixed childish irreverence with brilliant media manipulation; with other activists, he turned a march on the Pentagon into a communal exorcism and levitation of the building. He then founded the Yippies with a few other like-minded counterculture radicals, most notably his wife, Anita Hoffman, and another Digger acolyte, Jerry Rubin, in order to organize a peaceful protest and music fair at the 1968 Democratic National Convention.

Hoffman, sporting his afro, American flag shirts, and sunglasses, presented a sharp contrast to McLuhan, who took care not to display any distinguishing physical mannerisms. Hoffman would shout and swear to get attention. McLuhan kept his face as expressionless as possible during his lectures and even changed his tone of voice when he was being recorded. Hoffman tapped into people's emotions and desires for freedom, self-expression, and transformation. McLuhan avoided emotional

---

*To fill its ranks, Brandeis welcomed the leftist academics who had been blackballed at other schools as a result of McCarthyism. One of their greatest stars was Herbert Marcuse, who had just published *Eros and Civilization,* a radical synthesis of Marxist and Freudian theory that explored the possibilities of a nonrepressive society. Whereas Freud explained that civilization was necessarily driven toward repression and misery, Marcuse described a civilization with open sexuality and play, based on human instinctive drive toward happiness, as expressed in art and other cultural works. Abraham Maslow pioneered the movement in psychology away from the darkness of Freudianism and toward an Eastern-influenced, inner-potential self-actualization. He asserted that humankind's desires followed a hierarchy of needs, from basic ones such as food, sex, and sleep to complex ones such as art and beauty. If you want a society with art and beauty, you need to feed the people.

outbursts, and was pained when his friends expressed their feelings to him. While McLuhan was reserved and conservative, Hoffman uninhibitedly celebrated sex and drugs. McLuhan's world was that of thought, not feeling. Hoffman's was of the extremes of feeling as well as thought.

But in *Revolution for the Hell of It*, Hoffman raised McLuhan on a pedestal. McLuhan inspired Hoffman even more than the political revolutionaries Ché Guevara and Chairman Mao.

. . . .

Q. Do you read revolutionary writings?

A. Yes, Guevara, Debray, Mao, Giap, McLuhan. I find McLuhan and Giap the most interesting.*[11]

—*Revolution for the Hell of It*

. . . .

McLuhan and Hoffman shared an intrinsic understanding that the medium of communication determines how a message is understood. Hoffman hated the *New York Times* but loved the *Daily News,* because the Yippie movement was designed for television, and tabloids like the *Daily News* were the closest thing to TV in print. The *New York Times* treated the Yippies just like another straightforwardly radical political party, referring to them only as YIP, the Youth International Party, which made them sound like a humorless communist organization. The *Daily News* attacked the Yippies with the same tools the Yippies used to sell their message: short bursts of heightened language; big, iconic pictures; bold text. Although the political content of the Yippie message was not very different from that of the rest of the radical left, the medium of that message was humor, theater, and the sound bite. For the Yippies, the medium was very much the message.

MEDIA OF REVOLUTION

In January 1968, the Vietcong guerrillas launched the massive Tet Offensive, leaving thirty-seven thousand of their forces dead and killing

---

*Ché Guevara, Régis Debray, Mao Tse-Tung, and Vo Nguyen Giap were all Marxist revolutionaries who wrote about workers' rights and guerrilla warfare.

twenty-five hundred Americans. Militarily the Vietcong suffered greatly, but politically the American effort was mortally wounded. The Yippies invited people to have a festival in Grand Central Station, shutting down the heart of New York City's transportation system. The Grand Central Yip-In, intended to be peaceful, led to a near riot as police beat and arrested the thousands of youth who clambered all over the terminal. A few months later, Martin Luther King Jr. was assassinated and riots broke out across the country. Sirhan Sirhan assassinated Robert Kennedy, the last figure of political weight to offer a message of compromise and healing in a nation fracturing into conflict.

The Democratic National Convention, which anointed the candidacy of Hubert Humphrey, took place in Chicago in the last week of August 1968. Hoffman and the Yippies arrived on the first day. Antiwar demonstrators marched on the streets. Hippies made love and smoked dope in the parks. At first, it was peaceful, Soon, however, at the orders of Mayor Daley the Chicago police moved in with billy clubs and tear gas. Streets were blocked off with tanks and barbed wire. The cops showed no mercy in beating the demonstrators. Local, working-class kids, enraged by what they saw on the television, joined the protesters and fought back. The carefully mediated message of the Democratic politicians was overwhelmed by tribal theater played out with brutality and rage.

"We were an advertisement for revolution," Hoffman proclaimed in *Revolution for the Hell of It*. He understood that the real draw of television isn't the programming, which takes up ninety percent of the signal. It is the advertisements in the other ten percent. Commercials are fast-cut, loud, arresting images. The slow-moving soap opera provides the soothing context for the interesting soap ads. A figure of focus needs a grounding context. Only once a rhetorical environment is established can a message be expressed and the environment ignored. The hot message of the advertisement is effective in contrast to and in the context of the cool program.

Hoffman learned in his psychology classes what McLuhan taught: The figure–ground relationship allows the transmission of information. A bird's song becomes meaningful when it is heard in the context of the forest. When you hear the song, you identify it as coming from a bird—because of the pine needles below your feet, the trees stretching to the sky, the soft rustle of the wind, the faint, damp scent of earth. You don't consciously notice all the details of the environment, but they are necessary. The technique of propaganda transforms the subconscious by first inundating the environment with a steady, unchanging message, then blasting calls to action upon that environment. The staid, processed Democratic National Convention provided the rhetorical ground for what Hoffman called "the Cops vs. Yippies football game taking place on the streets of Chicago."

In 1968, Hoffman and Jerry Rubin, another Yippie ringleader and theatrical activist, were subpoenaed to appear in a House Un-American Activities Committee show trial. Rubin appeared in a uniform with elements from left-wing revolutionaries, including the Vietcong and Cuba. Abbie Hoffman tried to go in with an American flag shirt, but the Capitol police stopped him, and his shirt was ripped off in the ensuing fracas. In the trial, Hoffman stated, "I regret that I have but one shirt to give for my country." The old generation created political theater with long speeches and demagoguery. The new generation created political television with a single image or sound bite.

The Nixon administration indicted Hoffman, Rubin, and six others for the Chicago demonstrations. The trial of the Chicago Eight, the decadent height of Yippiedom, began in October 1969 and lasted four months. Every day brought a new level of disruption and chaos. The one black defendant, Bobby Seale, was bound and gagged in the courtroom, then taken away to stand trial separately. Abbie and Jerry's antics reduced the judge to incoherent sputtering. Wild rhetoric was exchanged by both sides—it was impossible to pretend that the trial was anything other than political railroading, an indictment not of what the defendants did but of what they stood for. Nightly news programs covered the trial as a comic counterpoint to the state of American politics.

WORK AND PLAY

Observing that most of the world participated in the 1960s only through their television sets, McLuhan stated that media transforms people into receptacles for information. Electronic media are the extension of our brain and nerves, and thus modify not only the way we use our hands or even our eyes and ears, but the very way we think.

> Electromagnetic technology requires utter human docility and quiescence of meditation such as befits an organism that now wears its brain outside its skull and its nerves outside its hide.[1]
> —*Understanding Media*

For this reason, electronic technologies have also transformed the way we work. In the industrial age, the entire business of humankind was the construction and distribution of materials—the transformation of raw materials into goods. In the information age, the factories and business processes that deal with physical materials are automated. Instead of handling goods we now handle *processes*. With electronic technology these processes are expressed as information. As everything becomes information, all of our business boils down to acquiring and using knowledge.

> Whereas in the mechanical age of fragmentation leisure had been the absence of work, or mere idleness, the reverse is true in the electric age. As the age of information demands the simultaneous use of all our faculties, we discover that we are most at leisure when we are most intensely involved, very much as with the artists in all ages.[13]
> —*Understanding Media*

The Industrial Revolution ushered in the age of specialization. Occupations became specialized, the sciences fragmented into specialties, and a person's day was broken into discrete fragments: time to work, time to rest, time to be creative. The factory worker did only one task without deviation—he could lose his arm trying to be creative. Specialization of the past era was due to this inflexibility of machinery. We simply, necessarily, mirrored our machines.

McLuhan stated that the electric age returned flexibility and adaptability to our environment and thus to our lives. In fact, to be successful in the information age, we must be adaptive and flexible. We must use all of our abilities at the same time. Leisure in the mechanical age could only mean rest and escape from work, but leisure intrinsically is getting to do what you want. We are at leisure when we participate in pursuits we enjoy, which have been relegated to hobbies and sports or the arts. Limits on what we may do restrict our comfort. The information age demands that we use all of our abilities, that we do everything we can—which means that there are no limits on what we may do. Without limits, we can live a life of creative expression. We can be at leisure. We can simultaneously work and play.

> One task we have is to separate the concept of productivity from work. Work is money. Work is the postponement of pleasure. Work is always done for someone else: the boss, the kids, the guy next door. Work is competition. Work was linked to productivity to serve the Industrial Revolution. We must separate the two. We must abolish work and all the drudgery it represents.[14]   —*Revolution for the Hell of It*

Hoffman believed in the promise of McLuhan's vision. He understood also that the divide between work and leisure has conventionally been the divide between competition and cooperation. Work is a power struggle. Leisure is not. The only kind of competition Abbie Hoffman believed in was artistic—the competition to be the most interesting, the most exciting, the most creative.

Industrial society is based on the concept of competition for resources. The advances of the Industrial Revolution, powered by mechanization and capitalism, came through the efficient application of accumulated power. Efficiencies of scale powered development, but created major inequities of resources. This becomes less of a factor as automation takes over manufacturing and business focuses on the process of acquiring and using knowledge.

> Cooperation will be the motivating factor in a free society. I think cooperation is more akin to the human spirit. Competition is grafted on by institutions, by a capitalist economy, by religion, by schools. Every institution I can think of in this country promotes competition.[15]
>
>   —*Revolution for the Hell of It*

Information is a potentially infinite resource. If someone shares or uses information, it is not consumed. Rather, its power and influence can grow. The instantaneous global network of electronic media offers the promise of the best of both worlds—where progress can be optimally efficient without the need for a maldistribution of power. The more that information is shared, the freer society is, the greater the potential is for cooperation. Perfect cooperation reaps the same results as perfect competition, and without losers.

This vision hasn't been realized yet, even though the information age has dawned. Is it a false dream? It is impossible to know while the mechanical age institutions still use political, social, and economic force to dominate.

STEAL THIS BOOK

On one issue in particular McLuhan and Hoffman agreed: the need to expose the corrosive influence of the powers that control the communication networks of the new global nervous system.

McLuhan, always seeking patterns out of chaos, created conspiracy theories about them. Like Wiener, he had a vicious streak of paranoia. He reveled in finding pieces of information, numerical coincidences, and arcane references to support his fears of takeovers and subversive Masonic plots. He kept these worries to himself and his closest friends, and spoke publicly only of his distrust of modern technology and bureaucracy.

Hoffman attacked the power structures, particularly the establishment media, directly.

. . . .

If you don't like the news, why not go out and make your own?
—*Steal This Book*

. . . .

Steal This Book (1971), his second manifesto, was a handbook for the new tribalism of the global village. It's based on a straightforward philosophy of an anarchistic society. Developed from an earlier pamphlet, *Fuck the System*, which Hoffman produced with funds from the city of New York and distributed for free, *Steal This Book* tells readers how to organize food cooperatives and shoplift from supermarkets; how to hitchhike and skyjack; how to start a radio station and grow marijuana. It's a strange collection of useful information about basic health care and techniques for jumping turnstiles. The underlying philosophy is that the governmental and corporate institutions that regulate society are unjust and arbitrary. Society should be free; people should have total freedom to express themselves, and products and goods should be free for the taking.

Hoffman went to numerous publishers with the manuscript for *Steal This Book*. They all rejected it, more because of the title than because of its radical content or instructions for pipe bombs and Molotov cocktails. No publisher wanted to distribute a book that told people to take it from the shelves. Finally, in 1971, after an unsuccessful attempt to self-publish, he found a small outfit willing to take it on. It quickly became a best-seller.

> To talk of true freedom of the press, we must talk of the availability of the channels of communication that are designed to reach the entire population, or at least that segment of the population that might participate in such a dialogue. Freedom of the press belongs to those that own the distribution system. Perhaps that has always been the case, but in a mass society where nearly everyone is instantaneously plugged into a variety of national communications systems, wide-spread dissemination of the information is the crux of the matter. To make the claim that the right to print your own book means freedom of the press is to completely misunderstand the nature of a mass society. It is like making the claim that anyone with a pushcart can challenge Safeway supermarkets, or that any child can grow up to be president.[17]   —*Steal This Book*

Hoffman had learned that we are only halfway into the information age as long as the industrial era establishments continue to control the media. Only the fixed institutions of publishing had the means to print, market, and distribute a message to enough people for the message to have immediate impact. The lesson was straight from McLuhan: The dominant senses of the mass public are not their eyes and ears, but the corporate-controlled communications networks: the television networks, the newspaper conglomerates, the book publishing industry, the banking networks.

This was the global information network before the Internet. A person without access to the media is a person without access to the foundations of society. Legal rights without the technological means are not true rights at all.

> Food conspiracies, bust trusts, people's clinics and demonstrations are all part of the new Nation, but if asked to name the most important institution in our lives, one would have to say the underground newspaper.[18]   —*Steal This Book*

In the 1960s the printing press was the technology of dissent, because, unlike TV, it was decentralized and somewhat easily available. All the groups of the counterculture movement organized and communicated via independent, underground newspapers. Stories, opinions, and ideas were sent electronically across the nation to independent publishers, who would then distribute newspapers in their towns and cities. Hoffman understood that while television influenced the mass public with arresting images, it was the power of print that communicated specific information and created activist coalitions.

Through the underground press, an inspired idea for organizing a rally or for giving away food could reach across the country—with the details to execute that idea. The newspaper combined the power of print and the immediate reach of the electronic network. Unlike most newspapers, the underground press shared their ideas and collaborated, so that their network was distributed.

The underground newspaper presaged the Internet and the World Wide Web. People would buy personal computers in the decades to come, and the battle would be the same—the people versus the powers that be. But the new battlefield would be online where, in theory, the ground could be more equal.

AFTERWARD

Despite their differences, McLuhan and Hoffman both understood the implications of electronic media and the new global village. They realized that corporations were the locus of power as much as governments. In the information age, all institutions broker in just one commodity: information. In the 1960s and 1970s, everything—military power, physical goods, entertainment—was becoming an aspect of the electronic media, of information.

McLuhan was the prophet, and Hoffman the revolutionary. McLuhan saw the change coming and attempted to communicate his knowledge to a world caught in paroxysm. Hoffman was riding the wave; he worked to build a new world as he fought to tear down the old. He understood that the dominant institutions were from a different era, but he welcomed the transformations. He fought with sound-bite politics for a free society that eliminated even the institutions of property.

They differed on the dangers of the information age, but they agreed on its promises, realizing, as Wiener and Doug Engelbart had earlier, that society could be built on the infinite, self-sustaining resource of information, which integrated work and leisure, utility and art, joy and efficiency. Hoffman lived the dream of total creativity. This philosophy is also reflected later in the works and writings of pioneers such as Alan Kay, Ted Nelson, and Jaron Lanier.

In the end, neither Hoffman nor McLuhan could escape the consequences of the communications technologies they exposed. Both were eaten up by the media machine, which distilled their messages until they were seen as low-definition cartoons. The feedback loop that mediated their message circled back to strangle them. Their words and actions were made into sound bites. Although they both loved fame, the greatest commodity in the information age, their lives were simply human. They discovered that they could not transcend the limits of the physical and emotional self—that which made them more than a flickering image on the television screen. A caveat for celebrities: Your message, when amplified throughout the global village, can loop back to subsume you.

During the 1970s, McLuhan continued to work with his McLuhanatics, producing more works as a collaborator, an idea generator, on further theories of media. He was fascinated by the right–left brain discoveries, and continued his interest in creating a curriculum for media studies for the young. In 1976, despite McLuhan's waning popularity in the media and academic worlds, Woody Allen gave him a cameo in *Annie Hall*, playing himself. His health soon decayed, and at the end of 1979 he suffered a massive stroke, which stripped his ability to speak, other than babbling and laughter. This caused vast grief to McLuhan, who had been a master of the spoken word, a man whose identity was constructed as an orator and debater nonpareil. He died on the last day of the following year.

Hoffman's life took an unexpected turn with the collapse of the counterculture in the early 1970s. He recklessly sold cocaine to undercover cops and, in 1974, avoided jail by going underground with his new girlfriend, Johanna Lawrenson, to begin a new life under the name Barry Freed. Freed was a different man from Hoffman, a diligent political organizer and environmentalist who didn't need or want to be the center of attention.

At this time, Hoffman underwent ever more severe mood swings, from manic violence to extreme depression. He had trouble maintaining his identity after so many years of being able to shock and amaze people whenever he felt the urge. With the election of Ronald Reagan to the White House sweeping the countercultural movement into an all but forgotten past, he resurfaced as Abbie Hoffman and served a reduced jail sentence. Although Hoffman then tried to inspire a new generation to fight battles against the CIA, random drug testing, and pollution, his established image as a violent radical was more powerful than any new identity. He could not escape the expectations built by the media. Wracked by manic depression, Hoffman committed suicide in April 1989 by consuming 150 doses of phenobarbitol, washed down by a half-pint of Glenlivet.

Hoffman's 1960s ideal of a free society, unfettered by the past, would later be applied to the Internet. It was John Perry Barlow, lyricist for the Grateful Dead, who first called this network "Cyberspace," from William Gibson's *Neuromancer*. In 1996 he posted a tract portraying it as a free, unpropertied world without privilege or prejudice. It is "where anyone, anywhere may express his or her beliefs, no matter how singular, without fear of being coerced into silence or conformity." In cyberspace, Hoffman's visions could be realized. Titled "A Declaration of the Independence of Cyberspace," Barlow's online manifesto begins:

> Governments of the Industrial World, you weary giants of
> flesh and steel, I come from Cyberspace, the new home of

Mind. On behalf of the future, I ask you of the past to leave us alone. You are not welcome among us. You have no sovereignty where we gather. . . . I declare the global social space we are building to be naturally independent of the tyrannies you seek to impose on us. You have no moral right to rule us nor do you possess any methods of enforcement we have true reason to fear.

EVERYTHING IS DEEPLY INTERTWINGLED

TED NELSON AND TIM BERNERS-LEE

> The web was built by billions of people simply be-
> cause they wanted it, without need, greed, fear,
> hierarchy, authority figures, ethnic identification, ad-
> vertising, or any form of manipulation. Nothing like
> this ever happened before in history. We can be blasé
> about it now, but it is what we will be remembered
> for. We have been made aware of a new dimension in
> human potential.   —Jaron Lanier

IN 1964, not long after Theodor Holm Nelson received an
M.A. in sociology at Harvard University, a manifesto was issued
by the Students for a Democratic Society (SDS). The SDS was the
largest, best-known, and most political New Left organization—
light-years apart from the prankish radicalism of Abbie Hoffman's Youth International Party. With the goal of a kinder and
gentler democracy, the SDS railed against racial injustices, the
threat of war, and violations of individual rights. Their work
"The Triple Revolution," written by W. H. Ferry et al., identified
"cybernation," "weaponry," and "human rights" as the three
fundamental, separate, and mutually reinforcing revolutionary
movements worth fighting for. (They were *against* nuclear
weapons, *for* human rights, and *neutral* about cybernation.)

On the "cybernation revolution," Ferry et al. asserted that
a new era of production has begun in which the computer and

the "self-regulating" machine shall create a system of unlimited and unprecedented productive capacity. The demand for human labor will decrease dramatically and, perhaps, disastrously. Because everything is *interrelated,* all already underprivileged citizens—black people, women, the poor, and the uneducated—would suffer even more. The owners of the means of production would get richer, and the dispossessed, now jobless, would have even less. The SDS implored the government to take necessary steps toward better education for better jobs and the benevolent regulation of "cybernation," so that everyone could benefit from its bounty. Under the right circumstances, they write, the revolution will make Americans (and eventually citizens of all countries) richer in democratic as well as material values. They end their essay with:

> Democracy, as we use the term, means a community of men and women who are able to understand, express, and determine their lives as dignified human beings. Democracy can only be rooted in a political and economic order in which wealth is distributed by and for the people, and used for the widest social benefit. With the emergence of the era of abundance we have the economic base for true . . . participation, in which men no longer need to feel themselves prisoners of social forces and decisions beyond their control or comprehension.[1]

A decade later, Ted Nelson, the sociology major, published a manifesto of his own. It was called *Computer Lib,* and its premise was that a person should be able to take a paragraph like the one above and make the word "wealth" synonymous with "knowledge" and "democracy" interchangeable with "the personal computer." In fact, Nelson advocated the concept of a home computer throughout the 1960s to mid-1970s—long before it actually existed. He saw computing machines as tools that could facilitate access to information, provide the ability to self-publish, and, as a result, empower anyone who could buy one.

Nelson was not a radical like his contemporary Abbie Hoffman or the leaders of the SDS. He was a liberal Democrat at the time, but a disgusted one. In *Computer Lib* (1974) and a second manifesto, *Literary Machines* (1981), he presented a few ideas about how to approach politics and power that involved running a network of nonhierarchical "hypertext" documents on personal computers. Hypertext, a term he coined, means nonlinear, nonhierarchical writing.

Nelson believes that a hypertext information system is the means to cultivate a vibrant culture of interdisciplinary generalists. Like both Bush and Engelbart, he imagined associative links as a powerful tool to model information. Like Kay, he wants the general population to understand that computers should be tools of personal empowerment. Like McLuhan, he distrusts the powers that control communication. And like Hoffman, he has thrown the fanatical force of his personality behind his convictions.

About twenty years later came another hypertext visionary, Tim Berners-Lee, an unassuming former physics major working as an information specialist at the European Particle Physics Laboratory (CERN). In "Information Management: A Proposal" (1989) he proposed an electronic hypertext network. He wrote two other manifestos, *Weaving the Web* (1999) and "The Semantic Web" (2001), which describe the social challenges of his creation, the World Wide Web. The Web is a working hypertext system that resembles Nelson's vision, but also differs from it dramatically.

PERSONAL COMPUTER LIB

Before the first (mass–produced) personal computer existed, Nelson told people it would be a tool for personal empowerment. In 1973, Xerox PARC had made the Alto, the first computer specifically designed to be used by only one person, but it wasn't available to the general public. Computers didn't have a very friendly reputation. Only in 1977, three years after *Computer Lib* was published, did the Apple II debut as the first popular, relatively inexpensive, and truly personal computer.

Nelson did his part to help people like Alan Kay and Seymour Papert introduce new technology to a reluctant or intimidated public. In *Computer Lib* he shocked, wheedled, cajoled, and blasted readers into believing that computers were going to be their new best friend. They are, he said, versatile gizmos that can be turned to any purpose, in any style.

- Don't believe that computers are rigid and deterministic like calculators—that computers won't *allow* certain things. Computers can do anything.

- Computers are not dehumanizing, just as the car is not dehumanizing. Cars, cameras, bicycles, and other technologies have become part of style, image, and individualism; culture. The computer can too.[2]

In his breathless fashion, he told his readers that the computer could help them simplify their life. It could generate or introduce whole new (simulated) worlds at their request. It could organize data and make databases. It could make art. New ways of accessing and viewing information are key to personal empowerment in a technological revolution that could swing toward either greater freedom and decentralization or command and control. The computer could mean personal freedom, a new occupation wherein the machine would do the dirty work and the person could exercise his or her creativity. It could transform work into fun.

> It is imperative for many reasons that the appalling gap between public and the computer must be closed. As the saying goes, war is too important to be left to the generals. Guardianship of the computer can no longer be kept to a priesthood. I see this as one example of the creeping evil of Professionalism, the control of aspects of society by cliques of insiders. There may be some chance, though, that professionalism can be turned around. . . . This book may suggest to some computer professionals that their position should not be so sacrosanct as they have thought, either.[3]   —*Computer Lib*

Nelson intended *Computer Lib* to defy the shadowy cabal of mathematicians, programmers, and other "professionals" who protected their privileged positions by representing themselves as the sole guardians of computers. *Computer Lib* was oversized (a coffee table book) and originally self-published. It had a flip side ("like the Italian/Polish joke book") with a separate title, *Dream Machines,* about understanding the new art of computer graphics. The front cover of the *Computer Lib* side featured a fist resembling the black power icon, set against a representation of a personal computer under which ran the tagline: "You can and must understand computers NOW!" The tone, he admitted, was inspired by a combination of Pete Seeger's banjo book, the *Domebook* (a guide to making geodesic domes), and automobile reviews in *Mechanix Illustrated*. It was the literal conjoining of hippie, hacker, and techie, and it became a cult classic, selling approximately fifty thousand copies between the first and second editions in 1987.

The design of *Computer Lib* was cribbed from rabble-rouser Stewart Brand's popular cybernetics-inspired the *Whole Earth Catalog*. Nelson painstakingly handwrote the entire first edition. Text of all sizes was placed into little boxes splayed throughout the book. It featured one-liners such as COMPUTERS BELONG TO ALL MANKIND, *Computing has always been personal,* and *Everything is deeply intertwingled*. Some lines were recurring. Nelson encouraged readers to read *Computer Lib* nonlinearly.

The layout, in fact, was an example of what Nelson termed "hypertext," which simply means nonsequential writing. Like Engelbart, Nelson had become familiar with the writings of Benjamin Whorf, who stated that the way we manipulate symbols, including language, determines the way we see the world. Nelson later realized that the way we use language to think is nonsequential. He had also read McLuhan, who wrote about the history of media technologies and asserted that the fallacy at the heart of Western thought is that ideas must be presented in a linear fashion. Nelson believes that the linearity of language combined with the old printing and binding technologies have trapped us into linear reading and thus linear thinking. Linearity = established hierarchy, and Nelson wanted to topple that hierarchy in all its incarnations.

Ideas can be expressed instead as a web, each crisscrossing to others. When Nelson first described hypertext in 1963 at the Association of Computing Machinery conference, his audience was responsive but nothing immediately came of it. Because no personal computer yet existed, it was difficult to carry out hypertext on anything but paper.

POLITICS, POWER, AND 'PUTERS

In *Computer Lib*, Nelson made the quest for the personal computer political. The power dynamic, as he saw it in 1974, was the people of the world versus the avaricious corporations. The particular defendant at that time: IBM. International Business Machines, "Big Blue," was anathema to everything in *Computer Lib*. If inertia and ignorance no longer held people back from experimenting with computers, then the corporation could. The computer world was, as Nelson termed it, an ibmocracy due to an ibmopoly (65 percent of the market in 1974)—a great ibmposition on personal freedom.[4] At the time, Nelson believed that IBM was purposefully, diabolically, preventing the debut of the personal computer.

. . . .

> If you are interested in democracy and its future, you'd better understand computers. And if you are concerned about power and the way it is being used, and aren't we all right now, the same thing goes.[5]   —*Computer Lib*

. . . .

Because IBM dominated the marketplace in mainframes, they had good reason to discourage the advent of the "minicomputer" or PC. The IBM operating system was best designed for bureaucracies—other large corporations—that trained people how to use the intricate operating systems and who could afford the (IBM) computers on which they ran. The IBM's operating system of the 1970s was complex—needlessly so, according to Nelson. Nelson called IBM a "concentration camp for information, where people were regimented and oppressed."

Nelson was always conscious of power—who has it, and how it's used. He was pre-beatnik, raised in New York City where he cultivated a hatred of what he calls middle-class stuffiness. As a kid he read science-fiction writer Robert Heinlein and later socialized with exiled anarchists who survived the Spanish Civil War. He received his B.A. from Swarthmore, where he conceived what he claims was the first rock musical and earned his degree in philosophy.

Nelson's lifelong idols are the likes of H. L. Mencken, Walt Disney, and Buckminster Fuller: renegade dreamers first, businessmen second. His vision was considered too unorthodox for most of the corporate world, but after he'd left Harvard he had taken on a few jobs in business. As a senior staff researcher to publishers Harcourt, Brace in 1966–1967, he doled out advice about electronic publishing opportunities using computers. He had taken William Jovanovich, president of HB, to see and discuss computer-aided text manipulation systems, but failed to persuade Jovanovich to fund his own ideas. At that same time, he tried to get a job working on Engelbart's oN-Line System (NLS). Engelbart treated Nelson to an all-expenses-paid recruitment visit, but didn't hire him, because they didn't see eye to eye on the model of a hypertext system. Engelbart did, however, compliment Nelson's abilities in a letter: "You write well, and it is certainly good service to be developing and presenting these things to the world."[6] Nelson, buoyed by the success of *Computer Lib,* kept on writing as he continued his career as an entrepreneur, educator, and software developer. He published a second edition of the book in 1987.

The major change in the second edition of *Computer Lib* is the acknowledgment of the first popular personal computers—Apple II in 1977; the IBM PC in 1981; and the Apple Macintosh in 1984. Nelson called the PC Big Blue's "great redemption." For its operating system, Big Blue contracted a wee company called Microsoft, which built its subsequent crushing success from the decision. The PC, unlike the Macintosh, had an "open architecture," meaning that small software and hardware vendors could improve on IBM's work. Open architecture (along with Ethernet, Bob Metcalfe's networking technology at PARC) was the foundation for what would become the networking of PCs, which would in turn facilitate the growth of the Internet.

With the IBM PC came cheaper and cheaper computing power. The PC was, in fact, cheaper than the Macintosh, which had better graphics and a better operating system (due to the ingenuity of people at PARC and Apple). With IBM's aggressive marketing and endorsement of the PC, corporations and individuals everywhere started buying them.

XANADU

The proliferation of PCs in the late 1980s fulfilled the first part of Nelson's vision. They could make possible the second, which was the hypertext system. Nelson imagined a global hypertext publishing system accessible on the PC. Its name would be Xanadu in honor of Kublai Khan's mythic paradise. Nelson's motives were very similar to Engelbart's. If it is assumed that life on earth is hell (what with all our problems of pollution, racism, poverty, etc.) Xanadu would be deliverance from the fate of repeating our mistakes. The system would link humankind to a better world through their PCs. It would be designed with "children, researchers, and heads of state" in mind.

. . . .

Hypermedia point the way to FREEDOM![7]   —*Computer Lib*

. . . .

Xanadu would also be designed for Ted Nelson. Nelson developed an early reputation for being as scatterbrained as he is brilliant. Rumors abound about how he has obsessively crammed storage lockers with books, papers, and tapes. He records everything for future reference. He is fanatically conscious of how easily information slips away, how entropic forces frustrate communication and control. Indeed, the alleged story behind Coleridge's poem "Xanadu" is that the poet, in an opium trace, wrote one hundred lines of the verse in his head. As he was busily transcribing them, he was interrupted by "a Person from Porlock," and promptly forgot the rest. Everything is intertwingled; the question is, who or what can remember it all? And when each one of us dies, where does it all go? Perhaps no one was more acutely aware of the need for an electronic prosthesis than Nelson, whose version of hell is seeing connections nobody else can see, but not being able to communicate them.

In 1981 Nelson wrote the first edition of *Literary Machines*—a manifesto for Xanadu, "the most audacious and specific plan for knowledge, freedom, and a better world yet to come out of computerdom; the original (and perhaps ultimate) HYPERTEXT SYSTEM" (as touted on the back cover of a later edition).* Like *Computer Lib*, *Literary Machines* is self-published (he says all publishing is vanity publishing) and nonsequential. The general structure of it, mapped out in the beginning, resembles an infinity loop, consisting of three basic parts. Part 2, the center, should be read repeatedly after (or while) reading Parts 1 and 3. Like *Computer Lib*, a taste of hypertext in paper form.

. . . .

The structure of ideas is never sequential; and indeed, our thought processes are not very sequential either. True, only a few thoughts at a time pass across the central screen of the mind;

Literary Machines was originally written in 1981 as an expansion on Nelson's paper "Replacing the Printed Word," presented at the 1980 World Computer Conference. It is a self-published work available as a hypertext online.

> but as you consider a thing, your thoughts crisscross it con-
> stantly, reviewing first one connection, then another. Each new
> idea is compared with many parts of the whole picture, or with
> some mental visualization of the whole picture itself.[8]
>
> —*Literary Machines*

. . . .

Nelson credits Bush and Engelbart as independently coconceiving the idea behind hypertext. He and Engelbart both read Bush's "As We May Think," and similarly built on Bush's idea of trails. In *Literary Machines*, Nelson presents readers with a full-text version of Bush's manifesto and dedicates the 1987 edition of the book to Engelbart, as the inventor of the text link.* An aspect of Engelbart's NLS that particularly inspired Nelson was the paperless instantaneous simultaneity of it all. Everything on the NLS was connected to everything else, references, comments, footnotes, etc.

Along with the NLS, Nelson credits other networked systems of the 1980s as "laudable attempts" at electronic publishing. Such efforts included word processing programs that shared text between users, community bulletin boards, and the U.S. Post Office's attempt to set up an "electronic mail system"—the ECOM service (which went under in 1985). The ARPAnet had been up and running for more than a decade by this point, connecting university and military posts around the world. USENET, a system for transmitting messages on the Unix operating system, likewise connected a community online. Other systems for text sharing among online communities included CompuServe, the Source, and the Well, also by Stewart Brand, creator of the *Whole Earth Catalog*. But all of these systems, according to Nelson, lacked standardization. None were compatible with the others, and they all lacked the sophistication and elegance that Nelson imagined possible. What the world needs, he insisted, is one uncomplicated, unified design.

Xanadu promised to be a way to save and share information that better represents the structure of our thoughts and the architecture of our brains. The reader could follow a thread or stream of thought through the system, or "docuverse," by clicking on links. The system would be a unified, standardized structure that would be shared and simultaneously

---

* "May his simple, honest, saintly devotion of the uplift and the empowerment of the human mind live forever," Nelson wrote.

organized by users. It would be a network of storage stations, thousands—even millions—of different computers linked by a shared repository of knowledge consisting of text, photos, drawings, videos, and audio files. Nelson figured that digital networks like CompuServe and the ARPAnet/Internet could be Xanadu's gateways.

Nelson imagined the following features for Xanadu:[9]

Links. The core of hypertext—and the key to understanding complexity—is links. Anybody can tag text in a document and make a link in any document. Indeed, a document may actually consist of many fragments of text distributed throughout Xanadu. Links would be stored separately from documents and would be evolvable. Each document could have comment, correction, translation, and quote links. Links in Xanadu *would not break,* even after a document has been revised or updated. Nothing would be lost.

Transclusion. The user could click on the link in a document, and the reference in the original document would pop up in an adjacent window (an idea that Vannevar Bush wrote about for the memex). Transclusion means that the original document is always usable and the reader can view any quote in its original context. Transclusion is implicit copyright permission, because, Nelson says, "As with the Hindu Lord Shiva, every manifestation the user sees of the document is the 'original.'"

Alternative versions. Anyone could create and publish an alternative version of any document. It could be transcluded next to the original.

Reader autonomy. Users could view and manipulate information in any way they want. Incorporating a front-end interface that resides on their computer, users could create their own links and marginalia. The links and notes would reside as a private file accessible only to the reader or as public information, if the user so chooses. Users could also use Xanadu's indexing facilities to organize private documents (personal media) that reside only on their PCs.

Royalties. Nelson believes that the original author should get not only credit for his or her work every time it pops up in a window, but also have the option of requesting royalties on either a per-view or unlimited basis. The proportion would be a percentage (ten to twenty percent) of the hourly fee to go online (which he figured to be about two to five dollars per hour). People could also sell private documents on Xanadu. The Xanadu system would keep track of royalties through franchises.

Franchises. The Xanadu franchisee would invest in computers with massive memory; they'd pay for the operating costs of Xanadu (about $50,000 for software and hardware and operational package). Franchises would ensure standardization of the back-end feeder software—what Nelson figures is the key to a united, workable system. They would all run the Xanadu software, and would be responsible for maintaining the integrity of the system. The franchises would collect royalties due for viewing of information stored on their computers and dole out percentages to authors accordingly.

Meeting rooms. Each franchise would also evolve as a stand where people could congregate online. Nelson imagined the stand to evolve into a "homey futuristic atmosphere" with meeting rooms, dining terraces, atriums, and the like. Nelson's vision here presaged the chat rooms and Internet cafés of the 1990s.

Books, magazines, and journals. These would still exist in Xanadu. They would offer authority and predictable quality of information. The difference is that this information would also transclude or link to other documents, other worldviews.

Nelson believed that only a distributed corporate model would succeed; first, because it was a way to raise money for a hypertext system and, second, it is a guaranteed way for such system to be standardized. Putting the interface aside, Nelson wanted to first develop the complicated back-end system that would make fancy features like royalties possible. This would prove to be a tremendous task.

To build such a system required elaborate programming, and Nelson believed people need to be paid for their contributions of code or content. His contribution to Xanadu was the vision and the publicity. As director and designer of Xanadu, he needed disciples. And they came, inspired by the word in *Computer Lib* and *Literary Machines*. One such consultant was K. Eric Drexler, later known for his work in nanotechnology. Drexler developed some key code, as did programmer Mark Miller. Nelson had one lasting collaborator: Roger Gregory, mathematician and chief programmer, who joined him in 1974. In the early 1980s the entire team sported black baseball caps with silver wings and the slogan: "Xanadu: the wings of mind."

Although equipped with vision and talent, Xanadu lacked funds for most of its early existence. Finally, at a hacker convention in 1987, Gregory met John Walker, founder of thriving Autodesk, which made AutoCAD, and Gregory inspired Walker to sponsor Xanadu with a budget of nearly $1 million a year. Walker believed that the motley team would introduce a product that would change the world by 1995. By 2020, Nelson mused in *Dream Machines*, the Xanadu network would consist of more than 100 million users uploading more than 100 million documents an hour to the system.

In 1987, a handful of PARC programmers came to work for Xanadu, discarded Gregory's old code, and rewrote a prototype with C++ and Alan Kay's Smalltalk. Smalltalk was so easy, so irresistibly flexible, that it proved ideal for experimentation. The final Xanadu code was to be written in C++. Everyone at Xanadu believed it would happen.

FREEDOM OF INFORMATION

One dedication in *Literary Machines* went to Engelbart. The other went to Eric Blair, better known as George Orwell, the author of *1984* and *Animal Farm*. Orwell's lesson was Nelson's motto: The way we manage information is *very political*. The way we approach it determines how free we really are.

> Whichever view you take, the questions are what these systems are to be like, what things are to be available; and to whom, and under what circumstances; and who may put things in, and who is responsible for their contents, and who may censor them, and who may protest the contents, and what gets thrown away on whose decision; and what is to be their relation to the archiving

of our heritage, and how accessible they are to be, and how reliably and accessibly the personal, national and human heritages are to be preserved. For rolled into such designs and prospects is the whole future of humanity, and indeed, the future of the past and the future of the future—meaning the kinds of future that become forbidden, or possible.[10]

—*Literary Machines*

Nelson leans toward a humanistic libertarianism—a creed that embraces the volatile pairing of individual freedom and social responsibility. Unlike the leaders of the SDS, he doesn't look toward government to regulate what they called the "cybernation revolution." He expects people to lead themselves toward the Jeffersonian ideal of idea propagation. He calls Xanadu populist, for it would be available to everyone at little cost and is open to all points of view. He wrote, "We have designed this network with no positions of superiority, rather in the way that the Constitution ruled out positions of nobility. It's not that we're modest, but rather that we want to put an emperor's resources as the fingertips of all users, especially children and scientists and poets."[11]

Nelson believed that Xanadu, unlike any existing corporation or militant government, could provide the tools for greater democracy, namely, a lack of bias. It would liberate the user from the traditional information power structures because anyone would be able to add [publish] a document that links to or quotes from any other [existing] document. Politics, science, history, art—could all be presented with points and counterpoints using hyperlinks. In fact, Xanadu could undermine all Western conventions of singularity, linearity, and necessary cause and effect. It would dismantle the traditional relationships that separate author from reader and producer from consumer.

Few people had ever aspired to make information so egalitarian. Cross-connections ideologically translate into greater tolerance and multiple perspectives. Xanadu was conceived to be cybernetic: flexible and responsive to change. Nelson wrote, "If you are not falsely expecting a permanent system of categories or a permanent stable hierarchy, you realize your information system must deal with an ever-changing flux of new categories, hierarchies and other arrangements which all have to co-exist; it must be a tolerant system . . . ."[12] The franchisers couldn't censor; the power would be in the hands of the people who post to it and interact through it. Xanadu would thereby defy the centralization (and authority) of the established publishing industry and mass media that Hoffman and the SDS both detested and exploited. Nelson believed Xanadu could transform everything from copyright law to education, independent of both government and corporation.

Whereas Hoffman had tried to change the system through the system, Nelson simply tried to introduce a whole new system.

> Rather than having to be run by the government, or some other large untrustworthy corporation, it can be dispersed under local ownership to serve entire nations and eventually the world.[13]
>
> —*Literary Machines*

WORLD WIDE WEB

Tim Berners-Lee met Nelson in 1992, three years after he wrote about a global hypertext-driven information system in a modest manifesto titled "Information Management: A Proposal." Within a year Berners-Lee had built the first version of what he called the World Wide Web.* He didn't know of Nelson's Xanadu back then, but he had heard of Nelson's ideas of hypertext and the docuverse, the heart and soul of his own idea. In the early 1990s Berners-Lee read up on Nelson and Xanadu and bought a copy of *Literary Machines*. Berners-Lee believes in the democratic, egalitarian ideals of Xanadu: that the resources of an empire should be at the fingertips of the common citizen. He believes it is possible to arrange information like neurons in the brain: decentralized, *semantically* linked, weblike. To do so is to "bring the workings of society closer to the workings of our minds."[14]

Tim met Ted for lunch on one of the worst days of Xanadu's existence. The stock of Autodesk, Xanadu's owner, plummeted in early 1992 and the new management dropped Nelson and Xanadu. Xanadu was henceforth exiled. All of the lead programmers except Gregory would

---

*Berners-Lee considered calling his system The Information Mesh: Mine of Information (TIM:MOI), but decided that was too egocentric.

abandon the project. From that day on, Xanadu, the mighty hyperlinked kingdom, would have to make do on a shoestring.

Berners-Lee's World Wide Web, on the other hand, was gaining widespread exposure in 1992. Unlike Xanadu, it was an operational system from the start, and it had more modest roots. Back in the early 1980s Berners-Lee was an information technology consultant at CERN, the European particle physics laboratory in Geneva, and there he developed a program called Enquire, which allowed the user to store information and link related bits together. Everything in Enquire was defined by what it was linked to and how the links were related. Enquire allowed multiple users to access the same information.

Inspired by the Internet, Berners-Lee imagined a set of protocols running on a network in order to provide hypertext to various types of systems—VAX/VMS machines, Unix, Macs, and PCs alike. "Information Management," his 1989 proposal, introduced the vision of a large hypertext database at CERN. In it, he noted the fact that the working structure of CERN resembled a "web" of interconnections that evolve over time. *Information is lost* in a traditional, tree-like hierarchical information storage structure. The system he proposed would link information without central control or coordination. Users would be able to annotate links and add private links. They should be able to look at the "topology" of the system—a model of all the information within it. He believed that ideas, interactions, and work patterns would be made discernable, which would facilitate problem-solving.

> Imagine picking up the structure and shaking it, until you make some sense of the tangle. Perhaps, you see tightly knit groups in some places, and in some places weak areas of communication spanned by only a few people. Perhaps a linked information system will allow us to see the real structure of the organization in which we work.[15]
>
> —"Information Management"

In 1990 Berners-Lee embarked on a mission to develop his knowledge organization project outside the walls of CERN. Against the advice of his friends, he decided to name it the "World Wide Web," or WWW— an acronym that is a tongue-tying nine syllables. The World Wide Web and Xanadu had a few ideals in common: (1) universality and standardization; (2) the ability to publish, link to, and read any document in the system; (3) no central control.

Berners-Lee built on those ideals, which are also those that underlie the development of the Internet itself. Whereas Nelson designed Xanadu as a complex system to assist the private, creative act of hyperlinking, Berners-Lee designed the Web as a simple system to encourage the public benefit of sharing information. The Internet succeeded because of open standards that linked different networks together. Berners-Lee wanted the Web to work in the same way, to link different documents and services together.

He didn't believe in Nelson's copyright pricing scheme—a single business model for paying for information. Nor would there be franchises where people bought servers. It would be free space, in both meanings of the word. The Web also differed from the Xanadu vision in that it lacked the capability to annotate and add marginalia or maintain a private document system within the larger public one. Unlike the Xanadu plan, the Web couldn't track versions of documents (historical backtrack)—documents could just disappear if pulled off the Web. Nor could users compare documents side by side or through "transcluded" windows peeping into documents. The Web would be simple and straightforward, which is why it, unlike Xanadu, would succeed.

By the end of 1990, Berners-Lee had written the Web software to allow users to create and view hypertext pages. The World Wide Web would be a service riding on the Internet—like email or newsgroups—that followed a set of protocols. He wrote the code to exchange hypertext documents— the Hypertext Transfer Protocol (http). And he wrote the program for the first Web server to hold Web pages and allow access to them at info.cern.ch. Universal resource identifiers, later to be renamed uniform resource locators, or URLs, indicated the virtual address of a document. The existing standard in the information technology community for hypertext documents, Standard Generalized Markup Language (SGML) was perfect for academics but nearly unusable. So Berners-Lee devised an extremely simple language, Hypertext Markup Language (HTML), which took only what was needed from SGML to get the World Wide Web started.

The World Wide Web system as Berners-Lee and his collaborator Robert Cailliau designed it, simple and flexible, *worked,* and it quickly flourished within CERN. There, Berners-Lee's program kept track of the relationships between people, projects, and machines. Notes, proposals, reports, meeting minutes, and half-baked ideas could all go up on the system, linked nonhierarchically.

To give the World Wide Web a head start in the "real" world, Berners-Lee ensured that it could incorporate existing Internet newsgroups and files—it encouraged hypertext files, but accepted all comers. A URL's header could point to any kind of document, for example, http, nntp, or mailto, for a hypertext, news, or email document, respectively. The World Wide Web spread like wildfire through treelike Internet newsgroups; particularly alt.hypertext. The cause was abetted by a telnet service that Berners-Lee set up on the CERN server so that people could get the software. The Web gave form and finesse to the fledgling Internet. The number of hits at CERN doubled every three months.

By 1993, the server at info.cern.ch was joined by about fifty others worldwide—five hundred by the end of the year. Other browsers for the Web were also being built, most notably by Marc Andreessen and his group at the National Center for Supercomputing Applications at the University of Illinois at Urbana-Champaign. Their free browser, called Mosaic (later Netscape), provided point-and-click access (and other upcoming fancy features like different types, colors and multimedia) to the Web and quickly became the browser of choice. Mosaic drove the popularity of the Web.

In 1994, with the commercialization of the Internet, Internet service providers emerged everywhere in the States. The number of WWW servers hit ten thousand as the Web continued its explosive growth. With the Web's early success came inevitable conflicts and complexities: To what extent does the development of nonstandardized features (like browsers) hurt or help the Web? Would CERN release the intellectual property rights to the Web's source code, allowing it to evolve just as the browser did?

OPENNESS

Because Berners-Lee never tried to keep the rights to his Web browser software, the question he's had to wearily endure is: Don't you regret that you never got rich off your invention? Exasperated, he'll admit how nice it would have been for his family, but that isn't the point. His values are different. The son of two mathematicians who worked on Alan Turing's Mark I, arguably the world's first commercial stored-program computer, Berners-Lee inherited the spirit of an academic pioneer, not an entrepreneur. He also believed the Web would take off only if it were free.

To Berners-Lee's relief, CERN *did* release all claims on the Web, which placed its code securely in the public domain. He believes that if CERN didn't make this magnanimous gesture, the Web could have suffered the same fate as the University of Minnesota's Gopher software. Gopher was an Internet-based information system that used treelike hierarchical menus. When the creators of Gopher decided to charge a licensing fee for corporations to use the software, industry dropped it. Berners-Lee called the licensing "an act of treason in the academic community and the Internet community."[16] Gopher died quietly.

Berners-Lee applied that lesson about openness and sharing to the World Wide Web. If CERN hadn't dropped the intellectual property rights, the Web might well not exist. Licensing fees—proprietary products—would have strangled it. The Web's development was open and collaborative. Xanadu, in contrast, was proprietary; at its core, a business. Nelson's vision was to present humankind with a fully functional, proprietary, sophisticated world in which the messiness of copyright would be solved, as well as most of the other trials and tribulations of building that world. The Web instead invited—*required*—its inhabitants to help build it. It was a World Wide effort.

THE W3C

The greatest challenge for Berners-Lee in 1994 was to ensure that the World Wide Web continued to straddle the fine line between chaos and order. On one hand, the Web should be free for improvisation. On the other hand, too much novelty could crush it. Berners-Lee wanted to ensure that it would remain stable so it could evolve. To do this he founded the World Wide Web Consortium (W3C).

The W3C is not a central authority. Nor is it a business. The Web consortium put Berners-Lee in the best position of all: to be able to think about what would be best for the *world,* not a corporation. As director of W3C, Berners-Lee determined that it would be vendor neutral and collaborative. The Advanced Research Projects Agency (ARPA) provided seed money for it because of its relevance to both industry and research. The European Commission supported it as well. It became established at http://www.w3.org. Businesses and research centers alike joined.

> Whether inspired by free-market desires or humanistic ideals, we all felt control was the wrong perspective.... Philosophically, if the Web was to be a universal resource, it had to be able to grow in an unlimited way. Technically, if there was any centralized point of control, it would rapidly become a bottleneck that the restricted the Web's growth, and the Web would never scale up. It's being "out of control" was very important.[17]
>
> —*Weaving the Web*

In *Weaving the Web* (1999), Berners-Lee recounts how the W3C took it upon itself to balance public and (new) private interests. To ensure equilibrium between technology, society, and politics, members would address and collaborate on certain issues—anything from access to pornography to domain name distribution. They would make recommendations and, in some instances, work to develop new technologies.

Berners-Lee feared governmental regulation over information. In 1996 the Communications Decency Act placed severe restrictions on Internet content in the name of preventing child pornography. Should the government decide what's decent or indecent? The W3C determined that the public should decide for themselves. They released the PICS software (Platform for Internet Content Selection) which enabled parents to block sites with certain ratings. Companies adopted the technology, and the Communications Decency Act was struck down in court. The lesson: The Web and related technologies allow us, in some cases, to create alternatives to government action.

> Bias on the Web can be insidious and far-reaching. It can break the independence that exists among our suppliers of

hardware, software, opinion, and information, corrupting our society.[18]   —*Weaving the Web*

. . . .

Ensuring that the medium can be separated from the message—as much as possible—is key to a truly democratic Web. Berners-Lee warns about the companies that create the hardware and software of the Web attempting to create biases that suit their own ends.

Understanding the architecture of the Internet and Web is key to preventing such bias. It consists of four horizontal layers of infrastructure: the transmissions medium, the computer hardware, software, and the content. Any of the first three layers may alter a user's access to content. Keeping each layer discrete is necessary to keeping information truly free. Corporations, however, would like to "vertically integrate" the infrastructure to their advantage—and are spending billions to do so. Microsoft's proprietary browser took over the market when it was bundled into their operating system monopoly. AOL and Time Warner merged to create a company that controls a dominant share in every layer but the computer hardware: Time Warner cable systems, Netscape, and AOL software and service providers, and the vast Time Warner media empire. Many users think AOL is synonymous with the Internet—they may soon be right. The global hypertext system Berners-Lee imagined would cease to exist if a single company achieved full vertical transmission and controlled every aspect of the Web.

. . . .

> The Web's universality leads to a thriving richness and diversity. If a company claims to give access to the world of information, then presents a filtered view, the Web loses its credibility.... Some might argue that the bias between layers is just the free market in action. But if I bought a radio and found that it accessed only certain stations and not others, I'd be upset.[19]
> —*Weaving the Web*

. . . .

Then there's the issue of domain naming. Control over desirable "top level" domain names such as money.com: Will people and companies with the most money get them? Berners-Lee believes that a degree of governance is necessary, and the responsibility has been assigned to ICANN, a regulating, neutral not-for-profit, non-US-centric body. ICANN is a prime example of how the Web community is attempting to govern the Web with the least amount of government intervention.

The W3C consortium, as Berners-Lee defines it, doesn't aspire to control the technology behind the Web. Rather, it mediates between industry and government. Its role is to educate. Its purpose is to keep the Web as free, open, and decentralized as possible.

> Technologists have to act as responsible members of society, but they also have to cut themselves out of the loop of ruling the world. The consortium deliberately does this. . . . It provides technical mechanisms, not social politics. And that's the way it will stay.[20] —*Weaving the Web*

A BETTER WEB

Nelson has been skeptical about the Web, asserting that it is not as robust, decentralized, or nonhierarchical as it should be, and that the difference between the Web and Xanadu is like that between plankton and the *Queen Mary*. "The Web displaced our principled model with something far more raw, chaotic, and shortsighted. Its one-way breaking links glorified and fetishized as websites are the very hierarchical directories from which we sought to free users. They discarded the ideas of stable publishing, annotation, two-way connection, and trackable change."[21] Nelson's concept of transclusion (side-by-side documents) would allow users to annotate and provide parallel commentary as well as provide agree/disagree screens to compare different documents. In Xanadu there would be fewer hierarchical documents and files unsuitable to connectivity.

Berners-Lee considers the Web to be in its first stages of evolution. Like Alan Kay, he thinks people aren't using computers to their own—or the computer's—full potential. The Web should also be about the ability to create. Or, as Berners-Lee deems it—to *intercreate*—meaning to interact and create with other people online.

The W3C is attempting to create new Web tools for interdisciplinary collaboration, bootstrapping-style. Berners-Lee would like to see tools that allow us to look up and compare, side by side, what politicians or defendants or accusers actually say, rather than what is revealed in the commercial media. The evolving Web would also incorporate annotation capabilities similar to those of the memex and Xanadu—a third-party service that would enable groups to share their comments on documents throughout the Web. Annotations would be superimposed on a page, point by point, rebuttal by rebuttal, agreement and dissent.*

Berners-Lee's ultimate Web is a social system that doesn't aspire to be *wise*; it simply functions as a social mediator—a neutral entity that handles the administrative aspects of human interaction. After all, in a world of ever-increasing information, people need a better way to process it and put it all to good use. To handle information overload would be to endow the Web with, if not wisdom, then the ability to make inferences between different concepts. In the future Berners-Lee envisions a new Web empowered with the capability to sort information through better association, stronger intuition. He calls it the Semantic Web.

· ·

> Information varies along many axes. . . . To date, the Web has developed most rapidly as a medium of documents for people rather than for data and information that can be processed automatically. The Semantic Web aims to make up for this. [22]
>
> —"The Semantic Web"

· ·

In an article in *Scientific American* titled "The Semantic Web," (2001) Berners-Lee states that the Semantic Web should be able to process data by *mapping all the relationships between documents,* as

---

*Some progress has been made on this front already, from organizations such as the Foresight Institute, which has introduced CritSuite.

he envisioned in his original manifesto, "Information Management."

Berners-Lee imagines software agents roaming from page to page that readily carry out sophisticated tasks for users, such as finding a dentist and making an appointment based on a set of personalized strictures. Like Kay, he envisions these agents to be part of the user interface, or user illusion. On the Semantic Web, the user could ask her agent to find a dentist who has a certified rating of "excellent" in root canal work, graduated from New York University, takes Aetna as an insurance carrier, has an office within fifteen miles of her apartment, and can see her on Wednesday at seven. Agents on the Semantic Web could buy stocks according to the user's preferences or negotiate with supermarkets to stock a fridge. The agents would have the ability *to infer,* use a degree of logic, to follow commands. If it succeeds, the Semantic Web would provide a sort of unprecedented global intelligence—an understanding based on an ability to find stronger relationships between terms and data.

The challenge for the researchers building the Semantic Web is the same that has plagued artificial intelligence researchers—how to work within Gödel's theorem, which declares that no knowledge representation system can answer everything correctly or ever be complete or perfect. But Berners-Lee insists that he is not developing artificial intelligence, at least not in the conventional sense of a machine with superhuman intelligence. The Semantic Web will be humanlike, but not human.

> Adding logic to the Web—the means to use rules to make inferences, choose courses of action and answer questions is the task before the Semantic Web community at the moment. A mixture of mathematical and engineering decisions complicate this task. The logic must be powerful enough to describe complex properties of objects but not so powerful that agents can be tricked by being asked to consider a paradox. [23]
>
> —"The Semantic Web"

For the computer to best analyze semantic relationships we need a language that will complement HTML—a language that will enable computers to compare hypertext. This language will enable the agent to access structured collections of information and sets of inference rules to conduct automated reasoning. The W3C project is developing the Resource Description Framework (RDF)—code that can be embedded in HTML pages to provide metadata on the document, including a template for authorship, version, content information, relations, translations, and legal information. A computer reading an RDF-enhanced Web page would be able to infer associative patterns between documents in a way that existing search engines can't. The other language the Semantic Web would read is XML (eXtensible Markup Language), which lets users create their own tags or labels such as <zipcode> to annotate Web documents.

Nelson scoffs at the Semantic Web and RDF and XML code. The Semantic Web, he says, is the "geeky illusion" that language and meaning can be matched easily. He believes that RDF and XML, meanwhile, enforce a hierarchical structure that undermines the virtues of hypertext.

Berners-Lee and the W3C, however, are considering some of the features of Xanadu as part of the Semantic Web. Members of the Xanadu project imagined a "certification link" (via a certifying agency or database) to ensure the legitimacy of a document. Berners-Lee likewise calls for a *trust engine* for the Semantic Web. These trust agents could attempt to mirror society in the Web world by embedding digital signatures in XML-coded documents. Cryptography will enable people to collaborate in small and large groups and facilitate commerce between corporate entities. The online community—individuals, corporations, etc.—can use existing tools such as W3C's free and open Jigsaw software platform to bootstrap toward greater collaboration and trust on the Web.

AFTERWARD

As an ideal, the Web should empower the individual and the entire human race. The more people use the Web, the more sophisticated and intuitive it gets, and the more promise it will have as a tool for collaboration and problem solving. In Engelbart's parlance, the human and the machine will *coevolve*.

> If we end up producing a structure in hyperspace that allows us to work together harmoniously, that would be a metamorphosis. Though it would, I hope, happen incrementally, it would result in a huge restructuring of society. A society that would advance in intercreativity and group intuition rather than conflict as a basic mechanism would be a major change.[24]
>
> —*Weaving the Web*

Nelson and Berners-Lee's visions of a global hypertext information system have driven the "cybernation revolution" prophesied by the SDS into the promised one, wherein more and more people around the globe benefit from its bounty. They also have a lot in common in seeing an increasingly evolvable, open, global system in the future. The two visionaries differ only in practice: Berners-Lee believes the Web will evolve into the Semantic Web. Nelson believes that Xanadu should rise from the ashes and prevail by following what seems to work best for software development: release into the public domain as an open project. The Web's success is a testament to a model in which no one entity has control.*

The personal and social advantages of the Web are tremendous. Berners-Lee relates it like this:

> The stage is set for an evolutionary growth of new social engines. The ability to create new forms of social progress

---

*In 1999, Nelson's Xanadu Operating Company, renamed Udanax, released a scaled-down version of Xanadu into the public domain. Xanadu is no longer proprietary. Nelson's hope is that open-code developers will create front-end software like browsers. The Xanadu system, even pared down, would be powerful enough to incorporate features such as two-way tracking (showing all links to and from documents), links that do not break (even after editing), and, importantly, tools for real-time collaboration. Skeptics remain dubious, Xanadu remains largely unknown, and yet Nelson and a community of enthusiasts remain optimistic.

would be given to the world at large, and development would be rapid, just as the openness of Web technology allowed that to bloom.[25]

Of shaping the future of a global hypertext system, Nelson says:

The problems are what they always were: freedom, pluralism, access. In all of this there will emerge a new humanism; in all of this we will find the new strengths and powers that we deserve, and freedoms that we require.[26]

SHARING THE SOURCE

RICHARD M. STALLMAN AND LARRY WALL

Electronic freedoms will be at the center of the whirlwind of the coming years. Either we will fight for them, or they will be taken from us like candy from a child.   —Ted Nelson

IDEAS ARE STRANGE AND MAGICAL. We can share an idea with someone else as easily as handing over a jacket. If two people share the jacket, only one of them can wear it at a time unless they rip it in half, rendering it useless. Unless both are the same size, it will fit only one of them well. When two people share an idea, however, they both can enjoy full use of it at all times. The idea shapes itself to fit each person. And it will never wear out; rather, the more a good idea is used and shared, the better it gets. People can learn, teach, and collaborate with ideas. No one can learn a jacket. Ideas inhabit the mental world; jackets inhabit the physical.

The Information Revolution is bringing the mental and physical worlds together. Not long ago, the primary way to store an idea outside the mind was in a book; now, it can be stored electronically with infinite variation. Marshall McLuhan recognized how profound the disjunction from the Gutenberg age to the electronic age would be, just by observing the changes wrought by the first electronic media: the telegraph, lightbulb, radio, television. They only presaged the arrival of the networked computer, the ultimate medium of ideas.

With computers, ideas are encoded as software, "code." The code inhabits the physical world, stored on punch cards, magnetic tape, a memory chip, a floppy disk, a CD. It can even be stored within the threads of a jacket. Software is both idea and object, mental and physical. The institutions of the Industrial Revolution, built around mastery of the physical world, treat software as if it were no different from a jacket. Individuals have been able to see the difference, but for their insight to matter to society, corporations and governments must adapt.

By the 1970s, the proliferation of computers had created a market for software development. Programmers, most famously Microsoft founder Bill Gates, realized that they could demand that people pay for the privilege of using code they wrote, or at least controlled, and could call anyone who just copied the software a thief or pirate. In 1975, Gates wrote the article "An Open Letter to Hobbyists," which led the charge to criminalize the once open, cross-pollinating programming community for sharing the BASIC interpreter he had written. He believed these hobbyists, who had sent him their thanks and suggestions for improvements, but no money, were stealing from him. At the time, the community thought Gates was contemptible for calling sharing stealing. But the Gates perspective allowed corporations to make billions of dollars, and it soon prevailed.

Once a few people became millionaires by forming companies to write proprietary software, thousands followed suit. The major corporations got into the act. In the early decades of computing, most code was proprietary, but bundled with the sale or lease of a particular system. By 1980, proprietary, licensed software was increasingly packaged separately as a stand-alone product, making programmers and businesspeople realize there were riches to be made. They realized that there was an increasing customer base willing and able to purchase software to enhance the systems they already had.

Two people, Richard M. Stallman and Larry Wall, embraced openness and collaboration and led the charge to establish a technological, social, and moral alternative to cutthroat commercialism. Stallman wrote "The GNU Manifesto" (1985) and the "GNU General Public License" (1989) for free software. Wall's manifestos are keynote addresses that summarize his years of developing the programming language Perl: "First Perl Conference Keynote" (also called "The First State of the Perl Onion," 1997), and "The Third State of the Perl Onion" (1999).

The Information Revolution, they believe, has wrought a "postscarcity" world wherein knowledge can be freer and better than ever before. Despite the encroaching corporate proprietary attitude, these revolutionaries attempt to hardwire social consciousness into the technologies of the next century.

EDEN

Stallman's fascination with computers and programming drove him to the famed MIT Artificial Intelligence Lab in 1971, when he was in his freshman year at Harvard University. Although he eventually earned a magna cum laude physics degree from Harvard, the computer center there was like most others then and now: heavily regulated, with a strong hierarchy that determined who was allowed to use the computing resources. At the AI Lab, Stallman discovered a completely different world, one in which hackers would and could literally break down the door if a professor dared lock up a computer terminal.

Stallman always had an extraordinary interest in computers. As a child growing up in Manhattan in the 1950s he scrounged up computer manuals and wrote down programs and algorithms, imagining the day he'd get to run them. At times that may have seemed like a fantasy. Although Stallman was extremely bright and self-aware, devouring science fiction books from an early age, he had trouble getting along with teachers and other children. After several years of devastating school experiences, he was sent to a special high school for troubled students. There he felt branded, trapped. He decided to figure out how to survive the system, and improved his grades dramatically. In 1969, the summer of the ARPAnet, he got a job at an IBM laboratory in New York and started programming a computer for the first time. In his last year of high school he transferred to the local public school, which enabled him to get into Harvard.

The AI Lab was Eden for the "happy hacker," the clever programmer who coded for the hell of it. This was the home of Minsky and Papert and a home to bevy of top computer scientists. The hacker there needn't be a student at MIT or even be past adolescence. He (or, rarely, she) just needed to have a passion for programming. When some would leave to get married and have a family, new hackers invariably took their place.

To be a hacker at the AI Lab meant that your ethical code was driven by the progress of the computer code—it was wrong, almost *evil*, to keep code or computing resources to yourself. Hackers respected one another because they were good at what they did, not because they had money or a title. This led to profound conflicts with other ethical systems, particularly ones that give supremacy to the individual ownership of ideas. From the hacker's perspective, keeping an idea or a new program to yourself was a spit in the eye of everyone else—you were obstructing progress and increasing waste, helping entropy instead. From the opposite perspective, hackers were constantly invading secrets and building systems without necessary security.

Everyone in Stallman's group celebrated creativity and individuality, diverse interests, and a sense of play. The hackers controlled their own time and, unlike the professors and graduate students, ignored the traditional rules and roles. With almost no official power at MIT, they maintained their status by being demonstrably the best computer programmers around. Stallman's days of programming code there were leavened by Bulgarian singing, folk dancing, and playing practical jokes. He felt safe within the confines of the MIT community, seemingly beyond the grip of the Vietnam War, which he considered wrongheaded. Despite having a low number, he wasn't drafted. The ninth floor of Tech Square remained his home, sometimes literally: There was one summer when he had no other residence, and slept next to his beloved computer.

By the late 1970s Stallman had established himself. Within the computing community the three initial log-in handle RMS was well known and well respected, in no small part due to the advanced text editor and programming environment he created, called Emacs.

Meanwhile, on the West Coast, Wall received an education in a completely different environment. He was raised in south Los Angeles as an evangelical Protestant; his father was a pastor, and both parents descended from a long line of preachers. The Walls moved to Washington state in 1963 and it was there, in 1972, where Wall first began programming on a school calculator. He almost managed to get a game of tic-tac-toe working on the machine, but couldn't quite fit the program into the 120 steps that was the calculator's limit.

Wall enrolled at Seattle Pacific University as a chemistry and music major. He switched to pre-med, but eventually became more interested in computer science and began spending a lot of time at the university's computer center. In fact, he spent three years working in the computer center, and attended classes only when he felt like it. There he helped a young Bill Gates, who, ever mindful of his cash flow, would schlep over from the nearby University of Washington to get cheap computer access. Eight years after Wall entered college, he finished his undergraduate degree with a self-made major in natural and artificial languages, in other words, linguistics and computer science. Like other information revolutionaries, his he had interests in a diversity of fields.

Wall intended to put his training in linguistics into the service of his religious convictions and become a Bible-translating missionary. He and his new wife, Gloria, moved back to California for graduate school in linguistics at Berkeley and the University of California at Los Angeles, while also studying at the missionary Summer Institute of Linguistics. They planned to go to Africa and learn unwritten languages, devise writing systems, and translate works including the Bible—work that would be simultaneously spiritual, unusual, and intellectual. But Larry had become allergic to everything from seafood to wheat, eggs, and tomatoes, and going to the far reaches of Africa might be detrimental to his health. He turned back to programming, which, as it turned out, was fortunate for the computer revolution ahead.

SURFING THE CODE

Programmers like Stallman and Wall have been on the front lines of the Information Revolution. They are among the most involved users of computers. They delve into the system, tweaking or even rebuilding it to serve their desires. They are creating the environment for everyone else.

Today, most programmers work inside of a preconstructed environment. In John von Neumann and Alan Turing's day, everyone who wanted to use a computer needed to know just how it worked, and had to flip switches or type in the numerical codes it could understand. Soon people designed systems to hide the complexity of the digital machinery. Today's operating systems have a graphic environment inhabited by virtual objects, represented on screens by icons, windows, menus, and buttons. The relationship between the virtual world on the screen and the bits flowing through the computer's processor is extremely arcane and complex. Alan Kay calls it the "user illusion."

A computer's processor is only able to comprehend a set of numeric codes, or *machine code,* specific to it. For example, the processor inside an IBM PC uses a language different from that inside a Macintosh. To avoid having to think only in numbers, programmers developed *assembly languages* with memorizable commands, like ADD or JMP, which the computer transcribes into the corresponding machine codes.

Then programmers developed languages in which one command would be the equivalent of dozens of assembler commands, allowing people to write their programs in something resembling English.* Software associated with the language, the *compiler,* takes the source program and translates it into machine code. These languages allow programmers to write complex programs quickly and reliably, letting the computer do the work of translating human thought to machine code.

Thus a program usually exists in two forms: the understandable *source code,* and the executable *machine code.* The source code, which consists of lines of text, is like a recipe; the machine code is the resultant dish. One can look at the machine code to try to determine what the

---

*Fortran, COBOL, LISP, and Algol all started in the first decade of computing. BASIC and Pascal were developed in the 1960s.

computer will do, but that is usually a near-impossible task, just as it's often difficult to exactly recreate a dish. And most programs are as complex as, say, a Twinkie, with dozens of ingredients and chemical additives and an industrial cooking process. It would be impossible to duplicate a Twinkie just by analyzing the finished product. The source code, however, is the recipe that allows you to create and modify your own Twinkies.*

UNIX

The university computing departments of the 1970s, where Stallman and Wall learned to program, were defined by the symbiotic growth of ARPAnet, the operating system Unix, and the programming language C. Unix and C were efforts to isolate simple "kernels" of necessary capabilities in a programming language and operating system. Flexible and powerful, Unix had the great strength of being portable, whereas previous operating systems were designed for a particular model of computer. Because implementations of C sprung up for nearly every hardware system, programmers could write code for large, complex programs that would remain comprehensible and flexible on various platforms but still compile almost as fast as if they had been handcrafted. As advances in hardware accelerated and new models proliferated, Unix became the dominant operating system for the networked computer centers across the country, and then the world. Unix and C also became the environment and the benchmark for Stallman and Wall to create their own work.

In that revolutionary year of 1969, as the ARPAnet went up, Ken Thompson and Dennis Ritchie of Bell Labs invented Unix. Following the lessons of the best in theoretical computer science, they designed Unix to be a collection of simple, complementary programs that could be linked together to perform complex tasks. The development of Unix was driven by the tool kit philosophy, which can be broken down into four principles:

- Write programs to be single-purpose tools. *reduction is!*
- Make the output of every program usable by other programs.

standardization

---

*Of course, this analogy breaks down in important ways; any program, be it source code or machine code, can be duplicated exactly, since it's pure information. There's no replicator machine for food—yet. See Chapter 12.

- Make a working program as early as possible.
- If a tool would help your work, use it. If it doesn't exist, build it.

This philosophy is well grounded in the real world—it's how carpenters use their tools to build a bookshelf or a house. It's also very similar to Alan Kay's object–oriented programming philosophy and the *Society of Mind* concept that Marvin Minsky was developing at the time. Computer scientists everywhere were realizing that systems of great complexity and creativity, from artificial intelligence systems to operating systems, can best be built by the symbiotic coordination of many simple parts. The only thing the Unix tool kit philosophy glossed over was that the programmer was required to handle all the coordination, an often arduous task, especially since the Unix tools actually weren't as simple as they should have been.

Thompson and the rest of the Bell Labs researchers in his team found that their approach was paying great dividends. They soon had a usable Unix system up and running. In 1973 a friend of Thompson's from UC Berkeley saw their talk and was impressed enough to ask for a copy of the system. Berkeley soon acquired a source license and became the second great center for Unix development, led by the graduate student Bill Joy. In 1975 Thompson came to Berkeley on sabbatical from Bell Labs. Under his guidance, Joy and another graduate student, Chuck Haley, began to improve and extend the Berkeley Unix system. By 1977, the year Apple began selling the Apple II, Joy had put together the computer tape with the Berkeley Software Distribution (BSD) of Unix, sending out thirty copies to those who had the necessary AT&T Unix licenses. Soon enough, Joy had become a one-man missionary for Unix, whose popularity was steadily growing. But the explosion was just around the corner, when PCs would converge with these professional tools.

A NEW PROPRIETY

As the 1980s rolled around Stallman and Wall became central players in the expanding computing universe. Suddenly, computing became part of the real world, which turned 180 degrees from the excesses and successes of the 1960s and 1970s. Ronald Reagan's election as the U.S. president marked the collapse of liberalism and the rise of the yuppie, replacing free love, the hippie, and the civil rights movement with corporate conservatism, the entrepreneur, and the Greed Decade. And thousands of those entrepreneurs were into computers. Whereas there once had been dozens of computer companies, now there were hundreds. The hottest companies in the world were computer companies that hadn't existed a decade before, like Apple and Atari. And while people had been making money by selling machines, this was the first time when millions, even billions, of dollars could be made just by selling software to run on those machines. It was the adolescence of the PC; commercial software; and, through Stallman and Wall, the birth of the free-software movement.

The development that shaped Stallman and Wall's careers began in 1980, as the popularity of Unix rose. They worked on the powerful computers that were using some variant of Unix as an operating system— they were outside the PC boom. The changes in the distribution and licensing of Unix changed their lives. AT&T realized Unix could be a commercial product and stopped contributing the Bell Labs developments to the rest of the Unix licensees—thereafter, Berkeley became the central focus of community advances. Meanwhile, the Defense Advanced Research Projects Agency (DARPA) wanted to consolidate their ARPAnet network on the same operating system, and chose Unix. Instead of going with AT&T's version, they supported the Berkeley development of Unix by Joy.

In 1982, Unix users from Stanford and Berkeley, including Joy, formed Sun Microsystems. Sun became an overnight success by selling, by the standards of the time, very inexpensive workstations running the Berkeley variant of Unix. The combination of the growth of the ARPAnet and the proliferation of Sun workstations ignited the Unix explosion. In 1984, the AT&T monopoly was split up; Unix emerged from its Bell Labs nest as a stand-alone commercial product. At the time there were three main variants of Unix: AT&T's Unix, Berkeley's BSD, and Sun's Unix, SunOS (later dubbed Solaris). They coexisted uneasily but peacefully, advancing steadily. All the versions were governed by AT&T's license, and for every copy of Unix sold, money was paid into AT&T's coffers.

A SYMBOLIC STAND

Meanwhile, the sea change to proprietary software hit the MIT AI Lab hard, and Stallman the hardest of all. The first glimmerings were in 1977, when Xerox gave the AI Lab one of the first laser printers out of Xerox PARC. Whereas earlier when Xerox had given them a graphics printer the hackers could hack around with its software, extending and improving its functionality and squashing bugs, this time the software was run by a separate, dedicated, inaccessible computer. The Lab lost functionality without any way of getting it back, since the hackers couldn't get at the code. Around the same time, Digital discontinued the PDP-10, the only system on which Stallman's system could run. The AI Lab would have to use a new operating system. And the only operating systems available were proprietary.

But it was the war between the hackers themselves that destroyed Stallman's world once and for all.

Led by the senior hacker Richard Greenblatt, the hackers at MIT had the dream of designing and selling a stand-alone machine that would run the operating system LISP. The LISP machine would not only be cool and hackable, but also represent the best of technology. They knew about the ideas of Kay and others, and incorporated them into the ideals of the AI Lab, planning to make the ultimate personal computer. But when in 1979, Greenblatt insisted that LISP Machine Incorporated (LMI) be a hackerish, small-scale company, most of the other hackers didn't go along. They instead decided to form a heavily funded company, Symbolics, with the goal of getting big, making money fast, and thus having a strong influence on the world.

In 1981, Symbolics hired the hackers en masse from the AI Lab. Soon all the hackers who were involved with either company had to resign from the AI Lab, leaving just Stallman to hold the torch. When MIT got a contract to use the Symbolics LISP machines, Stallman saw his opportunity to fight back. The LISP operating system had once been a joint endeavor between the AI Lab, Symbolics, and LMI, but Symbolics made their system proprietary. As a consequence, they forced the hackers to choose sides: for or against them.

Stallman stood alone against Symbolics. When new versions of the Symbolics system appeared at MIT, Stallman figured out how to reproduce the features with his own code. Since Stallman didn't hide his work, LMI could use it to keep up with Symbolics. Working on his own, Stallman out-hacked all of Symbolics' programmers for two years. While some at Symbolics simply saw Stallman as a wretched weasel, most of them could look past their corporate loyalty to be awed by one of the greatest hackers of all time. Stallman was John Henry to the steam locomotive of Symbolics.

Stallman knew he couldn't fight Symbolics forever, but he did it for long enough. He gave Greenblatt's company enough time to get a foothold in the LISP machine market. By 1983 it was time for Stallman to move on. Nondisclosure agreements were being shoved in his face. The hackers were gone. The bureaucratic, secret-laden, hierarchical, self-ish, institutional world had overtaken the AI Lab. The computer and the culture to which he pledged his life had died. But what to do next?

In 1984, Stallman decided to resign from MIT and begin his fight against the Orwellian forces that ripped apart his community. His plan: to develop a *free* Unix-compatible operating system, which he dubbed GNU (GNU's Not Unix, recursive acronyms being yet another AI Lab hacker tradition), in 1983.* He could see that Unix, although not his favorite operating system, considering its layers of hierarchy and passwords, was becoming the dominant system in the programming world. Since Stallman wanted to create a system that everyone would use, he knew that it would have to be compatible with Unix. GNU would be free to all—shared and enjoyed as the basis for an unfettered computing experience. His first idea was to get funding from hardware companies, who would benefit from a nonpro-prietary operating system. He argued the benefits of free software and was looking for a few investments of maybe $50,000 from a few different companies that could reap millions of dollars in benefits down the road. But every corporation thought it was a crazy idea. They wouldn't make an investment in a longhaired hacker's plan, however brilliant or however proven his skills. So he took his case to the community, by writing a tech-nomanifesto that defined a movement, the free software movement.

---

*GNU would be compatible with Unix, but none of the code would come from the AT&T-controlled Unix. Thus, GNU's Not Unix.

THE GNU MANIFESTO

Richard Stallman's "GNU Manifesto" was originally published in the March 1985 issue of *Dr. Dobb's Journal,* whose readers were the same types who read Stewart Brand's the *Whole Earth Catalog* a decade earlier. The "GNU Manifesto" is Stallman's manifesto, expressly named, which defined the GNU philosophy and established the free-software movement as a social, political, and moral cause. When it became clear that businesses rejected the idea of investing in free-operating system, Stallman rewrote the manifesto for a new audience: the community of programmers, his fellow hackers. He enjoined them to fight to preserve the way of life of the programmer. Moreover, he argued that it was immoral to not share code, and he would lead by example.

> I consider that the golden rule requires that if I like a program I must share it with other people who like it. Software sellers want to divide the users and conquer them, making each user agree not to share with others. I refuse to break solidarity with other users in this way.[1]   —"The GNU Manifesto"

What hurt Stallman the most about software companies was not that they profited by selling programs, but that by doing so they harmed the society of computer users. Without proprietary software, programmers have no reason not to work together, improving one another's lives by improving the code. They have no need to hoard ideas, because the only benefit comes from having others use them. Most important, working together creates the bond of friendship, respect, and love, while retaining the goad of competition; proprietary software means working against each other, which can lead to distrust, disrespect, and cynicism.

> The fundamental act of friendship among programmers is the sharing of programs; marketing arrangements now typically used essentially forbid programmers to treat others as friends.[2]
> —"The GNU Manifesto"

Stallman knew that the battle against proprietary software had to start at the bedrock of computing, the operating system. The operating system is the environment in which all other software operates; it is the world the programmer inhabits. In the real world, we all enjoy the benefits of public space—natural resources are common resources.

The idea of free (as in freedom) software certainly includes the idea that people are not obligated to pay money for the use of the GNU system. But money is not Stallman's central concern; rather, it is the health of the community and of all of society. The primary benefit of not having restrictions on breathing the air is not that we don't have to pay. The primary benefit is that we can breathe. The economic benefit of inexpensive software is a mere distraction, in Stallman's mind, to the societal benefits of a healthy, trusting, collaborative programming community that can share the source code of the system.

Stallman listed three primary benefits of free-system software: (1) Because the sources will be available, any user can make personal modifications; (2) schools will have a much more educational computing environment; and (3) the overhead and perniciousness of regulating use of system software will be eliminated.

> Consider a space station where air must be manufactured at great cost: Charging each breather per liter of air may be fair, but wearing the metered gas mask all day and all night is intolerable even if everyone can afford to pay the air bill. And the TV cameras everywhere to see if you ever take the mask off are outrageous. It's better to support the air plant with a head tax and chuck the masks.[3]   —"The GNU Manifesto"

By discussing such an economic system, Stallman wasn't ignoring the reality that programmers need to be paid. He was simply asserting that as computers become ever more important to society, they become natural resources like air and should be treated as such. System software becomes part of the societal environment and should have no restrictions or impediments to its free use. The prescience of his seemingly outrageous analogy of TV cameras everywhere to check on gas masks is chilling—this kind of Big Brother, round-the-clock, privacy-eliminating monitoring is endemic in today's world of proprietary operating systems.

DEVIL'S ADVOCATE

Just as Turing anticipated objections to artificial intelligence in his manifesto, "Computing Machinery and Intelligence," Stallman anticipated objections in his "GNU Manifesto." He knew that the prevailing wisdom was that free software couldn't work.

Objection: Nobody will use it if it is free, because that means they can't rely on any support, and you have to charge for the program to pay for providing the support.

Rebuttal: Stallman thought that if people would rather pay for GNU plus service than get GNU free without service, a company just providing service to people who have obtained GNU free ought to be profitable. This idea has been borne out. There are a number of companies now thriving by providing service to users of free software.

Objection: You need to advertise to reach lots of people, and there's no use in advertising something that's free.

Rebuttal: That objection can't work both ways: If GNU would benefit from advertising, a company could make a profit by advertising its services in distributing the system. If, on the other hand, the distribution of GNU is perfect without any outside help, it wouldn't need any advertising to reach lots of people.

Objection: My company needs a proprietary operating system to get a competitive edge.

Rebuttal: GNU will remove operating system software from the realm of competition. Stallman knew that if GNU was as good as any proprietary operating system out there, free-market economics would eliminate the proprietary systems. Just as there's no competition for the atmosphere in the breathable air market, there would be no competition for GNU, as the free software juggernaut took over.

Objection: Don't people have a right to control how their creativity is used?

Rebuttal: This has become the most lasting objection to Stallman's arguments. People who agree with everything else he says disagree with his feelings. Stallman made it very clear that he in particular felt the only moral choice one could make is to not control how his or her creativity is used. Many others are not as willing to be so saintlike, and simply resent his moral posturing. But Stallman didn't insist that others follow his lead. He reminded them that at least in the United States, individual control over creations isn't an intrinsic right. Rather, the U.S. Constitution gives control over the arts and sciences to society.

Objection: Competition makes things get done better.
Rebuttal: That objection is true for healthy competition, but Stallman believed that proprietary software, with its restrictions and lawsuits, made for unhealthy competition. Healthy competition is like a road race, where the victory goes to the swiftest. But competition can also include other strategies, such as attacking the other runners. When that happens, everyone finishes late or is crippled.

Stallman was personally wounded by what he experienced Symbolics doing, trying all they could to eliminate competition. The only good way to compete in software, he believed, was to write better software, not threaten your competitors, make customers sign restrictive deals, and hide your work. Those tactics allow software companies to make money fast, but it's money at the expense of progress.

At first the idea of banning high-paying organizations seems absurd, but historically it's a course society has taken. The greatest profits from the least effort are made by organizations that threaten direct violence, like protection rackets; or abuse a monopoly on a necessary product or commodity; or sell an addictive product, like drugs and gambling; or defraud their customers. Such organizations are illegal, because their profits come at the expense of the well-being of society.

The Ultimate Objection: I want to get paid for programming!
Rebuttal: Basically, money isn't everything. Stallman countered the reasoning that Bill Gates had professed in 1975 that the most important thing in software development is to prevent society from sharing software so that the individual developer can make as much money as possible. Plenty of people were programming, devoting their entire lives to

writing code, because of the pure joy of the task, and for fame and appreciation. The AI Lab hackers, while paid much less than if they had gone into corporations, were the most famous coders of the time. They are the ones whose names and exploits are remembered.

Stallman was certain that free software wouldn't mean that programmers couldn't earn a living. That, he felt, was an irrational fear. Programmers, like artists and musicians, would find ways to code even if they were paid little or less. When people do something useful, there's money in it somewhere, no matter what the particulars of the law. Speaking of the law, the legal code is free and available to all, but lawyers and judges, who use it and create new case law, are some of the highest paid professionals in the world.

THE GNU GENERAL PUBLIC LICENSE

The "GNU Manifesto" inspired enough people to join Stallman's crusade that the Free Software Foundation was born in 1985. While they began writing and distributing pieces of the GNU system, such as the Emacs text editor, a C compiler, and a debugger, each of which became favorites in the Unix world, Stallman also worked on figuring out how to formalize the manifesto's intentions with the power of law.

Stallman could simply have released his code into the public domain, without any copyright at all, where all works go when their copyright license expires. There are no restrictions whatsoever on what someone can do with a creative work that is in the public domain. You can chop out half the scenes in *Hamlet*, add some juggling and dialogue from Socrates, and still call it Shakespeare's *Hamlet*, without running afoul of the law (though it may be unwatchable). You could stick the entire text of *Hamlet* in the middle of a book such as this one without breaking the law. If GNU were public domain, software companies could take the source code and add whatever bits of it into their proprietary software. Stallman certainly didn't want to write a free operating system that would simply enrich the likes of AT&T or Microsoft. So he wrote the "GNU General Public License" (GNU GPL), which protects works with the power of copyright.

He knew that just as proprietary software developers used the strength of copyright to prevent users from sharing code, there must be a way for the Free Software Foundation to use the strength of copyright to ensure that users shared code. The first version of the GNU GPL debuted in 1985.* Although the "GNU Manifesto" proclaimed the free-software philosophy, it was the GNU GPL that was Stallman's sword. The license, which summarizes the GNU philosophy amid its legal clauses, establishes what Stallman coined "copyleft."

Stallman learned of the term "copyleft" from hacker Don Hopkins, who scribbled "Copyleft—all rights reversed," on an envelope he sent to his friend during the early years of the GNU project. The phrase was a brilliantly hackerish play on the standard phrase "Copyright—all rights reserved." Stallman, who appreciates puns with a childlike delight, latched onto it to describe his copyright innovation.

. . . .

When we speak of free software, we are referring to freedom, not price.[4]   —"GNU General Public License"

. . . .

By 1989, Stallman had learned that people were confused by the term "free software." They thought all he cared about was some kind of pinko, no-money-allowed software with which no one could get paid for their work. But that had nothing to do with what he cared about. He just believed that nonproprietary software was necessary to the exercise of intrinsic personal freedoms—free software for a free society.

The GPL protects what Stallman identified as the four freedoms necessary for a healthy programming community:

- The freedom to run the program for any purpose.

- The freedom to study how the program works and adapt it to your needs. Access to the source code is a precondition for this.

- The freedom to redistribute copies so you can help your neighbor.

---

*The initial incarnation was the GNU Emacs General Public License; then there was the GNU GCC General Public License, as well as GPLs for BISON, NetHack, and the other GNU applications. On February 1, 1989, the Free Software Foundation released the GNU General Public License, not tied to any particular application.

- The freedom to improve the program and release
  your improvements to the public, so that the whole
  community benefits. Access to the source code is
  a precondition for this.[5]

The GPL consists of two parts: requiring these four freedoms and guaranteeing the preservation of these freedoms in modified versions. The GPL states that if someone modifies or uses GPL-protected code in a new work, the new work must also be released under the GPL. Stallman dubbed this form of copyright protection "copyleft," since it uses copyright to *protect* the ability to copy, not *prevent* it. The protection is not against copying and redistribution, but against incorporation into nonfree works. If code is released under the GPL, people will always be able to look at it and tinker with it.

. . . .

The license agreements of most software companies try to keep users at the mercy of those companies.[6]
—"GNU General Public License"

. . . .

The GPL forces people to admit that their work rests on the shoulders of others; that progress is collective. They have to respect the wishes of other people in the community. And the free-software community values sharing. If copylefting leads to a bad system, projects released under the GPL will lose. People will just use alternatives, and development of the GPL-protected projects will wither away. But Stallman was sure that wouldn't happen: he believed that programmers with GPL-protected freedoms write the best code.

PERL

As Stallman was shaping the Free Software Foundation, Wall released Perl. The programming language was his master creation. To Wall, artistry is the crafting of order out of chaos, a beautiful whole out of individual brushstrokes or notes. He sees evolution as the most random, chaotic process of all—that God chose that as one of his tools is, to Wall, His ultimate artistry.

The genesis of Perl began in the early 1980s, when Wall was

working as a Unix support programmer at the cold war giant computer corporation Burroughs,* a job that gave him plenty of time to hack around writing his own programs. These hacks were intended to make his job easier and more enjoyable, and he released them for anyone to use to make their lives easier and more enjoyable. These programs—the newsreader *rn,* the programming tools *patch* and *metaconfig,* and a computer game, *warp*—along with his active participation in Internet newsgroups made his name quickly well known. *Patch* was especially popular, because it allowed people to easily share updates for programs over the low-bandwidth Usenet. Each of his programs was a great bit of code, but he still had plenty of free time and lots of coding zeal. He was ready to take on a real challenge, something that would really improve the way people used their systems.

In 1986, Wall's supervisor gave him a giant task with a tight deadline. Wall's division in Burroughs/Unisys was assigned to a National Security Agency project, codename "Blacker," which involved an encrypted, high-speed, bicoastal network—testing out a kind of top-secret, paranoid alternative to the ARPAnet. Wall was told to create a configuration and monitoring system for the network, which had both Digital and Sun Microsystems machines on either coast, in a single month. Using the Unix toolkit, including some of the stuff he wrote, he hacked together a solution, transforming the Usenet news system into a command distribution system. Problem solved.

The supervisor then told him to assemble reports from the jumble of log files on the different computers. Wall reached into the Unix tool kit and discovered that the tool he wanted to use, *awk,* wasn't up to the task. *Awk* had crucial bits missing and was too slow. Larry knew he had to write a new tool to do the job, but he was tired of making do with the kludgy jumble of the Unix tool kit, in which some tools were very good and others were awful. He wanted duct tape. He wanted a Swiss Army knife. He wanted to develop a tool that would continue to solve different problems in the future.

---

*When Wall first began at the company, it was the System Development Corporation, later bought by Burroughs. In November 1986 Burroughs merged with Sperry to become Unisys.

As Wall described his realization, he determined the three chief virtues of a programmer:

Laziness, impatience, and hubris.

This was a prankish play, the antithesis of the biblical virtues of an excellent wife (humility, forbearance, love, and diligence) (Philippians 4:2,3).

If Wall worked really hard, he probably could have figured out a way to get *awk* to do the job. But he was too lazy. Doing that work would take a long, boring time, and *awk* was a slow, slow program. He was too impatient. And he believed he could do the job better himself. He had the hubris.

Wall wrote a super text-processing tool, a complete programming language, which he soon dubbed *perl*. The story of how he came up with the name well conveys Wall's mind-set: His first thought was to name the tool after his wife, Gloria. Then he came up with *pearl*, which was both beautiful and obliquely scriptural, referring to Jesus' parable of a merchant "seeking goodly pearls, who, when he had found one pearl of great price, went and sold all that he had, and bought it" (Matthew 13:46). With that in mind, he came up with a phrase to justify the name as an acronym: Practical Extraction and Report Language. But Unix commands were rarely five letters long, and he heard of a process control language with the same name. So Wall changed the name to *perl*, which allowed him to keep the first acronymic expansion and come up with a second, hacker-humor one: Pathologically Eclectic Rubbish Lister.*

Throughout 1987 Wall worked on Perl, releasing the first version on December 18 to the comp.sources.misc newsgroup on the Internet. Perl embodied two precepts that Wall called the Perl slogans:

The first:

There's more than one way to do it.[7]

---

*Originally, *perl* was lowercase. Now, *perl* refers to the program and Perl the language.

Although that's certainly true in the real world, it is rarely true for computers. Programmers design their software to work in a very particular, logical way—and only one logical way. If your methods of thinking or problem solving are at all different, that's too bad. You have to learn to think the way the programmer intended you to think.

The second:

Easy things should be easy, and hard things should be possible.[8]

Wall adapted this maxim from the pronouncement Alan Kay made in "Microelectronics and the Personal Computer" in 1977. Wall understood that ninety per cent of most programs were relatively simple and straightforward tasks. The remaining ten percent posed the real challenge. Wall designed Perl to be the ultimate text-processing language, the ninety percent that is easy. C is the one hundred percent possible language, and Wall incorporated the C commands necessary to do bit-level hacking into Perl. But whereas a C program to print out "hello world" would take five or six lines of definitions and configurations, the equivalent Perl program looks like this:

```
print "hello world"
```

That's what he means by, "Easy things should be easy."

Together, the two credos reveal the power of Perl. By following the first one, Perl is able to follow the second one for programmers of different levels of ability. What is easy for a master hacker won't be easy for a novice. But Perl's multiple avenues allow programmers to learn new tricks and skills, developing new abilities and knowledge over time. Some of the tools in Perl are very straightforward; others are complex. Programmers who don't understand the complex tool, don't have to use it. But they may use it for a simple task at first, then steadily learn its nuances. Over time that which once was hard to understand becomes easy to understand—and therefore easy to program.

LINUX

In 1990, Stallman's Free Software Foundation had just about finished the GNU project. They had a complete, best-of-breed operating system, except for one detail: the kernel. The kernel, as the name implies, implements the core functionality of the system. It's what sits between a running application above and the computer hardware below. It was the last of the major essential components the foundation needed to build a working GNU system. But the GNU kernel development project was moving terribly slowly.

The GNU people wanted to build a superadvanced kernel with all of the greatest theoretical advances made practical, but doing so was incredibly difficult: A kernel has to not only work, but also work as fast as possible. And making something both complex and optimally efficient is a ferocious task. They worked on the kernel, which they dubbed the GNU Hurd, for years, struggling to make it work.

Like the lazy, impatient, and hubristic Wall, a Finnish graduate student named Linus Torvalds thought he could do the job. Torvalds, studying computer science at Helsinki University, just wanted to make something that would work. It didn't need to be perfect or beautiful or work on every machine ever made. In 1991 he released under the GNU GPL a kernel for the 386 platform that was designed to work as part of a complete GNU operating system. The kernel and the system became known as Linux. When Torvalds first released Linux, Stallman was still very gung-ho about the Hurd kernel. A lot of computer scientists thought the Linux kernel wasn't going to go anywhere. Stallman believed the consensus, and didn't really mind that Torvalds was calling the entire system "Linux," even though it was a GNU operating system.*

From the perspective of most computer scientists, Linux was awful, ignoring all the new ideas and using old, safe, boring ones. And it worked only on cheap computers.

---

*"GNU" here refers to the idea of such a system, protected by the GPL. The GNU idea was realized not solely by the Free Software Foundation project, but by many different hackers in disparate projects. The core projects of GNU, Linux, and BSD, which each comprised various essential programs, cross-pollinated with one another. Hackers collected the pieces they needed from each project, with other programs such as MIT's X-windows graphical interface, to build the operating system they wanted.

This book refers to that GNU/Linux/etc. operating system collection sometimes as "Linux," and sometimes as "GNU/Linux," reflecting the intended connotations of the author. While this may cause some consternation among the various advocacies, this book is primarily concerned, with respect to Linux, with how the principles of the "GNU Manifesto" and the intentions of the GNU GPL have entered society.

From the perspective of thousands of others, it worked! On cheap computers!

Linus had followed one of the number one rules that Thompson had followed in creating Unix: Make something that works as soon as possible—then start fixing it. The Internet, which had been open to commerce in 1991 and was growing at a remarkable rate, allowed people to contribute quickly and massively to the project, rapidly improving its reliability and power.

By 1993, the GNU system with Linux as its kernel was comparable to the commercial Unixes, and it and the free BSD projects killed off the smaller commercial Unixes. They were both growing, and growing fast. BSD Unix had been a combination of code owned by Berkeley and code owned by AT&T. In 1989, the Berkeley developers seperated out their work, releasing it without any licensing restrictions other than preservation of the copyright notice. It took them a few more years to write free versions of the AT&T code necessary for a working Unix system. When that happened, the 1990s saw numerous complete BSD systems as different developers "forked" the code: NetBSD, FreeBSD, and OpenBSD. Each fork was associated with a set of goals and personalities; the competition was by turns healthy and disruptive. In 1992, the AT&T-controlled Unix System Laboratories sued the commercial arm of the BSD distribution, Berkeley Software Design, to force the halt of any BSD sales. There were hundreds of pages of briefs, injunction requests, and countersuits. Only in January 1994 did both sides come to a settlement. The suit and the fractious forks considerably slowed the momentum of BSD. Linux, meanwhile, just kept gaining momentum and took an insurmountable lead, soon to be used by not thousands, but millions, as it paralleled the explosive growth of the Internet and the World Wide Web.

When corporations started getting involved with Linux, Stallman started to have a problem with Linux developers and users not giving credit to GNU. It became obvious that the companies that adopted Linux were deliberately avoiding mention of Stallman, the Free Software Foundation, the GPL, and GNU. The worst part, from Stallman's perspective, is that people began to forget the principles at the heart of the Free Software Foundation. Torvalds plays an important role in the development of one of the most widely used operating systems, but he is not necessarily an evangelist of the free-software movement. Whereas almost all GNU-related sites have pointers to the free-software philosophy, only rarely do the Linux sites. In response, Stallman began to push for the Linux system to be called GNU/Linux, a name slowly growing in acceptance by people who believe that the ideas and principles of the GNU project started it all.

PERLS OF WISDOM

Wall shares Stallman's belief in the freedoms of free software; Perl, of course, has always been free and nonproprietary. The essential difference is in how Wall goes about proselytizing these beliefs to others.

Wall, with some humor and humility, sees the similarities between his role as the leader of the Perl community and the prophets in the Bible. His most famous sermons have been his Perl Conference keynote addresses, which he came to call the "State of the Onion" speeches (combining an obvious pun on the annual presidential State of the Union address with the slightly more subtle, but no less painful, reference to pearl onions). In each one he reveals his own talents and interests, including the paths he could have gone down: linguistics, music, chemistry, missionary work. He famously wears Hawaiian shirts, or, for more formal occasions, neon tuxedos. While Stallman is stout with Jesus hair, Wall is slim, with unruly, fine brown hair, oversized glasses, and an infectious grin under a large, well-groomed moustache. He looks for all the world like an enthusiastic science teacher toiling away in a public high school, sticking with a sense of style developed in the 1970s but with humor and intelligence.

Like Stallman, Wall takes the stand to tell programmers that:

. . . .

It is better to give than to receive.[9]

—"First State of the Perl Onion"

. . . .

But he believes that Stallman pushes too hard, that his opinions are too extreme to make him the best kind of leader. Stallman, from the beginning of the GNU project, has antagonized people simply by living the nonprofit life. When the free software movement began, it was difficult to make money by programming other than to write proprietary software. There was no example to follow to build a commercial model for free software.

The only possibilities were to compromise, as Larry Wall did, and work for proprietary projects for a salary but write free software whenever possible, or make little money.

> Only if we have the fundamental right to own information do we also have the fundamental right to give information away, freely and without coercion. Simply because we want to, not because we have to.[10]   —"First State of the Perl Onion"

Wall understands the computing community as a system composed of the worlds of proprietary and free software. The many people who work and play in both worlds keep the two in orbit.

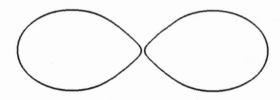

At one end of the free software world, pulling hard away from the proprietary world, is Richard Stallman. At the opposite end of the proprietary software world, pulling just as hard, is Bill Gates. Comparing this situation to an acetylene molecule, Wall says:

> Let me be specific. Some folks in this room are extremely leery of Bill [Gates]. Others are extremely leery of Richard [Stallman]. These people tend to be leery not only of the opposite hydrogen, but also the opposite carbon. They are supplying the repulsive forces, because they fear the opposite extreme.[11]
> —"Third State of the Perl Onion"

What Wall has found is that though he lives in the complexity of the free software world, he is more comfortable near the center. He felt that his relationship with Tim O'Reilly, who has created a publishing empire founded on proprietary materials for programmers (such as Wall's own Perl programming manual) is mutually beneficial and to his liking. He thinks O'Reilly represents the best of the proprietary world, encouraging the growth of free software, and even hiring Wall in 1996 to work on Perl. Any increase in the usage of Perl translates into increased sales of the O'Reilly-published Perl manuals. Wall wanted the Perl culture to include both the fanatics, the people who love Perl and work only with Perl, and the multiple joiners, the missionaries and merchants, who see simply Perl as a useful tool among many.

Maintaining all these virtues may seem paradoxical, but Wall asserts they are not. What is required is an ability to change one's perspective. There are times to ignore one's natural impulses, and be humble and patient. But there are also times to trust one's instincts. While this seems like common sense, most programmers rarely use common sense. They prefer logical systems that give only one right answer. By promoting a complex, paradoxical way of looking at things, Wall is challenging technologists to transform their philosophy of life. With Perl, he is promoting a balanced, flexible, and organic philosophy in contrast to the rule-driven, inflexible, and mechanical philosophy that has dominated both computing and theology.

> If there's a germ of an important idea in Perl Culture, it's this: that too much control is just as deadly as too little control. We need control and we need chaos. We need order, and disorder. Simplicity, and complexity. Carefulness, and recklessness. Poise, and panic. Science, and art.[12]
>
> —"First State of the Perl Onion"

To that end, Wall sees that everything is interconnected and even intertwingled. He admires messiness, complexity. After all, he designed Perl to be two things: a text-processing language and a glue language. Glue works because it is messy—because it is a complex chemical soup, able to interact and bind with all kinds of surfaces. Perl, with its complex and redundant design, fills in the cracks like glue. Neither glue nor Perl solves every problem, but each lets you bring things together.

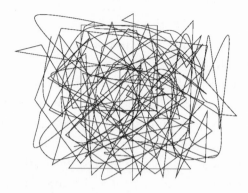

The secret Wall preaches is that as long as you can find patterns within complexity, messiness ceases to be a problem. You can try to follow all the air molecules bouncing around a room or you can understand them usefully in terms of temperature and pressure. You can try to understand the entire World Wide Web or follow your interests to get the answers you need. As long as you're given the tools to find what you need amid the messiness, as long as there are some rules, even if they're arbitrary or contradictory, you can navigate successfully. As Marvin Minsky tells us in *Society of Mind,* our minds can handle complexity by dint of agents that "unstick" it. This applies to everything from programming code to reprogramming our minds, to reprogramming our institutions.

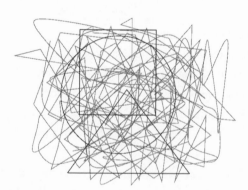

AFTERWARD

From the perspective of the outside world, Stallman and Wall seem identical. They are both programmers, organizers, and proselytizers of two of the largest and most popular free software projects in the world: GNU and Perl. They are popular speakers and prolific expositors of an alternative to the world of commercial software development. They love their work.

Yet the differences abound. While both attach the GPL to their work, Wall sees nothing wrong in supporting the proprietary model of the O'Reilly manuals, since they complement Perl's free, online documentation. Because good documentation is essential to the use of complex programs, Stallman thinks that making such documentation unshareable is wrong.

Wall believes that the coercive nature of Stallman's GPL is indicative of his atheism. He believes that a sense of morality and obligation derives from a belief in God, not from social pressures. He sees the corporate attempts to control individual behavior and the communist attempts to form collectives as two sides of the same coin. He has even called it a "hive mentality," a science fiction concept in which people lose all sense of identity and act like ants or bees in a colony, mindlessly fulfilling the goals of the collective. Wall finds Stallman's moral attitude to be impractical and polarizing, promoting conflict instead of peace. His own moral guidance comes from the Christian belief that every person is valuable in God's eye, but at the same time should strive to be humble. His measure of success, therefore, is intelligent cooperation and compassion, not just for those who agree with him but also for those who disagree. Whereas Stallman has drawn the battle lines in the sand, Wall strives to achieve redemptive subversion from the heart outward, whether subverting a bad person, a bad company, or a bad culture.

Stallman, motivated by the powerful emotions of the downtrodden, the dismissed, the disdained, has created a counterbalance to proprietary software in the GNU project and the Free Software Foundation. He doesn't believe his efforts support a hive mentality, or that people shouldn't be selfish or celebrate individuality. Rather, he is against giving individuals the power to dominate and divide others. In the course of his career this quiet and shy man has slowly come out of his shell, a near-religious figure in his own right, simultaneously loved and reviled.

Stallman's message about how free software can help government, business, and education has reached many corners of the globe. March 2001 marked the launch of Free Software Foundation Europe and, four months later, the opening of the Free Software Foundation India, the first affiliate in Asia. He believes that free software will help bridge the digital divide and also level the playing field for developing nations as they join the Information Revolution. Computer users in countries that struggle with oppressive regimes such as Burma (of particular interest to Stallman), can empower themselves by developing indigenous software communities and industries. Proprietary software mystifies technology, and this is a form of oppression; free software demystifies technology and makes it a tool of liberation.

Stallman also sees a direct connection between the free-software movement and the global protests against the trade agreements ruled by corporate interests and dehumanizing economic policies. He believes the forces that destroyed his hacker community, the placement of profit over people, are destroying communities all over the globe. Nike sweatshops in Indonesia, police brutality and racial profiling, first-world nations preventing poor countries from manufacturing inexpensive AIDS medication—are all abuses of power by institutions over people. He has nothing against entrepeneurialism and business—but he sees little good in the massive, unchecked power wielded by the gigantic multinational conglomerates with interests completely removed from that of the freedom of individuals.

Programming is primarily an artistic endeavor, an act of intellectual joy and love that Stallman and Wall want people everywhere around the world to realize and share. Both now spend as much time goading the free software community as they do coding, although Wall is currently leading the effort to build Perl 6, a complete rewrite of Perl.

The culture that is growing out of the free software movement is one that is learning to handle the complexities of both technology and human relationships. It empowers people with tools to create and contribute to the programming environment that increasingly affects us all.

THE ⓇEVOLUTION AND THE LAW

ERIC S. RAYMOND AND LAWRENCE LESSIG

> Undoubtedly, it would be very pleasant for us mice if
> the predatory cats of the world were to be belled,
> but—who is going to do it? Who is going to assure
> us that ruthless power will not find its way back into
> the hands of those most avid for it?
> —Norbert Wiener

THE PHILOSOPHY behind Richard Stallman and Larry Wall's free software has implications far beyond computers. It is a new model for the creation, distribution, and regulation of knowledge. It incorporates Norbert Wiener's belief in the circulation of information through regulatory feedback. It embraces J. C. R. Licklider and Doug Engelbart's theory that technology can help people communicate; that humankind will evolve by sharing problems and solutions. It supports Seymour Papert and Alan Kay's conviction that developing software is a joyful and creative act and that people think best when they are equipped to experiment freely. It holds the promise to be the infrastructure of Marshall McLuhan's global village and Abbie Hoffman's free society, transforming business, government, education, and technology alike. The software in our computers shapes the outside world.

Despite its promise, many forces oppose free and open development of software. The Internet is a testament to this, as it morphed from a center of research into a sphere of commercial activity. The code of the Net has changed, symbolically and in actuality, since Tim Berners-Lee introduced the Web in the early 1990s. Web businesses, the dotcoms, spontaneously generated into being, offering everything from books to cut-rate electronics, twenty-four hour junk food delivery, digital design, pornography, and dirt-cheap airline tickets. The corporations that own commercial territories like AOL and shopping sites can't—or won't—operate in the tradition of the free Internet. Users realized that corporate and governmental interests could threaten their rights of privacy and free speech by implementing architectures of control in the form of proprietary software.

When Norbert Wiener applied cybernetics to human systems—society— he came to the conclusion that information is meant to be shared, not held secret. He adopted the Greek word κυβερνετεσ, meaning "steersman," to imply the way in which a system must be regulated so that information (whether nerve cells in a body or electronic pulses in a machine) can flow optimally. It means that a system needs to be regulated in order to be free. Regulation can mean a degree of governmental control. Or it could mean a sort of free-market self-regulation, depending upon your point of view.

In the mid-1990s a legal scholar, L. Lawrence Lessig III, and a software activist, Eric S. Raymond, contemplated the regulation of the Net. Raymond and Lessig started to wonder: To what extent is the Web really free? In what direction are we headed? How does control, regulation, affect the Internet and the Web?

Lessig has aimed for openness on the Net through a balance between private and public interests and the enforcement of the rights of privacy and free speech through good governmental regulation. Raymond, who also calls himself a "wandering anthropologist and troublemaking philosopher," has adopted a development method on efficiency grounds. His belief is that the open Internet can fuel the open market, which translates into personal freedoms and the obsolescence of government. Raymond's and Lessig's manifestos—*The Cathedral and the Bazaar* (1997) and *Code and Other Laws of Cyberspace* (1999), respectively— express opposing and overlapping visions concerning the implications of open code on the Net. Both stand against the dramatic backdrop of the biggest power struggles of the Information Revolution to date, involving governmental regulation of information and the power of major corporations like Microsoft and AOL Time Warner.

THE BAZAAR

Raymond (best known by his handle "ESR") has a lot in common with Ted Nelson and Richard Stallman. All three realized early on that the way information is structured, delivered, and accessed on a computer can be intensely political. They believe knowledge should be shared and detest the idea of any authority barring access to information. They are extreme personalities who dabble in eccentric pursuits. Raymond, a balding, mustached, potbellied martial arts aficionado, writes epic Viking/Anglo-Saxon poetry for live-action role-playing games. Modeling himself after characters in Heinlein's science fiction, he provides a link on his Web page to his gun rights site where he rhapsodizes about the ethics of gun wielding—"It all comes down to you . . . No one else's finger is on the trigger but your own. . . ."

Raymond, Stallman, and Nelson are also master propagators of the hacker myth. In the tradition of the hackers in Stallman's AI Lab they have fortified ordinary computer users with a heroic mission: Defend your rights! They have written manifestos that have not only shaped the computer fanatic's self-image, but also, in so doing, the world's hardware and software environments. Between them, they have created the legend of the heroic hacker as a rogue individual who intrepidly fights against massive and menacing power, usually governmental or corporate.

In the 1987 update to *Computer Lib*, Ted Nelson asserted: NOW YOU CAN BE OPPRESSED BY COMPUTERS IN YOUR LIVING ROOM. To Nelson, the enemies were authoritarian companies like IBM, the government, and all others who had vested interests in either harvesting private information or forcing the public into one stagnant paradigm. To Stallman, the evil is the repression of the hacker community for the sake of proprietary software. To Raymond, the enemy is the monolithic entity—quintessentially Microsoft or the government.

Raymond's manifesto, *The Cathedral and the Bazaar,* addresses the folly of the hierarchical corporation (the "cathedral") and the viability of an open, decentralized alternative (the "bazaar").

> Linus Torvalds's style of development—release early and often, delegate everything you can, be open to the point of promiscuity—came as a surprise. No quiet, reverent cathedral-building here—rather, the Linux community seemed to resemble a great babbling bazaar of differing agendas and approaches ... out of which a coherent and stable system could seemingly emerge only by a succession of miracles.[1]
>
> —*The Cathedral and the Bazaar*

Eric S. Raymond published the first draft of *The Cathedral and the Bazaar* in 1997. A year later, he adopted an alternative name for free software, "*open source*," and founded the Open Source Initiative. In a planning session with Raymond and others, Christine Peterson, the executive director of the Foresight Institute, a nanotechnology think tank, coined the term. Bruce Perens drafted the Open Source Definition, the formative document of the movement, and announced it to the world. Like-minded free software advocates, including Tim O'Reilly and Larry Wall, enthusiastically supported the Open Source Initiative from the start. They thought "open source" would gain more than "free software."

Although Richard Stallman repeatedly said information wants to be "free" as in free speech—not free beer—outsiders were turned off by the Free Software Foundation's openly political mission to fight proprietary software. Raymond, although one of the first contributors to the GNU Project, stated, "In the battle we are fighting now, ideology is just a handicap. We need to be making arguments based on economics and development processes and expected return. We do not need to behave like Communards pumping our fists on the barricades. This is a losing strategy."[2] He and his colleagues considered Open Source a more marketable term than free software, with fewer anticommercial connotations. The open-source license, the OSD, offers companies more leeway than Stallman's GPL, because one may incorporate open source code into proprietary software. The GPL, meanwhile, ensures that free software remains free for all.

The two camps are functionally similar but philosophically distinct.

The open-source premise of the voluntary renunciation of copyright is justified by market economics (although not necessarily driven by economic factors). Free software is based on the argument that source code should be available because it harms society for it to be otherwise.

RULES OF THE BAZAAR

The leading open-source software of the late 1990s and early 2000s is GNU/Linux, jumpstarted by the Linux kernel of Linus Torvalds, who has led its development.* Before the tremendous success of Linux, Raymond thought major software could only be developed in "Cathedrals," by hacker-priests or arcane corporate bureaucracies. But a wild gaggle, the "bazaar," developed Linux—and it worked amazingly well. Somehow it tapped the collective IQ that Doug Engelbart sought through his NLS system, only now possible on the Net. Raymond sought to discover how the bazaar worked, against all expectations. He tried it with a free software project of his own (the *fetch-mail* program), and then proselytized it in "The Cathedral and the Bazaar." His manifesto features practical maxims:

> *"Release early. Release often. And listen to your customers."*
>
> *"Perfection (in design) is achieved not when there is nothing more to add, but rather when there's nothing more to take away."*(As adapted from Antoine de Saint-Exupéry) †
>
> *"Given enough eyeballs, all bugs are shallow."*

The Cathedral and the Bazaar made it clear that the bazaar method of development is plausible for any project hooked into the Net. Raymond disclosed that his fetchmail project alone fetched more than 600 contributors—1200 eyeballs. What closed-source developer could

---

*In his writings, Raymond simply calls the system "Linux."

†This is a direct gibe at Microsoft, whose applications are renowned for "featuritis," the phenomenon of adding as many features to a single application as possible, whether or not they're necessary or even barely useful.

compete with that? Microsoft wouldn't hire 600 "cathedral builders" to work on just one piece of a system—the equivalent of one stained glass window.

> In the cathedral-builder view of programming, bugs and development problems are tricky, insidious deep phenomena. It takes months of scrutiny by a dedicated few to develop confidence that you've winkled them all out. . . . In the bazaar view, on the other hand, you assume that bugs are generally shallow phenomena—or, at least, that they turn shallow quickly when exposed to a thousand eager co-developers pounding on every new release.[3]   —*The Cathedral and the Bazaar*

In cathedral-style development, the world is divided into two: developers and users. Only those inside the Cathedral, other developers, usually get to see and manipulate the secret source code—everyone outside must accept what is sent out. Although GNU Emacs, FreeBSD, and other free and open-source software have been developed Cathedral-style, most are developed in the Bazaar. In the bazaar everyone, from the master hacker to the newbie user, is allowed access to the source. Any user can be a developer. Everyone can contribute—and if the project is properly designed, everyone will. As a result of Raymond's manifesto bazaar-style software development became more popular while cathedral-style software became less popular and associated with proprietary projects.

Bazaar-style development is an organic process executed on an unprecedented scale; it works only under the proper conditions. The bazaar cannot be complete anarchy. For one, Raymond noted that an open-source project cannot be *initiated* in a ground-up grassroots style. A project must originate with a Stallmanesque or Torvaldian inspiration: one person (or group of people) with a kernel of a program and a vision for growing it. If he or she builds it—creates a stable foundation and guides the construction—they will come. After all, even a populist uprising must have its leaders. GNU wouldn't exist without Stallman and those who have been inspired by his ideas and code. The Linux kernel wouldn't exist if it weren't for both its humble, encouraging, creative Finnish leader. Nor would fetchmail (or perhaps the programmer-as-hero myth) exist without the flamboyant Eric S. Raymond.

On the other hand, the bazaar encourages ground-up work in project execution: testing, debugging, developing, and overall code improvement. As with Kay's Smalltalk, organic modularity is key to the process: Programmers can swap and switch organelles of code with ease. A hierarchy of sorts is implicit, at least in the sense that each project should have a leader/coordinator—a charismatic, modest, wise individual who can gently guide a community of free-thinking programmers willing to work for, well, free.

Raymond believes that in open source an *internal market* ultimately selects what leaders and projects will be successful. The community chooses its own leaders by only developing projects headed by the successful coordinators. This, he asserts, is a new leadership style that is based not on a power relationship, but on consensus.

> *"Treating Your Users as Co-Developers is Your Least-Hassle Route to Rapid Code Improvement and Effective Debugging."*

Just as the leader/coordinator of an open source project isn't a tyrannical master, the thousands of user-developers building it aren't drones. Nor are they completely altruistic, Raymond notes. Richard Stallman exhorts fellow programmers to write free code from moral incentives—a conviction that knowledge should be shared, not hoarded. Raymond emphasizes more selfish principles. His stand is that the pragmatic programmer is likely to not mind proprietary commercialism as much as Stallman. He or she simply supports open source to use and develop better tools than ever possible in a proprietary arrangement.

To many programmers, the fun of the collaborative coding challenge is incentive enough. The fun factor, after all, is what Ted Nelson and Alan Kay also emphasized. Using computers and writing code should be an enjoyable, deeply creative, and personally rewarding experience, as Papert found with Logo. Just as a fair guarantees better turnout than a Sunday church service, the bazaar atmosphere of an open source project attracts more people *because they have fun.* Marshall McLuhan and

Abbie Hoffman's dream that the information age would make drudgery and work obsolete is coming true.

> It may turn out that one of the most important effects of open source's success will be to teach us that play is the most economically efficient mode of creative work.[4]
>
> —The Cathedral and the Bazaar

The principle Raymond emphasizes the most is status or "egoboo"—a term meaning ego boost that he took from science-fiction fandom. A good programmer gets credit from his or her peers. Raymond, the amateur anthropologist, explains that the drive to compete for social status is hardwired into human culture. Programmers have a gift culture, not unlike aboriginal cultures that live in places where the climate is mild and the food is abundant. As a result, status is more important than ownership. And status is defined by what one gives away as a gift. In return for the best gifts, the best code, one gets egoboo, along with greater support and participation for one's own projects. Sometimes "gift-giving" translates into material reward. But egoboo is a currency unto itself— perhaps a more valuable one than monetary when other human needs are already fulfilled; most gift-giving programmers are gainfully employed in some capacity. The theoretical underpinning of this is straight from the 1960s: The question is no longer how one makes money, but how to satisfy one's psychological needs.

> By properly rewarding the egos of many other hackers, a strong developer/coordinator can use the Internet to capture the benefits of having lots of co-developers without having a project collapse into a chaotic mess.[5]
>
> —The Cathedral and the Bazaar

The Cathedral and the Bazaar was written so that a person with an MBA could appreciate the benefits of nonproprietary, bazaar-style software development. With this model, the code would benefit from thousands of contributors catching bugs and investing time, energy, and belief in the product. Accordingly, good software never dies—new contributors keep improving it year after year. You don't need management to cajole and interest their underlings—egoboo provides a stronger motivation than whip-cracking. Once the project becomes a must-have application, other people would do the work of porting it to new technologies.

The publication of *The Cathedral and the Bazaar* online and in book form (1999) resulted in a convincing and resounding triumph for the bazaar—and ESR himself. His supporters abbreviated it to "CatB." CatB's readership extended far and wide online and offline. On January 22, 1998, about eight months after the paper debuted, Eric Hahn, Executive VP and CTO of Netscape Communications, made an unprecedented announcement: They would give away, *reveal,* the source code for Netscape Communicator. Hahn emailed Raymond to thank him for the thoughts behind "The Cathedral and the Bazaar," informing him that CatB was an inspirational influence behind the decision. Netscape executives called him to hire him as a consultant (along with Torvalds and Stallman). Raymond hung up the phone in a daze.

That next month Raymond and his team of likeminded free software advocates came up with open source to describe bazaar-style open code software development and began the open source Initiative. With Netscape's decision, OSI got the proverbial key to the executive bathroom. But Raymond knew that if Netscape went down the toilet, so could any credibility for open source.

Either way, it was significant egoboo.

NETSCAPE

Jim Clark and Marc Andreessen, Netscape's founders, intended to develop a *commercial* browser for the Web. While Tim Berners-Lee's inspiration for the Web was pure research, Andreessen and Clark focused on business principles: development, marketing, and customer service. In 1994 they founded Mosaic Communications Corporation. Later that year they renamed themselves Netscape and changed their browser's name from Mosaic to Navigator. Navigator, downloadable for free, accelerated the development of the Web by many orders of magnitude. It rapidly became the dominant Web browser, and in 1995 it easily fended off even Microsoft's attempt at competition, Internet Explorer.

In 1998, Microsoft, initially behind the curve on the Internet, announced its intention to integrate Explorer 4.0 in its new operating system, Windows 98, making it a default part of the desktop on every personal computer that runs Windows. The move, if successful, could demolish Netscape. Clark and Andreessen hoped that going open source would gain Netscape a wider market share over Explorer.

Clark and Andreessen were convinced that they could harness the power of open source and still make a profit by becoming service based. This reflected Raymond's belief that software is inherently a service-based business that has been viewed and treated as a manufacturing-type business. The first major service-based business success was Cygnus Support, later renamed Cygnus Solutions, and finally acquired by Red Hat—a GNU/Linux distributor and service provider. Although Red Hat has no proprietary claim whatsoever on the code it is distributing and supporting—anyone can do the same thing—the company thrived by building its own reputation and brand. That reputation allows Red Hat to keep the best developers on its payroll, so that it won't fall behind any other company. With the new open-source-based business model, corporations like Red Hat are turning a profit and synergistically supporting open source software.*

While Microsoft bet on its monopolistic cathedral, Netscape threw open its gates to the bazaar. Netscape set up the nonprofit Mozilla.org, to coordinate the open-source development process both inside and outside the corporation and to maintain the source code. Netscape's paid engineers spearheaded the project, and the larger Web community contributed more as the process developed. The only way Netscape could compete with Bill Gates, Raymond reckoned, was to change the rules.

Just as Norbert Wiener asserted that information cannot be locked

---

*Other corporations have since embraced this model. In 2000, IBM's annual report announced, "We're betting a big part of IBM's future on Linux," pledging $1 billion and fifteen-thousand programmers to switch all IBM hardware and software to the operating system. Raymond was right—the Netscape deal got open source into even the most corporate of all boardrooms.

in secret vaults for long, Raymond insisted that Netscape's move toward open source would inevitably happen throughout the industry. In Raymond's opinion, closed-source Microsoft is doomed because its profit incentive is founded on trade secrets, not improved software. A company like Microsoft tries to spend as little as possible on supporting its software while making consumers believe they are getting his money's worth. Raymond, like Stallman, believes it's only a matter of time before consumers wake up and realize that they are being scammed—and that there is a better alternative.

LESSIG AND GOLIATH

The Netscape versus Microsoft story is quintessentially the struggle between the piranhic corporation versus the innovative small fish. By 1998 Microsoft's plan to integrate (to bundle) Internet Explorer into its Windows 98 operating system jumpstarted an antitrust case with the U.S. Department of Justice and nineteen states. Microsoft asserted that an integrated browser worked better with other Microsoft applications. The Justice Department believed it was a classic use of one monopoly, in operating systems, to establish another, in Web browsers—a violation of the Sherman Antitrust Law of 1890.*

Could all the promise of open source actually protect Netscape from extinction if more than 80 percent of all desktops were Windows systems and Explorer became part of the Windows code? What incentive would users have to download Navigator if Explorer were the default browser on their desktop, removable only by extreme measures? Customers couldn't really *choose for themselves.*

The person driving the case against Microsoft in the court of public opinion was the young, wiry, bespectacled Harvard University professor named Lawrence Lessig. Like Eric Raymond, Lessig studied philosophy at the University of Pennsylvania, and later entered a field dedicated to

---

*Sponsored by the brother of the Civil War general, the Sherman Antitrust Law of 1890 invoked in the Microsoft case was a populist backlash against the industrial monopolies of the late nineteenth century in oil, steel, and rail. Theodore Roosevelt and Edward Taft, his successor, used it to break Rockefeller's Standard Oil monopoly in 1911. Prosecutors accused Bill Gates of being the new Rockefeller.

revealing the effects of technology on society. Raymond decided to enter it through his work as a programmer. Lessig entered it as a lawyer.

Born in South Dakota, Lessig grew up in the small town of Williamsport, Pennsylvania, best known as the home of the Little League World Series. After graduating from Penn with a degree in economics, he followed Alan Turing, Marshall McLuhan, and Seymour Papert to Cambridge University, getting a master's in philosophy in 1986. He then went on to Yale Law School and quickly distinguished himself as a top constitutional lawyer, after graduating in 1989. He clerked for the Supreme Court justice Antonin Scalia as the token liberal surrounded by collegially hostile conservatives. At the age of thirty, he joined the faculty at the University of Chicago, later Harvard and finally Stanford Law School. With his involvement in the Microsoft case and related writings, Lessig became the definitive legal expert on the Internet and computing.

Lessig's life has shaped and reflected his beliefs about the role of government in society. In 1985, while at Cambridge, he smuggled a heart valve to a Jewish dissident behind the Iron Curtain in the Soviet Union. His wife, Bettina Neuefeind, investigated the genocidal crimes of the Yugoslavian government in Kosovo. Lessig has learned firsthand the lasting and personal effects of the cold war. He saw how political and legal doctrine is not a vague, impersonal theory but an architecture, lasting for generations, that can determine whether people live or die. He could see that the architecture of the future lay within the electronic musings of computers.

Lessig advised the Microsoft case's district court judge, Thomas Penfield Jackson, on the legal and technological issues of the case. He compared Microsoft to the Ma Bell monopoly, and declared Microsoft illegal for annihilating its competition in the browser market. He argued that Microsoft's browser and operating system should be regarded as two separate and discrete products, despite Microsoft's assertions to the contrary.

In 1999 Lessig published the best-selling *Code and Other Laws of Cyberspace*. In it the self-proclaimed constitutionalist argues that government should intelligently regulate the Internet to prevent evils such as monopolies and infringements of individual rights like privacy and free speech. He argues that the absence of regulation is *not* freedom. Lessig wanted the Internet to continue to be a place of freedom as Licklider and Berners-Lee intended—not a place of oppressive control, ruled by monopolistic corporations like Microsoft. We need laws for the Net that protect the freedoms of the people—to the greatest extent possible. We need the law to step in occasionally.

> Liberty in cyberspace will not come from the absence of the state.... Cyberspace, left to itself, will not fulfill the promise of freedom. Left to itself, cyberspace will become the perfect tool of control. [6]   —*Code and Other Laws of Cyberspace*

Lessig thought Microsoft represented every possible threat to a free Net. He joked in an email message about "selling his soul" by using Microsoft software. He accused the company of goading and threatening software rivals and hardware makers like Compaq by manipulating licensing agreements and access to codes needed to make non-Microsoft programs compatible with Windows. Microsoft ferociously attacked Lessig, declaring him biased and improperly appointed as "special master" to the judge. The judge rejected the charge.

In Lessig's "friend of the court" letter, he notes that the courts had been hesitant to apply centuries of legal doctrine to the software industry because they maintain the view that "code is different." Lessig believed that "it is a mistake to fetishize code in this way." Computer technology might seem like magic, but it isn't.

On June 7, 2000, with Lessig's counsel, Judge Thomas Penfield Jackson ruled that Microsoft did indeed violate the antitrust laws. He compared the corporation to a drug gang and likened Bill Gates to Napoleon. He ordered the company to be split in two and placed restrictions on its business practices. The breakup would have placed the Windows operating system in one company and created a second business for everything else, including software applications like Internet Explorer. Judge Jackson also set a long list of restrictions on Microsoft's conduct to last three years if the breakup order withstood appeal, and ten years if it didn't. Microsoft, of course, immediately appealed. On

June 28, 2001, the appeals court determined that Microsoft had violated the Sherman Antitrust Law and improperly commingled software code of the browser and operating system. They reversed the decision, however, to split Microsoft into two separate companies and reproved Jackson for opining to reporters about the case. They sent the case down to a new judge to determine the remedy for Microsoft's multiple violations.

NAVIGATOR LOSES ITS WAY

While Microsoft was on the stand for antitrust in the browser war, Netscape and Mozilla proceeded with its open source strategy. In 1999 Eric Raymond described Netscape and Mozilla as only a "qualified success" for open source. Mozilla, Raymond claimed, violated one of the foremost rules of open source outlined in CatB: Release early and release often. Jamie Zawinski, one of the key project leaders, resigned on Mozilla's one-year anniversary, declaring that Netscape was not a truly network-collaborative project because not enough outside programmers participated in project development.

What went wrong with open source? Zawinski feared it was the fact that, unlike other open-source projects, Mozilla was too much a subsidiary of Netscape, a corporate entity. In his tenure at Mozilla, Zawinski tried hard to convince hackers that he and his fellow Netscape Communications employees were just humble guides. The real Mozilla project existed in the hands of the community at large. But it wasn't exactly true.

In November 1998 the unthinkable happened: AOL, America's most popular Internet service provider and a corporate behemoth on the order of Microsoft, bought out Netscape Communications for $4 billion. The deal was good for investors, but not for users, who knew that large corporate mergers are detrimental to personal freedoms on the Net. Zawinski at first hoped that AOL would be enlightened about Mozilla, and not act as a "shambling inhuman beast of a corporation."[7] But his hopes were soon dashed. Thousands of Netscape employees followed the departure of Netscape founder Marc Andreessen. Zawinski, after tendering his resignation, fomented against Netscape for merging into AOL.

The Internet was changing from a place of freedom to a place of oppression:

> AOL is about centralization and control of content. . . .
> Everything that is good about the Internet, everything that
> differentiates it from television, is about empowerment of the
> individual. I don't want to be a part of an effort that could
> result in the elimination of all that.[8]

In January 2000, AOL became an even more shambling, inhuman beast with the acquisition of Time Warner, the world's largest media company and number one cable provider, for about $163 billion in stock. The deal was the biggest merger ever.*

By the time Microsoft's antitrust case was appealed in 2001, the browser war seemed over. As Mozilla slowly developed, Microsoft exploited its power to give Internet Explorer a dominating lead in market share. Netscape became a minor province in Time Warner's media empire, which spans magazines and movie studios, cartoons and cable networks.

In the aftermath of the merger, Zawinski voiced that AOL Time Warner is an atrocious example of centralization and control of all media, including electronic media. AOL, he feared, would become the primary channel by which the public receives information. It would bias the Net. Of this he said:

> It leads inevitably to a reduction of choices and a reduction
> of viewpoints that can become heard. That kind of control
> of the entire communication infrastructure, from content cre-
> ation, through marketing, to end-user delivery, is just a dis-
> aster as far as true Democracy goes.

---

*The AOL-Time Warner merger and Viacom's purchase of CBS mean that all TV networks, top film studios, major music labels, major cable channels, and most popular websites are under the control of just *seven* media conglomerates.

THE ARCHITECTURE AND THE MESSAGE

In 1948 Norbert Wiener warned us that it is when

> The Lords of Things as They Are protect themselves from
> hunger by wealth, from public opinion by privacy and
> anonymity, from private criticism by the laws of libel and the
> possession of the means of communication, that ruthlessness
> can reach its most sublime levels. Of all these . . . the con-
> trol of the means of communication is the most effective and
> the most important.[9]

Abbie Hoffman fought against the Lords of Things as They Are a generation later when television became the dominant means of communication.
Can the Net escape the same fate, of becoming under the control of totalitarian multinational corporations and governmental bureaucracies? How
are the Lords making the Net controllable, or, in Lessig's terms, *regulable*?

The institutions are making the Net regulable, Lessig discovered, under
the umbrella of *commerce*. Companies built commerce-enabling architectures
on top of and into the free Net of Licklider and Berners-Lee, ignoring or deliberately causing harm to individual freedoms. One way commerce-enabling
architectures affect the common citizen is through proprietary identification
technologies, such as "cookies." Companies prefer to deal with people they
can identify so they can tailor their product to consumers' spending patterns
and special interests. The more information they have about you, from your
favorite color to your birth date, fingerprint, and social security number, the
better. People, in the role of consumers, have reason to give away their information and lose anonymity—access to sites, secure transactions, and per-
sonalization. By selling products to you, companies get to own a bit of you.

The more powerful and prevalent the corporation, the more information
it can attain about you. Lessig provides the example of America Online. Users
must log into AOL using a password. AOL can identify who you are and
track your postings and purchases. AOL hires content police to ensure your
behavior is enforced. AOL can block communication between certain members. AOL can monitor your every move. AOL's code cannot be changed by
its members. AOL limits its crowds to twenty-three people at a time. AOL
is not a democracy; the management controls the space. Not to mention

knowing your spending patterns and special interests and applying them in commercially useful ways throughout the AOL Time Warner media empire. The software code is the legal code and it is a tool of control. In return, AOL provides conveniences to its members like informing them when other members are online and catering to individual interests. As Richard Stallman says, businesses will tempt you to give up your freedom by offering you gifts.

> Life will be easier for those who carry a [digital] ID than for those
> who don't.[10]   —*Code and Other Laws of Cyberspace*

Government, Lessig claims, may join forces with commerce to build this architecture of regulation on the Net. Although it may not regulate the Net directly, it can through commercial entities—by regulating *them*. A government could regulate gambling sites (by requiring that a digital ID verifies that the user lives in a state where gambling is legal), which in turn would force the market to regulate users on the Net. But why stop at gambling sites? All sorts of information pass over the Net that may interest governments—political opinions, classified data, even songs and mathematical equations.

Any sort of filtering or agent technology can operate hand-in-hand with digital IDs to cripple the tenets of democracy. W3C's PICs software for content selection, championed by Berners-Lee for parents to censor the Web for their children, is one such filter. It censors the Net just as an old-fashioned English butler would bar entry to an estate. Lessig realized the technology enables users to ban *anything* that doesn't match their personal ideologies (for example, only viewing sites approved by the Christian Right). A government or corporation could make filters part of the architecture of the Net. Such zoning and censorship could occur at any level—hardwired into the browser or into the ISP. The Net itself will become more fragmented, more subservient to special interests, less cohesive. If the Net is so corrupted, the technologies imagined and developed by Engelbart, Kay, and Nelson would actually work against their ideals. The Net wouldn't be a tool for dialogue, collaboration, and democracy. If precautionary steps aren't taken, the Net could actually become *anti*democratic.

> If there is speech the government has an interest in controlling,
> then let that control be obvious to the users. Only when

regulation is transparent is a political response possible.[11]
—Code and Other Laws of Cyberspace

. . . .

Corporations and governments can even regulate the Net geographically, by programming servers to discriminate against users from certain locations, as long as they can tell the location given the IP address or domain name. Countries like China could build a highly regulated Net to block access to politically charged information to outsiders. Corporations could bar certain people under certain ages from certain places on the Internet. Whoever has access to encrypted identification data can discriminate based on age, sex, medical status, political affiliation, race.

OPEN CONTROL

Lawrence Lessig, like Eric S. Raymond, is not against private enterprise. Neither the lawyer nor the open source activist is bound by ethical and moral imperatives to keep the Net wholly free of commercial interests. Lessig, as demonstrated by his stand in the Microsoft antitrust trial, believes in an active government, although he does voice his warnings and criticisms. What we must aspire to, he reasons, is a fine balance between regulation and freedom. Just as the framers of the U.S. Constitution aimed to ensure an equilibrium of power between the federal government and the individual states, industry, and individuals, so we need checks and balances on the powers that control the architecture of the Net. Lessig says that when commercial interests determine the architecture, they create a kind of privatized law. Although he is not against private enterprise, he does believe in limits to the free market. What is good for America Online is not necessarily good for America.

The limits to corporate and governmental power lie in the transparency of intention. Regulation isn't inherently wrong, Lessig argues; what is dangerous is *invisible* regulation. A closed, proprietary architecture hides commercial and governmental intent. If intent is hidden, the architecture can encourage any kind of wrong, such as covertly favoring one power, as in Berners-Lee's example of agent technologies that find only sponsors' products. The more code is open and available to the public, the more government and corporate power is constrained from abuse of power.

This all leads back to free software and open source. Lessig states that *open code is the crucial check on power on the Net*. There are several excellent reasons for supporting open code-software*: it's more robust, it's shareable, and its intent is transparent. For this reason he has praised Eric S. Raymond's *The Cathedral and the Bazaar* as *the* compelling essay that has defined the movement. "Open code is open control—there is control, but the user is aware of it."[12] Code developed in the bazaar makes it yet more transparent to the knowledgeable public. Each individual part is comprehensible to an individual who understands the principles of code.[†] Open code is, as Lessig deems it, a "A Freedom of Information Act for network regulation." He says it is the foundation to an open society.

> In a way that the American founders would have instinctively understood, ..."open code" ... is itself a check on arbitrary power. A structural guarantee of constitutionalized liberty, it functions as a type of separation of powers in the American constitutional tradition.[13]   —*Code and Other Laws of Cyberspace*

Yet, even if the code is open, how will the law be upheld? Lessig argues that the courts must determine constitutional values and must make constitutional choices about the Net. A dialogue begin—*now*—about what values the Net should have. To what extent does the U.S. Constitution guide us on the Net? What new values must we articulate for democracy and the rights of citizens? Who will make them lucid and enforceable?

Ideally, Lessig answers, the values of free speech, privacy, due process, and equality on the Net should be resolved in a responsible,

---

*Lessig calls it "open code," to avoid taking sides between "free software" and "open source."

[†]As society spends more time on computers, that is, within the architecture of code, it becomes ever more important that every citizen understand the principles of programming. Code is written for humans to read. Seymour Papert, Ted Nelson, and Alan Kay also explicitly argued that at least a limited ability to program computers is crucial to the preservation of democracy in the information age.

---

democratic forum. He fears that courts, in America and around the world, will step away from resolving these dilemmas because they are intimidated by the newness of the issues raised by the Net. But, then again, he asks: If there is no government or court system that represents and enforces these values, then who will? If code is law, who are the lawmakers? What values are being embedded in the code?

On these questions Lessig, the liberal and Raymond, the civil libertarian, part ways.

RAYMOND'S RETORT

In 1999, the society of Computer Professionals for Social Responsibility presented the Norbert Wiener Award to the open-source / free software movement. Eric S. Raymond, Richard M. Stallman, Larry Wall, and Brian Behlendorf (of Apache) accepted the award. Raymond wrote the following about liberty and law on the Net in his acceptance speech:

> All too often, people who invoke "social responsibility" are demanding that we give up individual liberty—that we accept just a bit more taxation, just a bit more regulation, just a bit more governmental intrusiveness, all for the supposed good of society. . . .We cannot leave the defense of our liberty to politicians . . . It is the duty of every citizen—and of every socially responsible programmer—not merely to passively resist the erosion of liberty, but to actively promote and extend liberty; to enlarge the private sphere; to take power away from government so that individuals and voluntary groups may peacefully work out their destinies.[14]

To Raymond, the libertarian, the Net will regulate itself, provided that the Net's users become like him: socially conscious and liberty driven. In general, he says, he doesn't argue from open source to politics, because he despises people who warp science to advance a political agenda. CatB was written without a directed political motivation. Despite this, his libertarianism allows him to see patterns between politics and open source.

The libertarian view is that the invisible hand of the marketplace will be enough to balance the interests of the individuals with that of the corporations. The reason: Most businesses will find it *necessary* to go open source. They won't have a choice. It's simply that open source works best. No closed-source company can possibly compete with the quantity of programmers working on a code; nor can such code be as valuable in the open market without being open. The Microsofts and AOL Time Warners will be ultimately restrained on the Internet by an architecture that will stay open source by default. No need for DJ intervention or any other governmental mechanism that may muck up free-market mechanisms.

The Open Source Initiative often works with other organizations such as the Electronic Frontier Foundation (founded by former Grateful Dead lyricist John Perry Barlow, along with Mitch Kapor and John Gilmore). The foundation is dedicated to acting as a defender of civil liberties on the Net by opposing initiating, and, defending court cases against misguided legislation; launching global public campaigns; introducing proposals and papers on electronic rights and providing a comprehensive archive of digital civil liberties information at www.eff.org. Its primary aim is to protect users of technology against wrongheaded laws, not to make new laws.

Raymond believes that free market capitalism is superior to any form of government intervention—even if the latter, through the letter of the law, intends to maintain open code on the Net. The libertarian ethic is that government should have limited power so that the people can have more. To Raymond and the founders of the EFF, the battle is often that of the noble, responsible individual versus a power-hungry governmental bureaucracy. Raymond writes:

> This battle needs to be fought on at least two fronts; technological (by developing technologies that empower individuals and put their activities and communications out of government reach) and political (by using provisions of the U.S.'s Constitution and analogous charters and traditions in other countries to head off government attempts to censor and control content).[15]

A JEFFERSONIAN BALANCE

Thus far the Net has been a democratic export worldwide in its facility for free speech, its distribution of secure encryption, and its resistance of censorship. Lessig invokes the spirit of Licklider and the intergalactic network as an example of how revolution and innovation is possible. The early Internet, after all, became popular only because of its generosity of spirit—privacy, free speech, free browsers, cheap access. Anyone with access to a computer—even at a local library—can get an e-mail account and an "emperor's library" at his or her fingertips.

But Lessig disagrees with Raymond that the Net will remain this way through free-market enlightened self-interest. Lessig argues that it will be regulated—controlled and abused—by companies, potentially monopolies, if no other regulation exists to counter such abuse. It is no more intrinsically free and open than Russia was after the Soviet Union fell and corruption filled the vacuum. He thinks even independent bodies of experts like W3C or the Internet Engineering Task Force (IETF) are subject to the interest of companies.* Markets need certain conditions, certain architectures, before they can succeed. They need governmental regulation. Lessig believes contract law, regulated property rights, and antitrust laws are examples of constructive regulation and insists that free markets won't function without them.

> Countries must come to an agreement about how law will regulate and about any norms that they will impose on private ordering. . . . It will require the nations of the world to come to a common understanding about this space and to develop a common strategy for dealing with its regulation.[16]
>
> —*Code and Other Laws of Cyberspace*

In an online debate on the website of the political journal *The American Prospect,* Lessig railed against Raymond's civil libertarian position:

> The techno-anarchist, self-congratulatory, fuck-the-government, give me code and Coke (-a-cola, that is) attitude is doing the movement harm. While the movement turns its energy away

---

*Indeed, the World Wide Web Consortium is considering a proposal to accept standards whose implementation requires licensing of patents for a fee.

from government, while it cocoons itself with this lullaby about how little from government we need, others less principled and others less convinced dominate the debate in Washington. While the open-source crowd has scorned those who would speak of regulation, regulations abound. Bad regulation, no doubt, but bad regulation is the product of a process where the good was not heard.[17]

Lessig believes that collective values ought to determine the architecture of the Internet and that those values can be embodied in intelligent law. Although U.S. law obviously cannot determine what happens abroad, it can and does set a precedent. Federal and state law can aspire to represent collective values. Lessig calls for nations of the world to come together to determine what regulation should be enforced and on what level.

How the Constitution deals with creative work—ideas—is the prime example of this public spirit. In 1813, Thomas Jefferson wrote "Ideas should freely spread from one to another over the globe, for the moral and mutual instruction of man . . . [They should be] incapable of confinement or exclusive appropriation." Constraint of ideas, Jefferson reasoned, harms society. Monopolists would hoard ideas to strengthen their own fiefdoms. Ideas belong in the "intellectual commons," the public domain—the same conclusion that people such as Wiener and Richard Stallman reached.

However, if there is no regulation, the authors of ideas suffer. An author tries to sell a book, and a giant publishing company can just sell their own version, without giving the author anything. A musician writes a beautiful song, and anyone can make his or her own record of it, again without paying the idea maker. If the author, the musician, and the artist can't get paid, they'll stop creating ideas. Society suffers if new ideas aren't created.

> If the law didn't protect the author at all, there would be fewer authors. The law has a reason to protect the rights of authors, *at least insofar as doing so gives them an incentive to produce.*[18]
> —*Code and Other Laws of Cyberspace*

The U.S. Constitution calls for copyright of creative work—including books, music, movies, and software—giving the authors a monopoly over the publication (the copying) of their works for a limited time, after which their works go into the public domain. Lessig believes that the law of copyright should be upheld—even on the Internet—emphasizing that the law stipulates *for a limited time and with the right of fair use.*

The limited time clause is crucial, because it makes copyright an incentive to produce, not a tool for monopolies over ideas.* While copyright seems to serve the interests of the authors, its real purpose is to serve the public. Copyright keeps authors from starving—but should remain brief to encourage the free flow of ideas among society.

UNFAIR USE

Lessig seeks salvation in the law, but not all law is good. Lessig cites the 1998 Digital Millennium Copyright Act (DMCA) as one of the most dangerous forms of regulation yet passed for the Net. It outlaws technologies designed to circumvent other technologies that protect copyrighted material, but doesn't allow the rights of limited time and fair use normally provided under copyright law. This, Lessig says to Raymond, is the result of "bad regulation" or "co-opted government" that threatens free markets if better regulation is not put into place instead. Lessig believes that if techies, hackers, and other proponents of the open source movement ignore the government, the powers that be will pass laws like the DMCA—ugly collaborations between government and business.

The worst infringement of the DMCA is to the right of fair use. Fair use in copyright law is as important as the limited-time clause. It stipulates that copyright law may not restrict the basic right of free speech. Although it's not conclusively defined, fair use indicates that copyright

---

*The current copyright duration for works created in and after 1978 is life of the author plus 70 years, or 95 years for works created before 1978. The Sonny Bono Copyright Term Extension Act passed in 1998 added 20 years to copyright protection for individual and corporate authors, including works already created. The plaintiffs in *Eldred v. Reno* (now Ashcroft) believe that this robs the American public of the rich and diverse public domain. Industries tend to benefit from it, not authors. Lessig argued its appeal in 2000; in February 2001 the U.S. Court of Appeals ruled against the plaintiffs; a year later the Supreme Court agreed to hear the case.

owners do not have the right to perfectly control how the public uses their work. Under fair use, citizens can make *limited* free use of copyrighted material for purposes of criticism, review, display, personal consumption, or teaching. People have the right to share a book with a friend, tape a television show, make a mix-tape of favorite songs, or present movie clips in a film criticism class. The DMCA restricts or forbids that right if the book, show, song, or movie is in digital form. Today only some creative works are mass produced in digital form (such as CDs), but in the near future, nearly all will be. Everything will be software, and the DMCA defines copyright law for software.

The DMCA criminalizes any behavior that could threaten technological methods that keep software proprietary. A person doesn't have to deliberately attack such "protection" to go to jail—she could simply explain why it's flawed, or even put up a website linking to someone else's explanation. The law prevents any exploration of weaknesses or violations of privacy in security and encryption programs. It fails to distinguish between capacity and action—it's like jailing chemists because they could build a bomb, gun owners because they could shoot someone, or car owners because they could drive over someone.

Raymond responds to acts like the DMCA with a confident shrug reminiscent of Yippie nonchalance. "We will fight these impositions through political actions, technical subversion, and other means because it is in our nature to do so. Often, we will win. When we lose we will route around the damage and carry on. . . . In the long run, technology shapes politics far more than the reverse."[19]

Yet Lessig is adamant that only the proper application of law can stand up to big business and bad regulation. When public interests are at stake, the collective should choose—through the mechanism of the law. He continues to rail against the DMCA through articles and arguments published in magazines and posted on the Net. The Electronic Frontier Foundation, likewise enraged, has filed an anti-DMCA lawsuit.

The DMCA is not the only legislation that threatens the distribution of information in the United States, which in turns affects developments abroad. The Security Systems Standards and Certification Act (SSSCA) of 2001 proposes that it would be a civil offense to create or sell any kind of computer equipment that does not include and utilize certified security technologies approved by the federal government. The same threats to the right of fair use imposed by the DMCA would also apply to the SSSCA. While the DMCA created the legal framework to punish people who by-pass copy protection, the SSSCA would force most Americans to buy only systems with copy protection mechanisms by default. If these laws are upheld, Lessig and others believe that researchers could flee America for countries such as Canada or Finland.

The future of the DMCA and the SSSCA remain to be seen.

AFTERWARD

As certain as Lessig is that courts and legislators must fight for fundamental rights and free speech on the Net, he acknowledges that the current system is not working to do so. He detects a weariness and wariness in the American people in regarding the government's ability to solve collective problems. Likewise, the courts have been reluctant to be judged political. The courts, he urges, *must* be political if they are to avoid becoming an enemy of the people. When the president and Congress, corrupted by a corporatized election process, fail to defend the principles of the Constitution, the courts must do so. And they must act fast, as ever more pernicious laws strip away Constitutional values.

> We stand at the edge of an era that demands we make fundamental choices about what life in this space, and therefore in real space, will be like. . . . The values of free speech, privacy, due process, and equality define who we are. If there is no government to insist on these values, then who will?[20]
>
> —*Code and Other Laws of Cyberspace*

Incidentally, the critical group most resistant to Lessig's ideas may be those to whom Raymond refers as "his people"—the motley programmers and hackers of the world, the very people who build the architecture of the Net. Raymond has bequeathed a theory, a language, and a mythic tradition to legions of programmers worldwide. His libertarian politics infuses this ethic. In his essay "How to Become a Hacker," Raymond reifies the hacker community (the bazaar) as a self-organized, independent, and conspicuously antiauthoritarian collective. Raymond believes that the selfishness of the libertarian programmer is superior to any claim to collective interest—better yet, the two meet as a form of mutual "enlightened self-interest." The open source society runs on a free market of egoboo.

> We may view Linus's method as a way to create an efficient market in "egoboo"—as to connect the selfishness of individual hackers as firmly as possible to difficult ends that can only be achieved through sustained cooperation. [21]
>
> —*The Cathedral and the Bazaar*

Although egoboo is not likely to be sufficient to foster the sort of democratic values that Lessig seeks, the efforts of the free-software and open-source community inspire what Lessig calls the transparency of intention, which is crucial to democracy on the Net. Raymond predicts that the infrastructure of the Net will remain all open source, as it was in the beginning with Tim Berners-Lee. It will continue to be moderated by consortia like ICANN and World Wide Web Consortium and service-based corporations like Red Hat Linux. Databases and development tools will be a mix of open and closed code. Applications, he predicts, will be the last to go open source, although "we can expect that the eventual destiny of any software technology is either to die or become part of the open infrastructure itself."[22]

The future of open-code software can be as unlimited as its human capital—the ultimate resource in a post-scarcity economy. It may lead to a reasoned resurgence of the free society fought for by the Yippies, expanding from software to become a new collaborative, nonproprietary, technology-enabled paradigm for education, science, and the arts. It may, as Raymond and Lessig hope in their separate ways, help limit the power of monopolies and oppressive government actions, problems that have plagued democracy since its inception. This battle of the Information Revolution, then, may be fought on more even ground.

PART IV

SYMBIOSIS

• K. Eric Drexler • Bill Joy • Jaron Lanier •

AT THE TURN of the millennium, information technologies seem to be everywhere. Every aspect of our existence is mediated—by cell phones, email, automated teller machines, computer-chipped cars, broadcast television. We live in human–computer symbiosis. If realized, new developments in nanotechnology, genetic engineering, and robotics will mean that information technologies will indeed be everywhere. Through molecular machines and DNA manipulation, we will be able to change physical reality as easily as we change our minds. The cybernetic paradigm is that complexity emerges through the dynamic interaction—feedback—of small, local entities. When robots the size of molecules communicate at the speed of light, the complexity that emerges will be difficult to fathom.

Communications and control remain at the heart of the Information Revolution. One revolutionary believes the future technologies can be regulated in a democratic fashion that depends to a degree on the morals of the technologists developing them. Another believes that only strict governmental regulation may forestall an apocalyptic scenario. Another believes that the threats to humankind are less detrimental than the mindset that has created them. Only one thing is clear: The success of the Information Revolution depends not on technological advances, but on the choices we make as a global society.

INFORMATION IS EVERYTHING

K. ERIC DREXLER

> Human beings are the sexual organs of the techno-
> logical world because the user of any medium is its
> content, just as the genetic code is the individual
> member of the species that manifests and transmits it.
> —Marshall McLuhan

A HANDFUL OF VISIONARIES believe that in the near
future we will manipulate atoms as easily as we manipulate
motors and gears today, and we will do this through nanotechnology, or technology at the scale of nanometers, one bil-
lionth of a meter. Nanotechnologists of the postindustrial era
would use computers to build nanoassemblers—molecular motors, bearings, and moving parts—that could manufacture almost anything, atom by atom, out of thin air. Material will
emerge from the collective assemblage of trillions of atoms that
we set into motion. Nanotechnology could provide the ultimate tools to eliminate human labor, disease, aging, and star-
vation. Nanoassemblers could read, repair, and alter the genes
of living cells. They could render unlimited amounts of food
for the world's population. They could inexpensively eliminate
pollution, reverse global warming, and renew our external environment—the air, the trees, the water. Humankind would
truly live in a postscarcity and postlabor age.

Nanotechnology is the convergence of the Industrial Revolution with advances in computer technology, artificial intelligence, biology, genetics, and engineering. It is a spectrum of computer technologies and technological ideas. It is the next stage of the Information Revolution, the cybernetics of the twenty-first century. Anything we dream, if nature permits it to be built at all, can become palpable reality once computers combine with nanotechnology. With these tools we will reshape our physical and mental worlds. They will facilitate human augmentation of body as well as mind.

Nanotechnology is the transmission of information across all boundaries: technological, physical, and biological. We will be able to communicate on a molecular level with our environment and with our own genetic information. Programming code will actualize itself as substance. As the distinction between technology and life blurs, everything can be manipulated, reproduced, decoded, analyzed, and accessed.

Everything will become information.

One scientist, K. Eric Drexler, has aimed to fulfill the promise of nanotechnology with the proper implementation of information technologies, a vision shared in his manifesto, *Engines of Creation* (1986).

SYNTHESIS: THE CONVERGENCE OF IT ALL

In the late 1970s Kim Eric Drexler, an undergraduate in interdisciplinary science at MIT, researched what many then thought was humankind's next frontier: outer space. He was born in Oakland, California, in 1955, and was a teenager when man first walked on the moon. Inspired, Drexler wanted to design technologies that would enable humans to someday live in space. Molecular biology and biochemistry courses led Drexler to contemplate what engineering would be like on the atomic scale. Molecular machine systems, he figured, could revolutionize not just space discovery, but everything from manufacturing to medicine.

Seeking support for a research paper, Drexler stumbled across a transcript of physicist Richard Feynman's famous speech to the American Physical Society in 1959. In "There's Plenty of Room at the Bottom," Feynman tackled the issue of how engineering and computing can be miniaturized.

He proposed that if content were displayed in a code of dots and dashes, each letter representing six or seven "bits" of information, and each bit a little cube of 125 atoms—then all the information ever written could be reduced to the size of a cube one two-hundredths of an inch wide—barely the size of a speck of dust. This is not news, he added. What, after all, is DNA but compressed information?* If a body can contain information so compacted, why can't, say, a computer? Vannevar Bush's memex was meant to store the record of civilization in a space the size of a room. Feynman saw no reason why, "in the great future," computers couldn't be shrunk to the molecular level, manipulated atom by atom. "The principles of physics, as far as I can see, do not speak against the possibility of maneuvering things atom by atom," said Feynman. He imagined a million tiny factories; chemists synthesizing any substance by arranging atoms: nanotechnology.[1]

Some fifteen years earlier, Feynman had worked on the Manhattan Project in Los Alamos, New Mexico, alongside the famous mathematician John von Neumann. It was while building that A-bomb that von Neumann conceived the idea that machines could self-replicate via another sort of chain reaction. In his posthumously published paper, "Theory of Self-Reproducing Automata" (1966), von Neumann proved that in a cellular lattice a universal Turing machine (a universal computer) could contain a program that directs the behavior of a universal constructor to build exact copies of itself. The cells change states and propagate in the tape of the Turing machine which, in turn, feeds duplicating instructions to the universal constructor, which uses the information to build another identical Turing machine and universal constructor. The automaton can build itself; it can reproduce.

Von Neumann wrote, "Self-replication would then be possible if the universal constructor is provided with its own description as well as a means of copying and transmitting this description to the newly constructed machine." As with DNA and the genetic code, he realized that any self-replicating system must function both as instructions and as data (self description). Errors in copying the data, he noted, could lead to evolution. The self-replicating machine could use information to create progeny, much as living cells, through DNA and RNA, synthesize enzymes and proteins and replicate themselves.

---

*The structure of DNA was discovered by James Watson and Francis Crick one year earlier, in 1958.

The field of cybernetics—communication and control in the organism and the machine—laid the groundwork for investigating how machines can reproduce and evolve like living entities. Von Neumann, participating in the early 1950s Macy meetings on cybernetics, often complemented Wiener's position; the two together found numerous analogies between machines and organic bodies. Von Neumann's work on cellular automata laid the foundations for the fields of artificial intelligence and artificial life.

Artificial intelligence pioneer Marvin Minsky received his Ph.D. from Princeton University during von Neumann's tenure there. Von Neumann was an early mentor of Minsky, who later worked with such visionaries as Claude Shannon and J. C. R. Licklider. Von Neumann's cybernetic idea that communication, or feedback, between simple cells of an automaton could result in complex, emergent properties was a major inspiration for Minsky's book, *Society of Mind*. The whole mind, because it is interconnected and interactive, becomes greater than the sum of its countless mindless neurons. In *Society of Mind* Minsky wrote,

> If you understand something in only one way, then you don't really understand it at all. This is because if something goes wrong, you get stuck with a thought that just sits in your mind with nowhere to go. The secret of what anything means to us depends on how we've connected it to all the other things we know. . . . And that's what we mean by thinking![2]

The greatest tribute to a person's intelligence would be to say his or her mind is "unstuck," which is exactly the praise Minsky gave to his mentor Feynman, after the renowned physicist passed away from cancer in 1988: "He was so unstuck and if something didn't work he would find another way."

Below are lines from a poem Feynman wrote shortly before his death about the interconnectedness of it all—DNA, atoms, neurons, particles, consciousness—all patterns of information from which a whole issues forth. The poem appears in the compilation, *The Pleasure of Finding Things Out* (1999).

. . . Growing in size and complexity living things masses of atoms

DNA, protein
dancing a pattern ever more intricate.
Out of the cradle
onto dry land
here it is, standing;
atoms with consciousness . . .

One of Feynman's spiritual heirs is Drexler, who in 1988 was a Ph.D. student at MIT, working with his adviser, Minsky. Drexler imagined a future technology that would do what nature already does, but quicker and with human purpose: to arrange atoms with computer-controlled self-replicating machines. Under Minsky's tutelage in artificial intelligence and engineering, Eric Drexler was the first student at MIT to receive a degree in nanotechnology, a new branch of technology that deals with the mechanization and manipulation of individual atoms and molecules—the stuff of the physical world that constitutes everything in and around us.

ASSEMBLERS AND REPLICATORS

In his foreword to Drexler's nanotech manifesto *Engines of Creation*, Minsky writes that the book "begins with the insight that what we can do depends upon what we can build." Drexler writes that what we can do with nanotechnology will "promise to bring changes as profound as the Industrial Revolution, antibiotics, and nuclear weapons all rolled into one massive breakthrough."

As described by von Neumann and detailed by Drexler, the concept of the universal replicator is based on biology. Viruses, bacteria, plants, and people use molecular assembly devices in the form of ribosomes that read information from DNA. Drexler imagines that a molecular replicator can also assume the form of human-made cell-sized factories of nanomachines with atomic conveyor belts. The nanomachine would bear hundred-atom-long assembler arms that could build replicas of themselves molecule-by-molecule. He thinks that these molecular factories could build one-hundred-million-atom large computers smaller than the synapse in the human brain and a million times quicker. The whole molecular factory, at fewer than a billion atoms large, could theoretically replicate itself in about the same time as a bacterium. Like bacteria, nanotech replicators could reproduce explosively. Working together, these fast-reproducing systems could manufacture houses, skyscrapers, spaceships, terraform for a civilization on Mars.

Order emerges from chaos. Drexler envisions the manufacture of an object using nanotechnology to begin the same way life begins, with a "germ cell," a "seed." The seed is a nanocomputer containing the equivalent of DNA—the blueprint. It is placed on a base plate in a vat surrounded by the proper heating and cooling infrastructure. A milky froth swarming with nanoassemblers is then poured over the plate. The assemblers tell the seed their location. Instructions from the seed travel through the network as the self replicating assemblers form a pattern, a crystalline scaffolding latticework, on which to build. Organic solvents fuel the system, as could self-made solar collectors. The first stages of the process of building a rocket, for example, would take just a few hours.

Then the communications network spreads instructions to some assemblers, which construct rods of interlocked fibers of carbon, in its diamond form. Other assemblers lay down other materials to make sensors, computers, motors, solenoids, and other parts.

. . . .

> Its creation has required less than a day and almost no human attention.[3]   —*Engines of Creation*

. . . .

Just as current personal computers are superior to Bush's mammoth Differential Analyzer, so miniature, self-coordinated, self-replicating machines will be superior to existing manufacturing technologies. These technologies will be cybernetic: interactive and responsive through feedback with their environment. Nanotech creations will not only leave the environment unsullied, but also consist of lighter, better designed materials than clunky machines could ever make. Nanotechnology could then make Drexler's undergraduate daydream of space travel possible. Spacesuits made of billions of nanocomputers will protect the human body with a three-dimensional diamond-based fiber that resembles a supple, strong second skin. A speck of material implanted in the suit could hold all the information ever written by humankind.

Through nanotechnology, Drexler seeks immortality for information—

both inorganic (textual) and organic (living bodies). In fact, he has made arrangements to cryogenically freeze himself after clinical death, to be later revived by nanobots that can repair cellular damage.* Nanobots can theoretically manufacture new eyeballs, kidneys, and skin using existing genetic information. Nanotechnology defies entropy, the process of breakdown and decay that Wiener so loved and feared. If realized, Drexler's science would transform the meaning of life itself.

> Assemblers will be able to make virtually anything from common materials without labor, replacing smoking factories with systems as clean as forests. They will transform technology and the economy at their roots, opening a new world of possibilities.[4]
>
> —*Engines of Creation*

In terms of the manufacture of physical things, Drexler imagines a time when AI systems, in conjunction with nanotechnology, will be able to fulfill human requests inexpensively and near instantaneously. "Genie machines" will produce what is asked for—food, toys, guns, houses, etc.—all on demand, thanks to millions of self-synchronized molecular devices, agents of construction.

THE SHAPE OF INFORMATION

With cybernetics, Norbert Wiener established that communications and control are fundamentally similar in both biological organisms and machines. The more interactive the machine—the better it responds to feedback with its environment—the more it resembles biological life. Ever since, researchers have been exploring other mechanisms of biology that can apply to machines, and vice versa. One is the notion of DNA: The blueprint of human life is analogous to the "seed" of a nanotech replicator. One replicates human beings, the other replicates "stuff," potentially anything.

The application of biological processes to technology (and vice versa)

---

*Drexler is a proponent of Extropianism, a worldview that seeks to defy entropy, that is, to cheat death.

goes further. In *Society of Mind,* Minsky introduced the idea that the mind contains an evolving system of communicative and cooperative agents, each mindless and useless by itself yet integral to the whole. The way Drexler imagines nanotechnology to work is the same way Minsky claims the mind works: mindless agents collaborating to create a whole greater than the sum of its parts.

In his work on nanotechnology, Drexler was strongly influenced by the biologist Richard Dawkins, who strengthened the idea that local interactions propagate themselves as the behavior of entire systems. The first part of Dawkins's vision is that animals and plants are composed of colonies of genes residing inside cellular societies. The organism acts as a coordinated whole only because its genes have, through evolution and coevolution, learned to act as an organized society rather than as an anarchy. Through reproduction, they replicate and propagate themselves.*

Dawkins was the first to popularize the notion that the genes of biological organisms are not the only *information replicators.* His conviction is that information in the form of science, religion, rumors, songs, fashion, techniques, etc.—self-replicates and propagates like genes. He calls these units of meaning or ideas *memes.* Dawkins, like the cybernetically inspired anthropologists Margaret Mead and Gregory Bateson, regards societal behavior as the product of millions of individuals exchanging information through a complicated feedback mechanism. This cultural information shapes human behavior as much as genetic information. Memes are to culture what genes are to bodies. Successful memes are repeated and spread among society, using human bodies as hosts. If the electronic network gives rise to a sort of global consciousness as Marshall McLuhan described, then

---

*In *The Selfish Gene,* Dawkins calls the body a "survival machine." Genes control the evolution of the survival machine, using it to sustain themselves from generation to generation. Genes have honed our brains, "fast executive computers," to anticipate—*simulate*—situations. This has culminated in a subjective consciousness, which is what separates humans from other animals and also "emancipates survival machines from their masters (their genes)." The "argument from consciousness" that Alan Turing discusses in "Computing Machinery and Intelligence" is the objection to computer intelligence that has held up the best. Minsky and his followers suspect that humans will replicate their consciousness in machines once we figure out the exact mechanisms of our own minds.

memes are the genes of the global organism. Our existing information technologies help memes transmit and replicate faster and farther than ever before.

Dawkins's *The Selfish Gene* (1976) contains a passage that foreshadows the rise of nonbiological information replicators, reminding us that genetic evolution is just one of many kinds of evolution:

> Whenever conditions arise in which a new kind of replicator can make copies of itself, the new replicators will tend to take over, and start a new kind of evolution of their own. Once this evolution begins, it will in no necessary sense be subservient to the old. The old gene-selected evolution, by making brains, provided the "soup" in which the first memes arose. Once self-copying memes had arisen, their own, much faster, kind of evolution took off.[5]

MATERIAL MEMES

Nanotechnology is in itself a meme that has successfully spread throughout the science and technology communities and, recently, to the public at large. As an idea it self-replicates and self-evolves as people talk and write about it. If researchers someday actually create nanobots, these nanobots may also self-replicate and self-evolve in the *physical* world. They'll cross easily from idea to actuality.

Feynman observed that scientific knowledge does not come with instructions on how to use it. He quoted the Buddhist meme, "To each is given the key to the gates of heaven; the same key opens the gates of hell." Drexler has launched the memes of nanotechnological heaven and hell.

Drexler admits it: Nanotechnology is dangerous. With every prospective benefit is a significant risk. Memes and machines can evolve faster than genes. Self-replicating nanobots could become like cancer cells and destroy our planet. Some technologists (other than Drexler) believe that they might learn to communicate with one another and form their own central nervous system or, as in Minsky's society of mind, their own emergent consciousness. There might be no way to control them from replicating indefinitely until everything becomes a "gray goo." For every promise of nanotechnology there is an equally strong objection:

Promise: Nanotechnology could extend human life and create an abundant food source without pollution.

Objection: More people, even with abundant resources, can dangerously alter the natural balance of human populations and ecosystems. Any living entity can be reengineered in a single lifetime rather than through thousands of years of evolution (if at all naturally).

Promise: All the world's information could be reduced to the size of a speck of dust.

Objection: Who will have access to it?

Promise: Nanotechnology could build enough computer power to make possible advanced AI systems that will have the ability to outthink human societies.

Objection: Such systems might displace humans and homogenize societies.

> Depending upon their natures and their goals, advanced AI systems might accumulate enough knowledge and power to displace us. And as with replicators, mere evolutionary "superiority" need not make the victors better than the vanquished by any standard but brute competitive ability.[6]   —*Engines of Creation*

Promise: Humans will be free from manual labor.

Objection: That means they might become disposable.

Promise: Nanotechnology can reprogram genes to rid of human ailments like cancer and the effects of aging.

Objection: The same technology can be used to wipe out populations of people with certain genes or create new cancers and exotic mutations.

Promise: We could try to control replicators by preventing them from self-evolving by incorporating redundant error (mutation) checking mechanisms.

Objection: It makes mechanisms heavier, bulkier, and more expensive. Besides, no approach is foolproof, either technologically or politically.

Promise: Individuals could grow and make anything. Social ills like world hunger and poverty would be eradicated. War and other problems that occur in economies of scarcity will cease to happen.

Objection: The technology could also be harnessed for the purposes of a totalitarian state. Or corporate entities, manufacturers of nanotech devices could become totalitarian entities, controlling everything by dint of surveillance devices or cell-mutating machines that could modify entire populations of people. We could be enslaved both biologically and environmentally.

> To destroy all life with replicators would require only a single speck made of ordinary elements.... Nanomachines and AI systems could be used to infiltrate, seize, charge, and govern a territory or a world.[7] —*Engines of Creation*

In addition to the promises and threats Drexler attributes to nanotechnology are those that result from existing advances in related information technologies such as genetic engineering. The question is always the same: *Who or what will have control over this information?*

The "bioinformatics" gold rush has inspired private corporations to mine the public database for patentable genes that they will sell in proprietary databases. Bioinformatics, a fusion of information technology with biology, is a $300 billion industry that promises to turn the raw genomic base-sequence data into knowledge for making even more lucrative new drugs. Hundreds of millions of venture capital dollars have likewise been sunk into proteomics projects to determine when and where genes are active and what are the properties of the proteins they encode. Although the human genome is available on the Internet, it is impossible to access the data or analyze the sequences without special software. Like other software, some programs are openly developed and made freely available in the public domain. But the databases of private companies are accessible only to pharmaceutical companies such as Pfizer and Eli Lilly who pay rates of up to several million dollars a subscription.

Information becomes much more powerful when it manifests itself physically. Will whoever has access to the new bio or nanotechnologies use them for the general good of humankind? Will they give the average citizen more free will or less? As with free software, will information be free and open? Or will corporations like Pfizer—or Microsoft—own the keys to humankind's heritage? What happens when a corporation has a patent on your health or your intelligence or your individual genetic information? Will these new technologies result in designer babies with superior genes for the wealthy, creating further and more detrimental class distinctions and different species of human beings? Will they alter the way humanity thinks about itself, reducing people to sequences of bits that can be stored in a database? Will they diminish our bodies, our volition, our individuality? What happens when human beings are just *information*?

SYNTHESIS: THE NETWORK OF KNOWLEDGE

Drexler feels responsible for the social consequences of the technology he wants to introduce to the world. He fears a concentration of power greater than any before in human history. In *Engines of Creation,* he quotes Bush who, in the face of atomic warfare, said, "Fear cannot be banished, but it can be calm and without panic; and it can be mitigated by reason and evaluation."

"Society needs better ways to understand technology," Drexler writes, and he has arrived at the same conclusions as Bush, Engelbart, Nelson, and Berners-Lee: Information systems must be developed that will help people sort, combine, spread, refine, and analyze knowledge. *Engines of Creation* was written before the Web, so Drexler was still on the cutting edge when he dedicated an entire chapter of his book to "the network of knowledge"—the idea that computer-based hypertext systems will shape our collective future.

Drexler sees a bio/nanotechnological information revolution happening only through a knowledge revolution. We can and must use the tools developed thus far in the Information Revolution. Since his days as an undergraduate at MIT he has believed that computing power will bring us the future. Drexler also sees computers as a tool for human communication. In his book he marvels over Nelson's Xanadu hypertext system, and in 1980 and 1981 he chipped in to the Xanadu effort, creating new data structure and algorithms for complex versioning and connection management in the system.

In *Engines of Creation* Drexler is enthusiastic about how hypertext will encourage people to publish more ambitious and better-conceived works.

In his 1987 essay "Hypertext and the Evolution of Knowledge," Drexler said that the medium would produce emergent benefits, helping to form intellectual communities, build consensus, and extend the range and efficiency of intellectual effort. "To gain valuable knowledge more rapidly, we must help it evolve more rapidly," he wrote. A hypertext system would particularly help the scientific community, because it would facilitate the "rigorous and reality-based" natural selection of knowledge through feedback.

ENGINES OF DEMOCRACY

In 1986 Drexler, his wife, Christine Patterson (who coined the term "open source"), and James Bennett founded the Foresight Institute, the sister to the Institute for Molecular Manufacturing.* Foresight is a non-profit organization dedicated to improving public and private policy decisions about nanotechnology, through hypertext systems that will enhance public knowledge exchange and critical discussion.

> We cannot do much to slow the growth of technology, but we can speed the growth of foresight. And with better foresight, we will have a better chance to steer the technology race in safe directions.[8] —*Engines of Creation*

On the advisory board of Foresight are several other information revolutionaries, including Stewart Brand, Minsky, and Engelbart. Now in his seventies, Engelbart remains a high-tech evangelist and humanist. Always ahead of the curve, he offers promises and warnings about the next stage of the Information Revolution:

> Fundamentally, I believe we are unprepared for the scale and
> pervasiveness of the technology changes ahead, and especially

---

*In 1986 a visionary businessman, John Walker, read *Engines of Creation* and became inspired by Drexler's enthusiasm for nanotechnology and hypertext. Walker, the founder of Autodesk, funded Nelson's Xanadu in 1988. In 1991 Walker donated $175,000 to help start the Institute for Molecular Manufacturing, where Drexler is a research fellow. Most of the Institute's grant money has gone to pay Drexler to work on projects such as computer simulations of molecular gears, bearings, and other parts.

the secondary effects of these technologies. Who is thinking about these second-order changes, which can be huge? And who is really aware of the forthcoming nanotechnology? This is for sure going to be there . . .

Like Lawrence Lessig, Drexler believes that we must understand the architecture of our emerging technologies. A lack of foresight and planning may indeed result in a "survival of the fittest" scenario. Evolutionary theory, applied to human societies, invites a force beyond public control to take over. If such a force is a repressive or totalitarian state or corporation, democracy has failed. The more advanced the technology and the less democratic its development and distribution, the greater the risk to humankind.

Naturally, the idea that nanotechnology could get into the hands of oppressive dictators or renegade terrorists is a concern of the Foresight Institute. Yet research suppression, Drexler adamantly insists, is not the answer. The need for controls should not hinder the development of new technologies; policies should ensure safety yet be nonthreatening. Drexler believes the answer lies in benevolent public institutions with effective checks and balances, and with purposes and methods that are open to public scrutiny and debate.

Such institutions, like the consortia that confer over the future of the Net (particularly Berners-Lee's World Wide Web Consortium), include the Foresight Institute as well as the press, research centers, and activist groups. "These decentralized institutions help us control the gray, bureaucratic machines," Drexler writes in *Engines of Creation*.

> The principles of representative government, free speech, due process, the rule of law, and protection of human rights will remain crucial. To prepare for the new burdens, we will need to extend and reinvigorate these principles and the institutions that support them; protecting free speech regarding technical matters may be crucial.[9]   —*Engines of Creation*

The best way to fortify our institutions, then, is to ensure that political entities can adequately judge complex technological facts. The more recondite technology becomes, the more it must, in the best interest of society and to the best of our ability, be publicly demystified. Experts must not control our lives. It is secrecy and mystification that beget totalitarianism.

Drexler calls for efficient, effective ways for experts to discuss technical facts and their application to public policy. His ideal of a rigorous and public debate about emerging technologies is related to the free-software activists' stance that all software code should be available to the public and Lessig's assertion that open code provides checks and balances on power. Issues should be aired and debated: How safe are replicators, really? Who gets access to the newest technologies, and under what conditions? How should laboratories be regulated? How should replicators be regulated? To what extent should knowledge be shared with nondemocratic countries? The best way to resolve such questions is through due process.

One idea is the "fact forum"—a procedure of argument, cross-examination, and negotiation regarding technical facts and direction mediated by a referee. In *Engines of Creation* Drexler quotes the anthropologist Margaret Mead as stating that existing institutions prostitute both science and the decision-making process. Foresight has proposed that a panel—a jury of sorts, if compared to a courtroom—should keep track of various positions and act as arbiters of technical controversies. All parties involved in the debate must agree on the panel. The fact forum wouldn't establish policies or have any governmental power, but it would guide and inform public policy. The process would be open to the public, but, unlike a government-instilled "science court," power would not be centralized. Fact forums, run out of universities (for example), are public debates that need not become mired in bureaucracies. Government agencies, in turn, could consult parties from the opposing sides of a fact forum before appointing members of an expert committee.

Just as the National Institutes of Health submitted guidelines for recombinant DNA, the Foresight Institute and Institute for Molecular Manufacturing have, in preparation for coming fact forums, established some preliminary guidelines on nanotechnology. Both industry and government are responsible for upholding them. Among the currently suggested controls and built-in safety mechanisms are:

- Develop nanotechnology to be absolutely dependent on a single artificial fuel source or artificial "vitamins" that don't exist in any natural environment;

- Make devices that depend on broadcast transmissions for replication or in some cases operation;

- Route control signal paths throughout a device, so that subassemblies do not function independently;

- Program termination dates into devices.[10]

These guidelines are just one safety gauge. The humane development of new technologies also depends on developing information-related technologies that enable participation in the larger public sphere. This remains Drexler's mantra. The Web has since materialized as a public forum for this sort of public debate. Its effectiveness as a democratic apparatus multiplies as people the world over cooperate. The implications of nanotechnology, after all, are global.

Drexler, like other information revolutionaries, strives to make the Web even more effective for enabling collectives of people to collaborate and circulate feedback. Peterson's origination of the term "open source" represents the Foresight Institute's commitment to developing information technologies along with nanotech ones. The Foresight Institute has developed annotation capabilities for the Web that are similar to those proposed in the original Xanadu project on which Drexler worked. Their technology, CritSuite (the first open-source inline annotation software on the Web), enables users to add and follow comments by routing any Web site through a Foresight Web server. Such tools, Drexler hopes, will invigorate the continuous debate about developing socially responsible technologies.

Just as memes often counter our genes (to temper our actions through consciousness), so regulatory forums—online and off—are meant to help counter the threat of social Darwinism that technological advance presents. If the power of nanotechnology is somehow outside the jurisdiction of rigorous and public debate, chances are its promises—a pollution-free environment, a disease-free population, and abundance for all—will be but the lost dreams of an annihilated race.

AFTERWARD: OPEN-SOURCE NANOTECHNOLOGY

The field of nanotechnology is still in its primordial stage. Drexler has credit for pioneering the vision of nanotechnology, and he has written a technical book, *Nanosystems* (1992), that details how scientists could power and direct assemblers. Other researchers in the field, however, have more modest ambitions. Much of the actual progress so far has been on the front of nanoelectronics—nanotransistors and nanowires. Researchers have incorporated nanocrystalline particles into substances such as ceramic and sunblock to make them tougher and more effective. They are working on ways to communicate between the nanoworld and the macroworld through laser beams and transducers. So far, however, the best technology has not been able to construct nonbiological nanomachines with molecular precision. Drexler and other theorists believe that powerful nanotechnology will be possible as soon as 2030. Skeptics think nanotech advocates are barking up the wrong tree— the machines of the future will come from genetic, not mechanical, engineering.

One great leap that Foresight had attempted to take toward transparent and socially responsible technology is to establish a safer, better legal environment for open-source programmers. Open-source initiatives—potentially in computer science crossover fields such as nanotechnology and bioinformatics—can benefit innovators and the public at large. As Wiener said of the A-bomb, sharing information can act as a public safety gauge. Information will leak out anyway—if it's bottled up, it may leak out in the worst possible way.

Incidentally, Foresight became embroiled in the open-source debate after another company attempted to patent an idea for annotation software that had already been implemented in CritSuite. So they took steps to protect open-source software from involuntary adoption or misappropriation by for-profit companies.

In 2001, Foresight established the PriorArt.org project, an offer to open-source programmers to inexpensively disclose their work as prior art in the intellectual property IP.com database. The public disclosure of previous inventions—known as "prior art"—is vital to the proper functioning of the patent system, since patents (and the monopoly rights that go with them) are, by law, supposed to be granted *only* to genuinely novel inventions. Patent attempts by companies like Microsoft could theoretically be squelched if part of the code were already filed as prior art. Foresight offered to help free-software programmers file their prior art so as to work within the patent system even as they work against it.

Foresight's proposal initially alleviated at least some software patent concerns; even Lawrence Lessig and Eric S. Raymond agreed on its usefulness. The project, however, was canceled because of lack of use. First, making patent disclosures is a lot of work, and many programmers don't have the time. Second, some in the open-source community feared that database entries would not succeed in preventing patents from being issued to third parties on their work, and could even be used by third parties to identify ideas they could patent.*

Despite the termination of Priorart.org, the Foresight Institute will continue to invent ways to support open-source efforts and reconcile proprietary interests with the ideals of openness and transparent intent. Even if not implemented across the board, open-source forays in bioinformatics and nanotechnology (as programming code or databases) will result in significant changes in the way we view commercial efforts. The free-software movement counters the proprietary production of everything from computer operating systems to the technologies that will cure/augment/mimic the human nervous system. There should be safeguards against the concentration of power by any given organization when it comes to the technologies that can directly affect human bodies or the organisms that humans rely on for food, shelter, or air. Likewise, there should be safeguards against misuse.

---

*Other grassroots intellectual property efforts are extending an open-source model to scientific publications. In 2000 a group of twenty-five thousand scientists founded the Public Library of Science—an initiative to persuade all scientific journals to agree to deposit all published articles in PubMedCentral or other free online resources within six months of their initial publication date. They believe traditional publishers of scientific information are inhibiting access to information by holding it hostage in proprietary databases.

The free-software movement, the society of mind, and nanotechnology have at least one concept in common: Their architecture is fundamentally based on communication between small, local entities. Once you can build from the bottom up, you can create machine systems capable of acting like organic entities. This applies to nanotechnology. Likewise to artificial intelligence. Likewise to open code. Likewise to democracy. Each individual is an agent, contributing to a whole, generating information, which translates to knowledge, which translates to action.

THE CIRCLE OF EMPATHY

BILL JOY AND JARON LANIER

The unfinished revolution is about what we can do to change the way we face the future so that we can better cope with all that is now happening.
—Doug Engelbart

IN 2000, Bill Joy, cofounder and chief scientist of Sun Microsystems, had certain fears concerning the future of the human race. One was twenty-first-century technology—genetic engineering, nanotechnology, and robotics (GNR). The second was unfettered global capitalism. Combined, they may mean that informational power in the hands of commercial entities and reckless individuals could backfire on the rest of the planet. Powerful new technologies could widen the gap between the rich and poor—not only financially and culturally, but also physically or *genetically*. He also feared a new species of machines that resemble biological organisms in their ability to communicate and self-replicate. Looking at the future of *Homo sapiens,* Joy concluded that at risk is the welfare of not just part of the human population, but all of humankind.

That same year, another influential technologist, Jaron Lanier, who coined the term "virtual reality," was likewise alarmed about the direction of technology. Lanier's concern, in contrast, was that the mass adoption of concepts such as memes and sentient self-replicating nanobots is in itself dangerous. Lanier calls it "cybernetic totalism," not as a slight against Norbert Wiener, but as a rebuke to what has become of cybernetics. Cybernetics foreshadowed the merger of biology, physics, and computing into a single science of information. Lanier believes that it is dangerous to explain everything—machines, bodies, thoughts, markets, species, etc.—as patterns of information. Human beings in particular are much more than streams of data encoded in genes.

Joy and Lanier are not Luddites. They are technologists, prominent leaders of the Information Revolution. A wild-haired and brilliant hacker, Joy had put together the Berkeley Software Distribution of Unix (BSD), the version of the Unix operating system that eventually enabled computers to be networked worldwide. With BSD, he pioneered the concept of open-source programming. As cofounder and chief technical officer at Sun Microsystems, Joy designed the company's advanced networking architecture, which escalated the company to fame and fortune. He also codeveloped Java and Jini, two of the most powerful programming languages to date. In 1997, President Clinton appointed Joy co-chairman of the Presidential Information Technology Advisory Committee, guiding the government and the country on information technologies of the future.

Lanier (rhymes with "career") has been a lifelong technophile, whose credentials begin with his childhood growing up in a Buckminster Fullerian geodesic house in New Mexico. At fourteen, Lanier dropped out of school because it wasn't challenging enough. Ten years later, he founded his own virtual reality company, VPL (Virtual Programming Languages), and pioneered the field of virtual reality. His early inspiration: Ivan Sutherland's Sketchpad, the same graphics software that awed Alan Kay back in 1969. Lanier developed the first implementations of multiperson virtual worlds using head-mounted displays and implemented "avatars," or representations of users within such systems. He also codeveloped the first implementations of virtual reality applications in the areas of surgical simulation and is working on virtual reality's newest incarnation, tele-immersion.

Why have these accomplished technologists suddenly turned against the popular ideas of technological progress and the wisdom of previous generations of computer visionaries, even those who likewise proclaim to be humanists? Why do they now seem like turncoats?

The answer is that before most others, Joy and Lanier saw the power of information technologies to alter and improve human realities. Now, as computers converge with life forms and follow biological models, they also foresee the abuses. They agree that we need a feedback loop to control technology and the way it is shaping our worldview. But they disagree about what choices we should make, and why. Joy fears the power, and wants to forbid it for the sake of humankind, as he discusses in his manifesto "Why the Future Doesn't Need Us" (2000). Lanier, in his essay "One-Half a Manifesto" (2000) expresses his fear that we're all too ready to abdicate our humanism with technological metaphors and, with it, the responsibility for moving ahead and making our own choices.

THE DEMOCRATIZATION OF EVIL

In "Why the Future Doesn't Need Us," Joy confesses that he was fascinated by K. Eric Drexler's *Engines of Creation* when he read it back in the mid-1980s. The concept of nanotechnology made him optimistic that molecular assemblers could someday cheaply correct damaged DNA, enable space travel, clean up the environment, restore extinct species, and create a postscarcity economy. The possibility seemed remote; it was fanciful enough to be safe. Fifteen years later, Joy read that nanoscale molecular electronics may actually be possible—and sooner than he anticipated. If advances in miniaturization continue at historical rates, superpowerful computers could realize Drexler's vision by 2020. Disturbed, Joy began to think about what nanotechnology might really mean for society.

. . . .

> Unfortunately, as with nuclear technology, it is far easier to create destructive uses for nanotechnology than constructive ones. Nanotechnology has clear military and terrorist uses, and you need not be suicidal to release a massively destructive nanotechnological device—such devices can be built to be selectively destructive, affecting, for example, only a certain

> geographical area or a group of people who are genetically
> distinct.[1]   —"Why the Future Doesn't Need Us"

. . . .

The nanotechnological capability for self-replication particularly concerns Joy. If nanomachines can copy themselves they can learn and evolve on their own. They have the power to run amok. Joy fears the "gray goo" scenario described by Drexler, the doomsday vision in which out-of-control assemblers and replicators consume all of the Earth's resources in unchecked reproduction, obliterating all biological life.

Joy believes that only World War II's atom and hydrogen bombs match the destructive absolutism of GNR technologies. In "Why the Future Doesn't Need Us," he quotes J. Robert Oppenheimer, who in 1948 stated that, "In some sort of crude sense which no vulgarity, no humor, no overstatement can quite extinguish, the physicists have known sin; and this is a knowledge they cannot lose." Oppenheimer made the transformation from the A-bomb's creator to the H-bomb's outspoken naysayer. Joy, midway through a career creating computer technology, has become a similar skeptic, worrying that his work might be applied to similarly sinful political ends.

To Joy, the prospect of a new and terrible arms race between nations is a strong incentive for early action. He finds Drexler's idea of a nanotech defense shield at best as naïve as the Republican Strategic Defense Initiative and, at worst, apocalyptic—the assemblers in the shield could self-replicate into the biosphere and destroy us all. Nor does he think much of attempts to resolve these issues through dialogue about collective ethics, such as the Foresight Institute's fact forums. We tried this with nuclear weaponry, Joy notes, and "We often spoke dishonestly to ourselves and to each other, thereby greatly increasing the risks." He adds that back then the dangerous information was contained in military labs under government control. Now information is driven by an essentially unregulated global capitalism, controlled by cash more than conscience. "There is no profit in publicizing the dangers," he concludes.

What makes the information age particularly dangerous is what also makes it so liberating: Information can circulate with unprecedented speed and scope. It has never been easier to access information—from a thousand uncontrollable sources or one of the giant institutional databases, all hooked into the global network. Most disturbingly, the three technologies Joy fears most—genetic engineering, nanotechnology, robotics—are basically just code—information—bits—and therefore can't be physically constrained. Joy maintains that they can be designed on any personal computer and spread around the Internet like a virus. Whereas an epidemic such as Ebola can spread only through actual physical contact, information can infect people around the world through global networks, as Joy described in an interview:

> Once the technology involved is fundamentally an information technology, it's much more difficult to control and the scale of the activity can be much smaller because you don't need a large laboratory. . . . There is the dematerialization of the information you need to do harm. It is becoming weightless—it's just bits.[2]

Visionaries like Alan Kay and Ted Nelson imagined that people with their PCs would be able to empower themselves to create new realities. This is the democratization of power. Joy is acutely aware of the power of the Internet for creating dangerous realities. As PCs and software become more powerful and sophisticated, one crazed and vengeful person can wreak more damage on society. Just as information technology has empowered an individual to improve or save the world, it also empowers him or her to destroy it. Joy calls this the "democratization of evil."

The potential for worldwide disaster is terrifying. Moore's law, which holds that processing power doubles every eighteen months, suggests that advances in molecular electronics could soon lead to a new generation of powerful computers that perform a calculation in eight hours that would take present-day computers a millennium. The nanotech vision is that a powerful computer in conjunction with an inexpensive assembly device can transform code into material substance in the average household. What if, for example, individuals can access genomic information and use nanotechnology to release entities into the world that search and kill all people based on age, race, or any other genetic factor? Unlike plutonium for nuclear bombs, there's no natural limit on the supply of information about nanotech designs or chromosomal engineering. An upload and a push of the button may be all that a megalomaniacal terrorist or organization needs to annihilate the world, real and virtual. Computer viruses and worms that cripple businesses and markets have already foreshadowed such crisis. What would happen if these computer viruses could also invade our bodies?

For these reasons, Joy calls us a more conservative approach to the Information Revolution; a new balance between communications and control.

> We are being propelled into this century with no plan, no control, no brakes. Have we already gone too far down the path to alter course? I don't believe so, but we aren't trying yet, and the last chance to assert control—is rapidly approaching.[3]
>
> —"Why the Future Doesn't Need Us"

His conclusion: *No one* should develop dangerous technologies. The hazards of a decentralized global capitalist system outweigh its virtues. Following Wiener's analogy to thermodynamic entropy, Joy maintains that secret knowledge will always leak out. However, whereas Wiener believed that the preemptive release of information is beneficial to humankind, Joy believes it is dangerous. Knowledge in the hands of the specialist can easily end up in the hands of the terrorist. Just as the effort to abolish nuclear weapons is underway to avoid a global arms race, he insists that we should abolish other dangerous technologies—preferably before they exist in a dangerous form.

Joy's solution is that scientists and engineers should adopt an oath of ethical conduct, swearing that they will cease and desist working on technologies that will be implemented for mass destruction.

> We have, as a bedrock of our society, long agreed on the value of open access to information, and recognize that problems that arise with attempts to restrict access to and development of knowledge. In recent times, we have come to revere knowledge.... But despite the strong historical precedents, if open access to and unlimited development of knowledge henceforth puts us in clear

danger of extinction, then common sense demands that we re-
examine these basic, long-held beliefs.[4]

—"Why the Future Doesn't Need Us"

. . . .

Joy states that *governments* should ensure that precautionary principles
are established and followed through. Like Lawrence Lessig, he chastises
Americans for their overwhelmingly anticollective attitude. Our only
hope against collective hazards, he believes, is the collective will of the
people. The purpose of government, delineated in the Declaration of
Independence, is to give citizens the legal and institutional mechanisms
to express their collective will which, he believes, is to halt the development of dangerous science no matter the costs.

> With their widespread commercial pursuit, enforcing re-
> linquishment will require a verification regime similar to
> that of biological weapons, but on an unprecedented scale.
> This, inevitably, will raise tensions between our individual
> privacy and desire for proprietary information, and the
> need for verification to protect us all. We will undoubtedly
> encounter strong resistance to this loss of privacy and free-
> dom of action. . . .Verifying the relinquishment of certain
> GNR technologies will have to occur in cyberspace as well
> at physical facilities. [5]

"Why the Future Doesn't Need Us" received mixed reaction from Joy's
peers in high tech. Technologist and author Raymond Kurzweil, whose
vision of "spiritual machines" includes the bio- and nanotechnologies
that Joy rebukes, agrees that some level of relinquishment will be necessary, but said that arresting the arrow of progress in midflight is in itself reckless. He calls instead for more time to develop the necessary
defensive technologies. After all, there are people who are dying of cancer and other terrible diseases who may benefit from these technologies
and to relinquish them is to extinguish hope. John Gilmore, cofounder
of the Electronic Frontier Foundation, argues that making new technologies illegal will simply drive them underground, thereby increasing

the danger. Because of the decentralized nature of technological research, he says, Joy's call for total relinquishment is a pipe dream.

Linus Torvalds applies the framework of evolution, stating that technology provides the means for humankind to keep evolving and, with it, the definition of what it means to be human. "Everyone always thinks that being different is inhuman because right now we are human. But as we continue to evolve with whatever happens, in 10,000 years we will not be human according to today's standards. We will just be a different form of human."[6]

John Seely Brown, former director of the Xerox Palo Alto Research Center, and researcher Paul Duguid admonish Joy, claiming that the controls to technology already exist—"technological and social systems shape each other . . . evolv[ing] together in complex feedback loops, wherein each drives, restrains, and accelerates change in the other."[7] Joy's manifesto, they write, is part of the regulatory feedback loop that keeps technological development in check.

SYNTHESIS: ACCEPTING THE THREAT

Joy was correct when he surmised in his manifesto that there would be critics who'll read his warning and dismiss it, claiming that "nothing is new." Indeed, there have been many precedents of "Why the Future Doesn't Need Us," including a panoply of science fiction tales in which AI beings supplant human beings. All ethically minded scientists, physicists, engineers, and software designers have likewise pondered the big question that defines their livelihood: *At what point does technology endanger humankind?*

Technologists who regard themselves as humanists have sought to ensure that their creations would help more than hinder the plight of humankind. Many have aimed to create technologies that will accommodate human beings and lead toward growth and behavior in accord with the highest values. However, they can never ignore the obvious and painful realization that technology, no matter how well intended, is a double-edged sword.

In 1950, in an essay titled "Atomic Knowledge of Good and Evil," Wiener acknowledged that this amoral nature of knowledge is as old as human civilization, as accounted for in our biblical tale of the Garden of Eden:

> Neither the laws of physics, nor the inventions of man appear to us with definite and unremovable moral labels. The fire that burns underneath our boilers is after all the same fire that levels our forests and our cities. The electricity with which we execute our criminals also serves to move the wheels of industry.

Just as Joy wants to apply the brakes to GNR technologies, so Wiener questioned whether we can really control our creations. In *Cybernetics* (1948) he wrote, "The mere fact that we have made the machine does not guarantee that we have the proper information to stop it."[8]

As machines become more cybernetic—more humanlike—they threaten to supplant human intelligence and volition. Wiener balanced between the two edges of the blade; he simultaneously developed cybernetic technologies for the "machine revolution ahead" and insisted that these machines will *not* replace human values.

Around the same time, Alan Turing argued in "Computing Machinery and Intelligence" (1950) that computers will soon be thinking and conscious; that "the use of words and general educated opinion will have altered so much that one will be able to speak of machines thinking without expecting to be contradicted."[9] Turing's argument for computer consciousness is that when computers behave as if they are intelligent and conscious, when they pass the Turing Test, it will be petulant to argue that they are not in fact intelligent and conscious.

Several visionaries have adopted humanistic outlooks on the virtues of technologies for democratic and social purposes, but also maintain the belief that these technologies will in the end usurp us. J. C. R. Licklider found hope for humanity in the prospect of becoming partners with our tools. In "Man-Computer Symbiosis," (1960) he envisioned a period of great promise as humans and computers joined in a symbiotic relationship, both dependent on the other, acting as one cybernetic organism, before computers take over.[10] Marvin Minsky and other researchers in the field of artificial intelligence have likewise adopted this outlook, believing that humanistic values can transcend human beings if we use them in how we shape or apply our technologies.

Other visionaries, such as Doug Engelbart, believe that our emphasis should be not on worrying that technologies will supplant us but on developing technologies that will augment us. Humans have always evolved with their tools, but the tool should be subordinate to the human. Accordingly, Engelbart's oN-Line System required the human to learn and adapt to the tool rather than to make the tool intelligent enough to preclude the human learning process.

To the same effect, Alan Kay asks, "When is technology an amplifier and when is it a prosthesis?" A prosthesis would cause a healthy limb to atrophy; an amplifier would make it more robust. Kay was inspired by Seymour Papert, who developed Logo not to build intelligent computers, but to stimulate the physical, visual, and symbolic faculties of the human brain.

Humans and their technologies will continue to develop a fuller and more evolved symbiosis, as evidenced by the free-software and open-source movements that harness technology to share and develop knowledge based on human behavior. Although GNR technologies threaten to be prostheses, they also promise to be amplifiers. They can augment our individual and collective consciousness, our intelligence, our health, and our standard of living. Those at the forefront of the Information Revolution hope this is worth the risks.

Joy's reaction to the question "At what point does technology endanger humankind?" is grounded in fear. But the decision to simply stop and turn back may be foolish, if not impossible. The real answer lies in walking the difficult path, by eating from the Tree of Knowledge, by opening Pandora's box. If we avoid knowledge because we fear its possibilities, we avoid ourselves. We've been dependent on our technologies since Prometheus brought fire down from the gods. Our path depends on how we apply the technologies using our other tool set: human values.

LANIER'S LINE

A few months after Joy's essay debuted in *Wired,* Jaron Lanier, virtual reality pioneer, wrote a rebuttal titled "One-Half a Manifesto" (2000) and posted the nine-thousand-word piece on the World Wide Web.* A technologist-artist known for his bearish burliness, dreadlocks, and *khaen* playing[†] almost as much as for his virtual reality software, Lanier has taken a unique stand on the future of technology.

. . . .

> . . . The motivation for our predecessors to embrace the Enlightenment and the ascent of rationality was not just to make technologies more quickly. There was also the idea of Humanism, and a belief in the goodness of rational thinking and understanding. Are we really ready to abandon that?[11]
>
> —"One-Half a Manifesto"

. . . .

Lanier thinks that what's wreaking havoc on the world is not our technologies, but the assumptions that have driven Joy and others to madness. He believes the real threat behind computing technology is our exaggerated and misleading view of its promises and perils; the attitude that "computers will become the ultra-intelligent masters of physical matter and life." This is the paradigm that has pervaded our cultural and scientific thinking since World War II. Lanier outlines the misled beliefs:

- Cybernetic patterns of information provide the ultimate and best way to understand reality.

- People are no more than cybernetic patterns.

- Subjective experience either doesn't exist, or is unimportant because it is some sort of ambient or peripheral effect.

- What Darwin described in biology, or something like it, is the singular, superior description of all creativity and culture.

- Qualitative as well as quantitative aspects of information systems will be accelerated by Moore's law.

---

*The unwritten second half of his manifesto, Lanier writes, would be about the real promise of the technology, namely the "lovely flowering" of computer culture evidenced by the hacker community.

[†]A *khaen* is a free-reed bamboo mouth organ from Laos and northeast Thailand.

- Biology and physics will merge with computer science (becoming biotechnology and nanotechnology, resulting in life and the physical universe become mercurial); achieving the supposed nature of computer software. Furthermore, all of this will happen very soon! Since computers are improving so quickly, they will overwhelm all the other cybernetic processes, like people, and will fundamentally change the nature of what's going on in the familiar neighborhood of Earth at some moment when a new "criticality" is achieved— maybe in about the year 2020. To be a human after that moment will be either impossible or something very different than we now can know.[12]

Lanier sees it like this: "Cybernetic totalism," beginning with the ideas of Wiener, Claude Shannon, and Turing, has created a situation in which people regard all culture and being as a "shuffling of bits." He believes that as well intentioned as the original circle of cyberneticists may have been, the *transformation or reduction of everything to information*— human, machine, ecosystem, society, etc—threatens humankind. Just as Darwinism inspired the Nazi-related phenomenon of social Darwinism, Lanier believes cybernetics has spawned a limited and deterministic model of human reality.

. . . .

Cybernetic Totalists look at culture and see "memes," or autonomous mental tropes that compete for brain space in humans somewhat like viruses. . . . Once you have subsumed something in its cybernetic reduction, any particular reshuffling of the bits seems unimportant.[13]   —"One-Half a Manifesto"

. . . .

The cybernetic mind-set infers that humans and computers are alike in that they can be expressed in informational terms. From the Turing Test (the "creation myth") on, Lanier argues, we have begun to treat computing technology as if it has achieved the "moral and intellectual status of personhood." In effect, he argues, we have reduced ourselves to the philosophical and physical level of computers: We're both bits, one DNA and the other programming code. Evidence that we have stooped to the level of our computing technology is simple: We conform ourselves to badly designed software. Computers were originally modeled after human brains. In a striking reversal, humans have started to think of themselves as specialized computers, or, at least, we have adapted to computers in our own minds.

Lanier argues that the prevailing paradigm also suggests that computers are subject to the same forces of evolution as biological life forms. If DNA is information and DNA is shaped by a (seemingly) linear, progressive force of natural selection, then we assume that all other forms of information are evolving similarly. That includes computer code, microchips, artificial intelligence, etc. In fact, Lanier says, we have begun to believe that computers will soon become so complex as to assume an emergent consciousness, even common sense.

Lanier's intent is to test our sensibilities when he then poses the question: Do they belong within our circle of empathy?

It's an absurd question to most people, yet its intent is to emphasize the absurdity of our dilemma. Of course computers are not our equals, yet; despite Turing's predictions, no machine has yet passed the Turing Test. Until they do—a prospect Lanier finds dubious—humans deserve empathy and computers don't.

> On the inside of the circle [of empathy] are those things that are considered deserving of empathy, and the corresponding respect, rights, and practical treatment as approximate equals. On the outside of the circle are those things that are considered less important, less alive, less deserving of rights.... My personal choice is not to place computers inside the circle.... My position is unpopular and even resented in my professional and social environment.[14]
>
> —"One-Half a Manifesto"

Lanier defends his stand by invoking an "extra-rational" faith that humans are unique and entitled to special rights and privileges as sentient, emotional beings. He claims this belief is no longer self-evident, particularly in the high-tech circles for whom his manifesto is written.

If faith isn't reason enough to maintain that humans are intrinsically separate from their creations, then Lanier presents evidence that the belief that our technologies are progressing toward some transcendent or cataclysmic reality is a fallacy. AI has failed its early promise. Software, rather than becoming simply more sophisticated, is getting bigger, bulkier, and clumsier. Lanier says it is hardly evolving, and certainly not toward some emergent consciousness that will preempt ours.

This is where Lanier claims his authority, for he has spent his career developing software. Most recently, he has been the Lead Scientist of the National Tele-immersion Initiative, a coalition of research universities studying advanced applications for the future of the Internet. He is also the codirector of Project GUMBO, based at Caltech, an exploration of how scientists evaluate and collaborate on very large scale scientific simulations. He cowrote VPL, the virtual reality programming language. In his deep past he was mentored by Minsky at MIT.

One reason why Moore's law doesn't mean anything, Lanier claims, is that software cannot keep up with hardware. His VPL crashes all the time. Software has taken up more and more space as developers attempt to incorporate previous versions (legacy code to ensure compatibility). Furthermore, an increase in processing power doesn't mean a corresponding algorithmic increase in other parts of the system. This creates bottlenecks.

> It is the fetishizing of Moore's Law that seduces researchers into complacency. If you have an exponential force on your side, surely it will ace all challenges—who cares about rational understanding when you can instead rely on an exponential extra-human fetish? But processing power isn't the only thing that scales impressively; so do the problems that processors have to solve. [15]
>
> —"One-Half a Manifesto"

As a result, he concludes, Joy and other doomsayers have nothing real to fear. After all, the ability to create software that will model and manipulate everything from atoms to human beings is at the root of Joy's terror. Lanier believes that such capabilities are not around the corner, but at some distant and dubious point in the future—nature is much more incomprehensibly complex than the code we write. An ironic upside to this reality, however, is that applications will require more and more humans to build and fix them. If Moore's law remains in force, Lanier claims, the full employment of human beings around the globe will be necessary to keep computers, the reality and the fantasy, up and running. This, in the end, could fulfil the vision of people from Abbie Hoffman to Ted Nelson to Alan Kay: A livelihood working with or through computers could be more creative, flexible, participatory, and rewarding than any other.

> Scenarios that predict that biotechnology and nanotechnology will be able to quickly and cheaply create startlingly new things under the sun must imagine that computers will become semi-autonomous, superintelligent, virtuoso engineers. But computers will do no such thing if the last half century of progress in software can serve as a predictor of the next half century....[16]
>
> —"One-Half a Manifesto"

The feedback Lanier received from his peers in high tech was as mixed as the response to Bill Joy's article. His critics on the Edge.org website have taken bits of the manifesto, especially Lanier's assertion that software is doomed, and argued against them. A few have pointed out that new and better ways of coding are underway and have criticized Lanier's work as a software designer. To the issue of machine intelligence, Rodney Brooks, director of the MIT AI Lab, implored Lanier to simply get over his fear of being a machine and said that unless one believes in spirituality, people are matter and obey the same physical laws of the universe as anything else. To the issue of inept software, physicist George Dyson invoked what Lanier would deem the seductive "cybernetic totalist" paradigm to prove that code is evolving by *virtue* of its sloppiness, which is like the primordial soup of life. He wrote, "It is lousy code that is bringing the digital universe to life, rather than leaving us stuck in some programmed, deterministic universe devoid of life."

AFTERWARD: PROGRESS

Joy may believe in technological threat and Lanier may scoff at such fears, but the two have a great deal in common. They're both self-proclaimed humanists. They both maintain that people possess reason and free will and are worthy of compassion. Keenly sensitive to the power dynamic between corporation, government, and individual, they side with the individual.

But their differences may be more profound. Joy hopes that we will turn our backs on technologies that may be more dangerous than nuclear weaponry, but certainly have more complicated possibilities—possibilities that include great hope. His vision offers a warning but no real solutions. Lanier sees the hope and promise in future information technologies. He wrote only half a manifesto—the unwritten second half would describe his hope for the future. Lanier finds fault not in technology but in technologists. Many are all too ready to talk about the future as if our actions make no difference, as if just because tragedies will happen we should not strive to avoid them, and just because advances will be made we don't need to solve today's problems.

Joy's fear and Lanier's skepticism haven't prevented them from continuing to develop their projects. In late 2001 Lanier was the chief scientist of the animation company Eyematic and chief scientist of the National Tele-immersion Initiative. Tele-immersion, similar in spirit to Ivan Sutherland's virtual world, will project individuals into a virtual space, tracking their motions and mouthings. It is a new medium for human communication on the Web that creates the illusion that the user is in the same room as the others with whom she is interacting. With tele-immersion, scanning cameras will sense people and their environment as if they are three-dimensional animated sculptures.

Lanier has high hopes that tele-immersion, when it is fully realized around 2010, will help humankind. He believes it is fundamentally a tool to help people connect better, stating in a *Scientific American* article that, "communications technologies increase the opportunities for empathy and thus for moral behavior. Consequently, I am optimistic that whatever role tele-immersion ultimately takes on, it will mostly be for the good."

Since the early 1990s, Bill Joy has lived in Aspen, Colorado where he runs his own research and development lab, Sun Aspen Smallworks. As he pledged in his manifesto, he continues to develop software—cautiously.

Software is a tool, and as a tool builder I must struggle with the uses to which the tools I make are put. I have always believed that making software more reliable, given its many uses, will make the world a safer and better place; if I were to come to believe the opposite, then I would be morally obligated to stop this work. I can now imagine such a day will come.[17]

—"Why the Future Doesn't Need Us"

One idea borne out of Joy's lab in late 1999 is the Jini distributed computing technology—software to facilitate the communication of cell phones, pocket-sized computers, pagers, and other devices over computer networks. This, Joy says, is the new paradigm for networking: extremely simple-to-use computing power, distributed across a diverse collection of devices connected to a network, each able to share the other's resources. While the promise of Java, Sun's popular object-oriented language, is to get programs to operate on any computer, Jini's promise is to run in any gadget. Anything and everything will be connected to the Net and represented by an agent in the network, as envisioned by J. C. R. Licklider, Alan Kay, and Tim Berners-Lee among others. It's nomadic, ubiquitous computing.*

Joy's other plans for distributed computing are for an initiative called Juxtapose (Jxta). Jxta is Sun's contribution to the much-hyped "peer-to-peer" (P2P) technology made famous in 2000 by file-swapping programs such as Napster. Like Napster, Jxta would enable networked computers to communicate directly with each other—instead of going through a central server for communication, as is common.† Napster is actually an

---

*Under the Jini license anyone can gain access to the Jini code. Unlike proper open-source agreements such as the GNU General Public License or the Open Source Definition, however, developers keep a level of proprietary control over their contributions. This stipulation has piqued the ire of open-code advocates like Raymond and Stallman, who flatly state that Jini is not open or free code. By late 2001 attempts to develop Jini under such conditions have been half-hearted, compounded by the limits of band width on the Net.

†Napster is not quite true P2P—though the music files are distributed among all Napster users, the software requires a call to a central directory to return search results. The centralized directory allowed the number of Napster users to grow rapidly without the need for complicated P2P algorithms; however, if Napster had been truly decentralized, it couldn't have been shut down.

amalgam of P2P and central-server networking; Jxta is intended to be totally decentralized and distributed. Jxta is developed under the Apache open-source license and development model, a truly free, open, and collaborative model.

The promise of P2P, distributed computing, is a more democratic Net of the future—a much more complex network in which individual computers, wireless phones, powerful servers, and databases all work together to offer new kinds of Web features, whether they are software services offered remotely or interactive sharing programs such as Gnutella. More P2P applications will eliminate bottlenecks on the Web caused by too many hits to a site. Once gadgets become networked, they will all be able to speak to one another directly, without going through a central site. Distributed computing means the emergence of a new global village in which everything—the pubs, the roads, the square, the lights, the vehicles—can communicate with each other and with the villagers.

Distributed computing, P2P, could fulfill the promise of cybernetics: ubiquitous interactivity. Its proponents imagine that it would be irrepressible, replacing the central servers and clients of the Web with cheap personal computers and appliance implants, each simultaneously autonomous and part of the great body of information. It could be the natural extension of Berners-Lee's Semantic Web, in which agents could take on laborious tasks that require a sort of common sense. Cars could haggle with gas stations for the lowest prices, refrigerators could order food, and houses could conserve energy and sell excess wattage to neighbors. Distributed computing could satisfy Vannevar Bush, Doug Engelbart, and Ted Nelson's dream of a world in which information is never lost. It may present us with better ways to process it all, each chip a mindless agent contributing to an emergent intelligence—Minsky and Papert's society of mind.

Most of all, distributed computing could alter the power dynamic. There would be no unobtrusive way to control information if it can be passed from individual to individual. The concept of publication, crucial to the premise of copyright, would require a transformation. It may necessitate alternative payment (and credit) models for the swelling ranks of writers, artists, programmers, and others who create information for a living instead of filling slots in bureaucracies. These models remain to be seen, although possibilities point to a Xanadu-like direct payment plan that reduces the necessity and viability of large corporations.

If all goes wrong, this new vision could mean that widespread P2P surveillance, censorship, and malevolence compromise our rights. We can imagine it as a venue for vicious self-replicating nanobots, terrorism, or rampant global commercialism. More likely, we hope, is that it means a greater power to the people and a means to spread humanistic values. The distribution of computing is the distribution of information is the distribution of power. Each of us, equipped and informed, will have better tools to augment our knowledge, our creativity, our free will, our empathy—our best qualities.

A world of thoroughly distributed computing and tele-immersion would fulfill Norbert Wiener's vision. Streaming from implants and appliances and intimate computers, the vision is of ubiquitous information in all its manifold forms, incessantly flowing and feeding back over airwaves and brainwaves. It illustrates our connected and communicative world, internal and external, best stated by Wiener himself:

> To live effectively is to live with adequate information. Thus, communication and control belong to the essence of man's inner life, even as they belong to his life in society.[18]

1930s

'36 Abbie Hoffman and Ted Nelson are born

'37 Alan Turing publishes "On Computable Numbers"

1940s

'40 Alan Kay is born

'44 The Macy Conferences begin

'45 War II ends with the dropping of the atomic bomb on Hiroshima and Nagasaki.

   —John von Neumann publishes the "First Draft of a Report on the EDVAC"

'46 Alan Turing publishes "Proposed Electronic Calculator"

'48 Norbert Wiener publishes *Cybernetics*

1950s

'50 Turing writes "Computing Machinery and Intelligence"

   —Norbert Wiener publishes *The Human Use of Human Beings: Cybernetics and Society*

'53 Richard M. Stallman is born

'54 Larry Wall is born

'55 Tim Berners-Lee, K. Eric Drexler, Eric S. Raymond, and Bill Joy are born

'57 John von Neumann dies

　—J. C. R. Licklider publishes "The Truly SAGE System, or, Toward a Man-Machine System for Thinking"

'58　Marshall McLuhan coins "the medium is the message"

　—The United States enters the space race with the launch of the satellite Explorer

　—ARPA is founded

1960s

'60 Jaron Lanier is born

　—J. C. R. Licklider writes "Man-Computer Symbiosis"

　—John McCarthy develops the timeshared computer

'61 Lawrence Lessig is born

　—Doug Engelbart writes "Special Considerations of the Individual as a User, Generator and Retriever of Information"

'62 Doug Engelbart writes "Augmenting the Human Intellect A Conceptual Framework"

　—Marshall McLuhan writes *The Gutenberg Galaxy: The Making of the Typographic Man*

　—J. C. R. Licklider starts the Information Processing Techniques Office at ARPA

'63 Seymour Papert joins Marvin Minsky at the AI Lab

　—Ted Nelson coins the term "hypertext"

'64　Norbert Wiener dies

　—Marshall McLuhan writes *Understanding Media: The Extensions of Man*

　—Ivan Sutherland succeeds J. C. R. Licklider at the Information Processing Techniques Office

　—Bob Taylor at NASA funds Doug Engelbart with $85,000

　—The Augmentation Research Center develops the mouse

'65 J. C. R. Licklider writes *Libraries of the Future*

　—Donald Davies coins the term "packet switching"

　—Ivan Sutherland brings Robert Taylor from NASA as deputy director of the IPTO

'67 Vannevar Bush publishes "Memex Revisited"

—Seymour Papert and BBN engineers led by Walter Feurzeig create the first version of Logo

—Larry Roberts presents his idea for the ARPAnet to the Intergalactic Network

—NBC airs "This is Marshall McLuhan"

—Abbie Hoffman tosses dollar bills into the New York Stock Exchange pit

'68 J. C. R. Licklider and Bob Taylor write "Computer as a Communication Device"

—Abbie Hoffman publishes *Revolution for the Hell of It*

—Doug Engelbart presents the NLS at the Fall Joint Computer Conference

—Abbie Hoffman organizes a Yippie celebration/protest at the Democratic National Convention

—Alan Kay meets Seymour Papert at the AI Lab

—The Vietcong launch the Tet Offensive

—Martin Luther King Jr. and Robert Kennedy are assassinated

'69 Alan Kay writes "The Reactive Engine"

—The ARPAnet goes online

—Robert Taylor hands the directorship of the IPTO to Larry Roberts

—Ken Thompson and Dennis Ritchie of Bell Labs develop Unix

—NASA successfully sends astronauts to walk on the moon

—The trial of the Chicago Eight begins

1970s

'70 Xerox PARC opens

—The Mansfield Amendment, passed in 1969, restricts ARPA funding

'71 Abbie Hoffman publishes *Steal This Book*

—Gary Starkweather invents the laser printer at Xerox PARC

'72 ARPA is renamed DARPA

'73 The Alto, arguably the first machine designed to be a personal computer, is built at PARC

—Bob Metcalfe develops Ethernet

'74 Vannevar Bush dies

—Ted Nelson publishes *Computer Lib*

—The Altair, the first commercially available personal computer, is sold

'76 Steve Jobs and Steve Wozniak found Apple Computer

'77 Alan Kay publishes "Microelectronics and the Personal Computer" and, with Adele Goldberg, "Personal Dynamic Media"
—The Stanford Research Institute dismantles the Augmentation Research Center
—Apple Computer begins selling the Apple II
—Bill Joy puts together the BSD version of Unix

'79 Xerox PARC demonstrates the Alto and Smalltalk to Steve Jobs

1980s

'80 Marshall McLuhan dies
—Seymour Papert publishes *Mindstorms: Children, Computers and Powerful Ideas*
—Apple Computer goes public

'81 Ted Nelson publishes *Literary Machines*

'83 Richard Stallman conceives the GNU project

'84 Alan Kay writes "Computer Software"
—Apple Computer debuts the Macintosh
—The AT&T monopoly is broken up and Unix becomes a stand-alone commercial product

'85 Marvin Minsky publishes *Society of Mind*
—Richard M. Stallman writes "The GNU Manifesto"

'86 K. Eric Drexler publishes *Engines of Creation* and founds the Foresight Institute

'87 Larry Wall releases Perl
—Autodesk begins sponsoring Xanadu

'89 Tim Berners-Lee writes "Information Management: A Proposal"
—The Free Software Foundation releases the GNU General Public License
—Abbie Hoffman commits suicide

1990s

'90 Tim Berners-Lee build the prototype of the World Wide Web
—J. C. R. Licklider dies

'91 Alan Kay writes "Computers, Networks and Education"
—Linus Torvalds releases Linux

'92 Autodesk drops the Xanadu Project

'93 The World Wide Web grows to 10,000 servers

—The team at the NCSA led by Marc Andreessen develops Mosaic; Andreeson and Jim Clark found Netscape

—Commerce is allowed on the Internet

'95 Microsoft releases Internet Explorer

'97 Eric S. Raymond writes *The Cathedral and the Bazaar*

—Netscape announces that it will open the source code of its browser

—Larry Wall gives the "The First State of the Perl Onion" address

—AOL buys Netscape for $4 billion

—Microsoft integrates its Explorer browser with its operating system

—The Digital Millennium Copyright Act and Sonny Bono Copyright Term Extension Act are passed

'99 Larry Wall gives "The Third State of the Perl Onion" address

—Lawrence Lessig publishes *Code and Other Laws of Cyberspace*

—Tim Berners-Lee publishes *Weaving the Web*

—Bill Joy develops Jini and Juxta

—Udanax releases a public domain version of Xanadu

2000s

'00 Bill Joy publishes "Why the Future Doesn't Need Us"

—Jaron Lanier writes "One Half a Manifesto"

—Thomas Penfield Jackson rules that Microsoft violated anti-trust laws and orders a break-up

—AOL and Time Warner merge and, with Viacom's purchase of CBS, nearly all corporate media are under the control of seven global corporations

—IBM pledges $1 billion to Linux development

'01 Tim Berners-Lee writes "The Semantic Web"

—The U.S. Court of Appeals determines that Microsoft violated anti-trust laws but reverses the break-up order

I AM DEEPLY GRATEFUL to those participants in the front lines of the Information Revolution who have lent their time to answer interview questions and/or read and comment on relevant sections of the manuscript. Particular thanks go to Doug Engelbart, Richard Stallman, Alan Kay, Eric S. Raymond, Larry Wall, Seymour Papert, Ted Nelson, Lawrence Lessig, Christine Peterson, Len Kleinrock, and Terry Winograd. I am grateful to many of these visionaries who have given direct permission to excerpt from their important writings.

Many thanks also go to those who have reviewed and commented on the manuscript, in whole or in part: Paulina Borsook, James Craig Burley, Ryan Campbell, Lois Dachary, Catherine Heins, Kannan Jagannathan, Douglas Johnson, Bill Kerr, Alexandre Oliva, Diana Merry-Shapiro, Cynthia Solomon, Sam Steingold, John Sweeney Jr., and Dan Velleman.

Big props go to Shepard Fairey, culture jammer, for designing the cover art.

Thanks also go to the people who have been particularly helpful and supportive in the research of this project, or in the acquisition of photos and permissions: Amanda Ayala, Mary Coppernall of the Bootstrap Institute, Amy van der Hiel at the

W3C, Marlene Mallicoat, Denise Ondayko, Greg Poschman, Susan Stambaugh, Derrick Story, Ka-Ping Yee, and the archivists at MIT and Stanford.

I also would like to thank Myles Thompson for his enthusiasm and support of this project from its inception. Thanks also go to Victoria Larson and Renea Perry at TEXERE, Deborah Kletnotic, and The Book Design Group.

Last but not least are the friends and family who have supported me through the process of writing this book. Thanks for all the e-mail.

Visit http://www.technomanifestos.net for a comprehensive list of references and recommended readings.

Technomanifestos

Berners-Lee, Timothy. *Weaving the Web* (Great Britain: Orion, 1999).

—"Information Management: A Proposal." 1989. http://www.w3org/history/1989/proposal.htm.

—with J. Hendler, and O. Lassila. "The Semantic Web." *Scientific American,* 284 (5): 34–43, 2001.

Bush, Vannevar. "As We May Think." In *Endless Horizons.* (Washington, D.C.: Public Affairs Press, 1975); First published in *Atlantic Monthly,* July 1945.

—"Memex Revisited." *Science Is Not Enough.* (New York: William Morrow, 1967).

Drexler, K. Eric. *Engines of Creation.* (New York: Doubleday, 1986).

Engelbart, Douglas C. *Augmenting Human Intellect: A Conceptual Framework.* Summary Report AFOSR-3223 under Contract AF 49(638)-1024, SRI Project 3578 for Air Force Office of Scientific Research, Stanford Research Institute, Menlo Park, Calif., 1962.

—"Special Considerations of the Individual as a User, Generator, and Retriever of Information," *American Documentation,* 12, no. 2: (1961) 121–125. First presented at the Annual Meeting of the American Documentation Institute, Berkeley, Calif., October, 1960.

Hoffman, Abbie. *Revolution for the Hell of It.* (New York: Dial Press, 1968).

—*Steal This Book.* 1971. http:///www.tenant.net/Community/Steal/Steal.html.

Joy, William. "Why the Future Doesn't Need Us." *Wired,* April 2000. www.wired.com/wired/archive/8.04/joy.html.

Kay, Alan and Adele Goldberg. "Personal Dynamic Media," *Computer,* March 1977.

—"The Reactive Engine." Ph.D. thesis, University of Utah, Salt Lake City, 1969.

—"Microelectronics and the Personal Computer." *Scientific American,* 237, no. 3, (1977).

—"Computer Software." *Scientific American,* 251, no. 21 (1984).

—"Computers, Networks and Education." *Scientific American,* (1991).

Lanier, Jaron. "One-Half a Manifesto." *Edge,* September 2000. http://www.edge.org/3rd_culture/lanier/lanier_index.html.

Lessig, Lawrence. *Code and Other Laws of Cyberspace.* (New York: Perseus, 1999).

Licklider, J. C. R. and Robert Taylor. "Computer as a Communications Device," Archives, Massachusetts Institute of Technology, Cambridge, Mass., 1968.

—*Libraries of the Future.* (Cambridge, Mass.: MIT Press, 1965).

—"The Truly SAGE System, or, Toward a Man-Machine System for Thinking." NAS-ARDC Special Study, Archives, Massachusetts Institute of Technology, Cambridge, Mass., 1957.

—"Man–Computer Symbiosis." *IRE Transactions on Human Factors in Electronics,* HFE-1, (March 1960): 4–11. http://memexorg/licklider.html.

—"Man–Computer Symbiosis: Part of the Oral Report of the 1958 NAS-ARDC Special Study, presented on behalf of the Committee on the Roles of Men in Future Air Force Systems," 20–21, November 1958.

McLuhan, Marshall. *The Gutenberg Galaxy: The Making of the Typographic Man.* (Toronto: University of Toronto Press, 1962).

—*Understanding Media: The Extensions of Man.* (Cambridge, Mass.: MIT Press, 1964).

Minsky, Marvin. *Society of Mind.* (New York: Simon & Schuster, 1985).

Nelson, Theodor. *Computer Lib.* (Seattle, Washington Microsoft Press, 1987).

—*Literary Machines.* Self-published by the author 1981, 1987.

Papert, Seymour. *Mindstorms: Children, Computers, and Powerful Ideas.*

(New York: Basic Books, 1980).

Raymond, Eric S. *The Cathedral and the Bazaar.* (Sebastopol, Calif.: O'Reilly & Associates, Inc., 1999).

Stallman, Richard. "GNU Manifesto." 1985. http://www.gnu.org/gnu/manifesto.html.

—"GNU General Public License." http://www.gnu.org/licenses/gpl.html. 1985.

Turing, Alan. "On Computable Numbers, with an Application to the Entscheidungs problem," *Proceedings of the London Mathematical Society* (Series 2) 42, (1936): 230–265

—"Computing Machinery and Intelligence." *Mind,* vol. 59, no. 236, 1950: 442–458.

—"Proposed Electronic Calculator." National Physical Laboratory report (1946). Published in B. E. Carpenter and R. W. Doran (eds.) *A.M. Turing's ACE Report,* (Cambridge, Mass: MIT Press, 1986).

Von Neumann, John. *First Draft of a Report on the EDVAC.* Contract W-670-ORD4926, Morse School of Electrical Engineering, University of Pennsylvania, Philadelphia, 1945.

Wall, Lawrence. "First Perl Conference Keynote." http://www.wall.org/~larry/keynote/keynote.html. 1997.

—"Second State of the Onion." http://www.wall.org/~larry/onion/onion.html. 1998.

—"Third State of the Perl Onion." http://www.perl.com/1999/08/onion/talk.html. 1999.

Wiener, Norbert. *The Human Use of Human Beings: Cybernetics and Society.* (New York: Anchor Books, 1950, 1954).

—*Cybernetics* or *the Control and Communication in the Animal and the Machine,* second edition (Cambridge, Mass.: MIT Press, 1948).

Other Manifestos and/or Works Directly Quoted

Barlow, John Perry. "A Declaration of the Independence of Cyberspace." http://www.eff.org/~barlow/Declaration-Final.html. February 8, 1996.

Brand, Stewart. "SpaceWar." *Rolling Stone,* December 7, 1972. http://www.wheels.org/spacewar/stone/rolling_stone.html

Dawkins, Richard. *The Selfish Gene.* (New York: Oxford University Press, 1976, 1990).

Ferry, W. H., et al. "The Triple Revolution." *The Sixties Papers: Documents of a Rebellious Decade,* edited by Judith Albert (New York: Praeger, 1984).

Laurel, Brenda. *Computers as Theatre.* (Menlo Park, Calif.: Addison-Wesley, 1991).

Lessig, Lawrence. *The Future of Ideas: The Fate of the Commons in a Connected World.* (New York: Random House, 2001).

McCulloch, Warren S., and Walter Pitts. "A Logical Calculus Immanent in Nervous Activity," *Bulletin of Mathematical Biophysics* 5 (1943): 115–133.

McLuhan, Marshall, and Quentin Fiore. *The Medium Is the Massage* (New York: Bantam, 1967).

Otlet, Paul. *Traité de Documentation: le livre sur le livre.* Théorie et practique. Editiones Mundaneum, IIB Publication No. 197, 431–450. (Brussels: Palais Mondial, 1934).

Rinzler, Alan, ed. *Manifesto: Addressed to the President of the United States from the Youth of America.* (New York: Macmillan, 1970).

Rubin, Jerry. *Do It! Scenarios of the Revolution.* (New York: Simon & Schuster, 1970).

Shannon, Claude E. "A Mathematical Theory of Communication," *Bell System Technical Journal,* 27, (July and October 1948): 379–423, 623–656.

Sutherland, Ivan E. "Sketchpad—A Man-Machine Graphical Communication System," Presented at the Spring Joint Computer Conference, Detroit, Mich., May 1963. Available as Technical Report no. 296, Lincoln Laboratory, Massachusetts Institute of Technology, Cambridge, Mass., 1963.

Teilhard de Chardin, Pierre. Bernard Wall, trans. 1955 *The Phenomenon of Man.* (New York: Harper, 1975).

Torvalds, Linus. *Just for Fun.* (London: Texere, 2001).

Von Neumann, John. *The Computer and the Brain.* (New Haven, Conn.: Yale University Press, 1958, 2000).

Wiener, Norbert. "Communication and Secrecy in the Modern World" Massachusetts Institute of Technology, Cambridge, Mass., 1951.

—*I Am a Mathematician.* (Cambridge, Mass.: MIT Press, 1956).

References

Abbate, Janet. *Inventing the Internet.* (Cambridge, Mass.: MIT Press, 1999).

Bardini, Thierry. *Bootstrapping: Douglas Engelbart, Coevolution, and the Origins of Personal Computing.* (Stanford, Calif.: Stanford University Press, 2001).

Brand, Stewart. *The Media Lab: Inventing the Future at MIT.* (New York: Viking Penguin, 1987).

DiBona, Chris, et al., eds. *Open Sources: Voices from the Open Source Revolution.* (Sebastopol, Calif.: O'Reilly & Associates, Inc., 1999).

Gillies, James, and Robert Cailliau. *How the Web Was Born: The Story of the World Wide Web.* (Oxford: Oxford University Press, 2000)

Goldstine, Herman H. *The Computer from Pascal to von Neumann.* (Princeton, N.J.: Princeton University Press, 1972).

Hafner, Katie, and Matthew Lyon. *Where Wizards Stay Up Late: The Origins of the Internet.* (New York: Simon & Schuster Inc., 1998).

Halberstam, David. *The Fifties.* (New York: Random House, 1993).

Heims, Steve J. *John von Neumann and Norbert Wiener: From Mathematics to the Technologies of Life and Death.* (Cambridge, Mass.: MIT Press, 1980).

Hiltzik, Michael. *Dealers of Lightning: Xerox PARC and the Dawn of the Computer Age.* (New York: HarperCollins, 1999).

Hodges, Andrew. *Alan Turing: The Enigma.* (New York: Walker, 2000).

Levy, Steven. *Hackers: Heroes of the Computer Revolution.* (New York: Doubleday, 1984*).*

—*Insanely Great: The Life and Times of Macintosh, the Computer That Changed Everything.* (New York: Viking Penguin, 1994).

Marchand, Philip. *Marshall McLuhan: The Medium and the Messenger.* (New York: Ticknor & Fields, 1989).

Poundstone, William. *Prisoner's Dilemma.* (New York: Doubleday, 1992).

Segaller, Stephen. *Nerds 2.0.1: A Brief History of the Internet.* (New York: TV Books, 1998).

Sloman, Larry. *Steal This Dream: Abbie Hoffman and the Countercultural Revolution in America.* (New York: Doubleday, 1998).

Waldrop, M. Mitchell. *The Dream Machine: J. C. R. Licklider and the Revolution That Made Computing Personal.* (New York: Penguin Group, 2001).

Recommended Readings

Borsook, Paulina. *Cyberselfish: A Critical Romp Through the Terribly Libertarian Culture of High Tech.* (New York: Perseus Books, 2000).

Brin, David. *The Transparent Society: Will Technology Force Us to Choose Between Privacy and Freedom?.* (Reading, Mass.: Perseus Books, 1998).

Gladwell, Malcolm. *The Tipping Point: How Little Things Can Make a Big Difference.* (Boston: Little, Brown, 2000).

Jones, John Chris. *The Internet and Everyone.* (London: Ellipsis, 1999).

McChesney, Robert W. *Rich Media, Poor Democracy: Communication Politics in Dubious Times.* (Urbana, Ill.: University of Illinois Press, 1999).

Raskin, Jef. *The Humane Interface: New Directions for Designing Interactive Systems.* (Menlo Park, Calif.: Addison-Wesley, 2000)

Rheingold, Howard. *Virtual Reality.* (New York: Simon & Schuster, 1991).

Shapiro, Andrew L. *The Control Revolution: How the Internet Is Putting Individuals in Charge and Changing the World We Know.* (New York: Perseus Books, 2000).

Chapter One

1 Norbert Wiener, *The Human Use of Human Beings,* (New York: Anchor Books, 1950; 1954), 17, 18.

2 Norbert Wiener, *Cybernetics,* 2nd ed. (Cambridge, Mass.: MIT Press, 1948; 1961), 33.

3 Wiener, *Human,* 33.

4 Ibid., 12.

5 Wiener, *Cybernetics,* 58.

6 Wiener, *Human,* 116.

7 Ibid., 17.

8 Ibid., 26–27.

9 Claude E. Shannon, "A Mathematical Theory of Communication," Bell System . . .

10 Ibid., 79.

11 Ibid., 96.

12 Ibid.

13 Ibid., 132.

14 Wiener, *Cybernetics,* 177.

15 Wiener, *Human,* 181.

16 Ibid., 185.

17 Norbert Wiener, "Communication and Secrecy in the Modern World" 1951: MIT Archives, Cambridge, Mass.

18 Wiener, *Human,* 129.

19 Ibid., 120.

20 Ibid., 40.

21 Ibid., 28.

22 William Gibson, *Neuromancer* (New York: Ace Books, 1984), 51.

Chapter Two

1 Norbert Wiener, *I Am a Mathematician* (Cambridge, Mass.: MIT Press, 1956), 75.

2 Ibid.

3 Vannevar Bush, "As We May Think," 1945 *Endless Horizons* (Washington DC: Public Affairs Press, 1975); originally published in *Atlantic Monthly,* July 1945.

4 Ibid., 19.

5 Ibid., 12.

6 Ibid., 13.

7 Ibid., 11.

8 Ibid., 11.

9 Wiener, *Mathematician,* 75.

10 Vannevar Bush, "Memex Revisited," *Science Is Not Enough* (New York: William Morrow, 1967), 89.

11 Ibid., 75.

12 Vannevar Bush, "Man's Thinking Machines," 1963; Massachusetts Institute of Technology Archives, Cambridge, Mass.

13 Ralph Waldo Emerson, "The Poet," 1844, *Selected Essays* (New York: Penguin, 1982).

14 Bush, "Memex," 75.

15 Ibid., 100.

16 Ibid., 96.

17 Ibid.

18 Wiener, *Cybernetics,* 2nd ed. (Cambridge, Mass.: MIT Press, 1948; 1961), 158.

Chapter Three

1 Alan Turing, "On Computable Numbers with an Application to the Entscheidungsproblem," April 1935, *Proceedings of the London Mathematical Society* (series 2) 42, 250.

2 Ibid., 253–254.

3 John von Neumann, *First Draft of a Report on the EDVAC* Contract W-670-ORD4926 30 June 1945, Morse School of Electrical Engineering, University of Pennsylvania, Philadelphia, Pa., 5.

4 Ibid., 2–3.

5 Alan Turing, "Computing Machinery and Intelligence," October 1950 *Mind* 59, no. 236, 438.

6 Alan Turing, *Proposed Electronic Calculator,* 1946, Department of Scientific & Industrial Research 10/385, April 1972.

7 Ibid.

8 Turing, "Computing," 433.

9 Ibid., 434.

10 Ibid., 442.

11 Turing, Report for National Physical Laboratory, July/August 1948; *see* Andrew Hodges, *Alan Turing: The Enigma* (New York: Walker, 2000).

12 All quotations in section from Turing, "Computing," 443–452.

13 Turing, "Computing," 456.

Chapter Four

1 J. C. R. Licklider, "Man-Computer Symbiosis: Part of the Oral Report of the 1958 NAS-ARDC Special Study, presented on behalf of the Committee on the Roles of Men in Future Air Force Systems," 20–21 November 1958, MIT Archives, Cambridge, Mass.

2 Ibid.

3 Licklider, "Man-Computer Symbiosis," *IRE Transactions on Human Factors in Electronics,* HFE-1, March 1960, MIT Archives, Cambridge, Mass., 2.

4 Ibid., 1.

5 Ibid., 8.

6 Ibid., 3.

7 Licklider, "The Cerebral Frontier. A preliminary draft of a report to the Basic Research Panel of the AFSAB by the Committee of AI, Bionics, and Man-Computer Symbiosis," 24 April 1961, MIT Archives.

8 Ibid.

9 Licklider, *Libraries of the Future* (Cambridge, Mass.: MIT Press, 1965), 33.

10 Ibid., criteria 1, 16, 5, 14.

11 Ibid., criteria 9, 13, 15, 7, 8, 17, 25.

12 Licklider, "Memorandum to members and affiliates of the intergalactic network," 25 April 1963; MIT Archives.

13 Licklider and Robert Taylor, "Computer as a Communications Device," *International Science and Technology,* April 1968; MIT Archives, 21.

14 Ibid., 32.

15 Ibid., 21.

16 Ibid., 40.

17 Ibid.

Chapter Five

1 Douglas Engelbart, "The Augmented Knowledge Workshop." In *A History of Personal Workstations,* Adele Goldberg, pp. 187–214. (New York: ACM Press, 1988), 192.

2 Douglas Engelbart, "Special Considerations of the Individual as a User, Generator, and Retriever of Information," *American Documentation* 12, no. 2, pp. 121–125, April 1961. Presented at the Annual Meeting of the American Documentation Institute, Berkeley, Calif., 23–27 October 1960, 121.

3 Ibid.

4 Ibid.

5 Douglas C. Engelbart. Letter to Dr. Vannevar Bush. May 24, 1962. http://www.histech.rwth-aachen.de/www/quellen/engelbart/ Engelbart2Bush.html. May 24, 1962

6 Douglas C. Engelbart, (1962c). *Augmenting Human Intellect: A Conceptual Framework.* Summary Report AFOSR-3223 under Contract AF 49(638)-1024, SRI Project 3578 for Air Force Office of Scientific Research, Stanford Research Institute, Menlo Park, Calif., 131.

7 Ibid., 1.

8 Ibid.

9 Ibid., 17.

10 Ibid., 21.

11 Ibid., 8.

12 Ibid., 21.

13 Ibid., 14.

14 Engelbart "Knowledge," 191.

15 Douglas Engelbart (1986/87), interviews conducted by Judith Adams and Henry Lowood on 19 December 1986, 14 January 1987, 4 March 1987, and 1 April 1987 for the Stanford Oral History Project. Transcript of tape recording, Stanford University Archives, Stanford, Calif. http://www.sul.stanford.edu/ depts/hasrg/histsci/svoral/engelbart/start.html March 15, 2001.

16 Engelbart "Knowledge," 193.

17 Norbert Wiener, *Cybernetics,* (Cambridge, Mass.: MIT Press, 1948, 1961), 32.

18 Engelbart, *Augmenting,* 105.

19 Ibid.

20 Loren Stein. "Doug Engelbart's Unfinished Revolution." *Palo Alto Weekly,* December 23, 1998, 7.

21 Engelbart, *Augmenting,* 123.

22 Ibid.

23 Douglas Engelbart, interview conducted by David Bennahum on October 3, 1996 "Doug Engelbart: The Interview." http://www.memex.org/meme-3-01.html 5 August 2001.

Chapter Six

1 Marvin Minsky, *Society of Mind* (New York: Simon & Schuster, 1985), 22.

2 Ibid., 308.

3 Ibid., 102.

4 Ibid., 229.

5 Ibid., 236.

6 Seymour Papert, *Mindstorms: Children, Computers, and Powerful Ideas* (New York: Basic Books, 1980), 4.

7 Ibid., vii.

8 Ibid., viii.

9 Ibid., 5–6.

10 Ibid., 5.

11 Ibid.

12 Ibid., 26.

13 Ibid., 36.

Chapter Seven

1 Joanne Kelleher, "Alan Kay: Prophet of Intimate Computing," *Computerworld,* June 22, 1992, 30.

2 Alan Kay, "The Reactive Engine," Ph.D. Thesis, University of Utah Salt Lake City, September 1969.

3 Bob Ryan. "Dynabook Revisited with Alan Kay," *Byte* 16, February 1991, 205.

4 Kay, "Engine."

5 Stewart Brand, *Whole Earth Catalog,* 22 December 1968, 75.

6 Stewart Brand, "SpaceWar," 7 December 1972. http://www.wheels.org/spacewar/stone/rolling_stone.html 15 August 2001.

7 Ibid.

8 Alan Kay and Adele Goldberg, "Personal Dynamic Media," *Computer,* March 1977, 31.

9 Ibid., 31.

10 Kay, "Microelectronics and the Personal Computer," *Scientific American* 237, no. 3, September 1977, 231.

11 Ibid., 239.

12 Ibid., 238.

13 Ibid., 244.

14 Kay, "Personal," 32.

15 Alan Kay, "Computer Software," *Scientific American,* 251, September 1984, 54.

16 Ibid., 57.

17 Ibid., 59.

18 Tod Newcombe, "Expression and Interface: An Interview with Alan Kay," *Government Technology,* February 1998. http://www.govtech.net/publications/visions/feb98vision/kay/phtml.

19 Alan Kay, "Computers, Networks and Education," *Scientific American,* September 1991, 138.

20 Ibid., 143.

21 Ibid., 140.

22 Ibid., 140.

23 Ibid., 140.

24 Ibid., 148.

25 New Perspectives: Interview with Alan Kay. http://www.npq.org/issues/v12/p14.html. 6 May 2001.

26 Kay, "Networks," 148.

27 Kelleher, "Intimate," 30.

28 Kay, "Microelectronics," 244.

Chapter Eight

1 Marshall McLuhan, *The Gutenberg Galaxy: The Making of the Typographic Man* (Toronto: University of Toronto Press, 1962), 130.

2 McLuhan, *Understanding Media: The Extensions of Man,* 1964 (Cambridge, Mass.: MIT Press, 1999), 7.

3 Ibid., 22.

4 McLuhan, *Gutenberg,* 141.

5 Ibid., 31.

6 Wyndham Lewis, *America and Cosmic Man* (1948), 21.

7 McLuhan, *Understanding,* 61.

8 Ibid., 57.

9 Pierre Teilhard de Chardin, Bernard Wall, trans. 1955 *The Phenomenon of Man,* (New York: Harper, 1975), 110.

10 McLuhan, *Gutenberg,* 32.

11 Hoffman, *Revolution for the Hell of It* (New York: Dial Press, 1968), 70.

12 McLuhan, *Understanding,* 57.

13 Ibid., 347.

14 Hoffman, *Revolution,* 57.

15 Ibid.

16 Hoffman, *Steal This Book* (New York: Pirate Press, 1971). http://www.pieman.org/stealthisbook.html 3 April 2001.

17 Ibid.

18 Ibid.

Chapter Nine

1 W. H. Ferry, et al., "The Triple Revolution" 1964. *The Sixties Papers: Documents of a Rebellious Decade* ed. Judith Albert.(Praeger: New York, 1984), 197.

2 Ted Nelson, *Computer Lib* (Seattle, Washington: Microsoft Press, 1987), 21.

3 Ibid., 7.

4 Ibid., 136.

5 Ibid., 5.

6 Letter from Doug Engelbart to Ted Nelson; Stanford Archives, Stanford, Calif.

7 Nelson, *Lib,* 21.

8 Ted Nelson, *Literary Machines* (Self-published by the author: 1981; 1987), 5/9.

9 All ideas on the Xanadu system as depicted in *Literary Machines* and other writings on and about Xanadu, and from personal interview with Nelson.

10 Nelson, *Literary,* 3/19.

11 Ibid., 1/23.

12 Ibid., 1/24.

13 Ibid., 0/6.

14 Tim Berners-Lee, *Weaving the Web* (Great Britain: Orion, 1999), 1.

15 Tim Berners-Lee, "Information Management: A Proposal" 1989, May 1990. http://www.w3org/history/1989/proposal.htm 31 May 2001.

16 Berners-Lee, *Weaving,* 79.

17 Ibid., 106.

18 Ibid., 135.

19 Ibid., 144.

20 Ibid., 149.

21 Ted Nelson, "Xanalogical Structure, Needed Now More than Ever" May 2000. http://www.sfc.keio.ac.jp/~ted/XUsurvey/xuDation.html

22 Tim Berners-Lee, James Hendler and Ora Lassila, "The Semantic Web" May 2001. http://www.sciam.com/2001/0501issue/0501berners-lee.html.

23 Ibid.

24 Berners-Lee, *Weaving,* 224.

25 Ibid., 189.

26 Nelson, *Lib,* 24.

Chapter Ten

1 Richard Stallman, "The GNU Manifesto," *Dr. Dobb's Journal of Software Tools* 10, no. 3, March 1985. http://www.gnu.org/gnu/manifesto.html.

2 Ibid.

3 Ibid.

4 Richard M. Stallman, "GNU General Public License," 1989. http://www.gnu.org/licenses/gpl.html.

5 Stallman, *The Free Software Definition,* 1996. http://www.gnu.org/philosophy/free-sw.html.

6 Stallman, "License."

7 Larry Wall, *Programming Perl* (Sebastopol, Calif.: O'Reilly & Associates, 1991), 4.

8 Larry Wall, *Programming Perl,* second edition (Sebastopol, Calif.: O'Reilly & Associates, 1996), ix. Though this slogan first appeared in the second edition of the Camel book, the idea was expressed, albeit more diffusely, in the first edition.

9 Larry Wall, "First Perl Conference Keynote," 1997, also known as the "First State of the Perl Onion." http://www.wall.org/~larry/keynote/keynote.html 6 May 2001.

10 Ibid.

11 Larry Wall, "Third State of the Perl Onion," 1999 http://www.perl.com/1999/08/onion/talk.html 6 May 2001.

12 Wall, "First."

Chapter Eleven

1 Eric S. Raymond, *The Cathedral and the Bazaar* (Sebastopol, Calif.: O'Reilly & Associates, 1999).

2 Andrew Leonard, "Let My Software Go!" http://www.salon.com/21st/feature/1998/04/cov_14feature.html April 1998.

3 Raymond, *Cathedral,* 41.

4 Ibid.

5 Ibid., 66.

6 Lawrence Lessig, *Code and Other Laws of Cyberspace* (New York: Perseus, 1999), 5.

7 Jamie Zawinski, "Fear and Loathing on the Merger Trail" 23 November 1998. http://www.mozilla.org/fear.html 6 May 2001.

8 David Streitfield, "An Awkward Anniversary" 17 March 2001. http://www.washingtonpost.com/wp-srv/WPlate/2000-03/17/1191-031700-idx.html 6 May 2001.

9 Norbert Wiener, *Cybernetics,* second edition (Cambridge, Mass.: MIT Press, 1948; 1961), 160.

10 Lessig, *Code,* 42.

11 Ibid., 101.

12 Ibid., 107.

13 Ibid., 7.

14 Eric S. Raymond, "On Socially Responsible Computing."
http://www.tuxedo.org/~esr/writings/cpsr-speech.html 6 May 2001.

15 Eric S. Raymond, "Defending Network Freedom."
http://www.tuxedo.org/~esr/netfreedom/index.html October 19, 1999.

16 Lessig, *Code*, 206.

17 Lawrence Lessig and Eric S. Raymond, "TAP Controversy: Should Public
Policy Support Open Source Software?" 27 March 2000.
http://www.prospect.org/controversy/open_source/lessig-l-2.html 6 May
2001.

18 Lessig, *Code*, 153.

19 Lessig and Raymond, "TAP."

20 Lessig, *Code*, 220.

21 Raymond, *Cathedral*, 65.

22 Ibid., 194.

Chapter Twelve

1 A transcript of Feynman's 1959 speech "There's Plenty of Room at the
Bottom" at the Annual Meeting of the American Physical Society at
Caltech can be found at http://www.zyvex.com/nanotech/feynman.html.
First published in the February 1960 issue of Caltech's *Engineering and
Science*.

2 Marvin Minsky, *Society of Mind* (New York: Simon & Schuster, 1985).

3 K. Eric Drexler, *Engines of Creation* (New York: Doubleday, 1986), 27.

4 Ibid., 63.

5 Richard Dawkins, *The Selfish Gene*, 1976 (New York: Oxford University
Press, 1990), 34.

6 Drexler, 173.

7 Ibid., 174.

8 Ibid., 203.

9 Ibid., 200.

10 Foresight Institute, "Foresight Guidelines on Molecular Technology,"
June 4, 2000. http://www.foresight.org/guidelines/current.html.
June 4, 2000.

Chapter Thirteen

1 Bill Joy, "Why the Future Doesn't Need Us," *Wired* 8 no. 4, April 2000. http://www.wired.com/wired/archive/8.04/joy_pr.html 6 May 2001.

2 John McIntyre, "Interview with Bill Joy," September 6, 2000. http://www.ciber.gatech.edu/workingpaper/sun.html.

3 Joy, "Future."

4 Ibid.

5 McIntyre.

6 Linus Torvalds, *Just For Fun* (London: Texere, 2001), 154.

7 John Seely Brown and Paul Duguid, "Ideas to Feed Your Business: Re-Engineering the Future." April 24, 2000. http://www.thestandard.com/article/0,1902,14013,00.html.

8 Norbert Wiener, *Cybernetics,* second edition (Cambridge, Mass.: MIT Press, 1948; 1961), 34.

9 Alan Turing, "Computing Machinery and Intelligence," *Mind,* October 1950, 442.

10 Licklider, "Man-Computer Symbiosis," *IRE Transactions on Human Factors in Electronics,* HFE-1, March 1960, MIT Archives, Cambridge, Mass., 60.

11 Jaron Lanier, "One–Half a Manifesto," *Edge* 74, September 2000. http://www.edge.org/3rd_culture/lanier/lanier_index.html 1 May 2001.

12 Lanier, "Manifesto"

13 Ibid.

14 Ibid.

15 Ibid.

16 Ibid.

17 Joy, "Future."

18 Norbert Wiener, *The Human Use of Human Beings: Cybernetics and Society,* second edition (New York: Houghton Mifflin, 1950; Doubleday, 1954), 18.

About TEXERE

TEXERE seeks to become the most progressive and authoritative voice in business publishing by cultivating and enhancing ideas that will illuminate the global business landscape. Our name defines the spirit of our vision: TEXERE is the ancient Latin verb "to weave." In an increasingly global business community, we seek to create an intersection where authors and readers can share the best thinking and the latest ideas. We want to leverage the expertise and insights of leading thinkers by weaving them with TEXERE's capability to deliver them to the marketplace.

To learn more and become a part of our community visit us at:

www.etexere.com

and

www.etexere.co.uk